Oahu's
NORTH SHORE

A Guide To Its
Treasures And Beauties

A Complete
Guide to the
Best Part of
Oahu

Patricia O'Rorke

ISBN: 1-4392-3771-9
Library of Congress Control Number: 2009903954
EAN13: 9781439237717

**Visit www.OahusNorthShore.com to order additional copies.
Also available on Kindle.**

Photos and Maps by Edward Asmus

For Ted

CONTENTS

1. WHAT TO KNOW BEFORE YOU GO

ABOUT THIS BOOK

There are many guidebooks to the island of Oahu, but the few pages they devote to the northern part of the island omit a treasure trove of fantastic places and activities. This handbook goes beyond their superficial glimpse, taking you to sensational beaches, mountain trails, waterfalls, and attractions that most visitors never see. It gets you off the main highway to experience the amazing beauty, charm, and aloha of a special place where the spirit of "Old Hawaii" remains strong.

Northern Oahu is truly unique. Although it lies less than an hour by car from the hustle and bustle of Honolulu, its iridescent beauty remains surprisingly undisturbed. Verdant mountains descend to breathtaking sandy beaches, coral reefs teeming with sea life, and fabulous surf. The North Shore extends from Kaena Point on the west to Kahuku Point, the northernmost tip of the island. This handbook covers not only the North Shore, but also the Windward Shore from Kahuku Point to Kaaawa.

While it is a legendary playground for ocean lovers, this lovely part of the island has many other dimensions. It is an ideal place to explore Hawaii's unique culture, history, and environment. In addition to endless water sports, numerous other activities are readily available. This guide aims to enhance your visit, whether you come to sightsee, swim, surf, snorkel, scuba dive, kayak, golf, hike, bike, birdwatch, ride horses, play tennis, camp, skydive, bike, shop, visit, or just plain loaf.

HOW TO USE THIS GUIDE

Chapter I tells you in a nutshell what you should know before you arrive. It begins with a quick overview of northern Oahu and "Ten Commandments" for a safe and enjoyable visit. "Short Lists" identify the top ten tourist attractions and the best spots for beachgoers, surfers, families, foodies, nature lovers, history buffs, lovers, and daredevils. Suggested itineraries provide a game plan for those with only one day, one weekend, or one week to spend, and some wonderful things to do on a rainy day or a full moon. "Travel Tips" address climate, clothing, culture, and the wide range of activities available in northern Oahu. A brief history provides a basic understanding of the unique environment and culture of the area.

Chapter II is a comprehensive Drive Guide. After describing how to get there and some handy pitstops along the way, it takes you on a circle tour of northern Oahu, telling you the story of each area and the interesting things to see and do there. Reading it in advance will help you decide where to go and what to do in the time you have available. If you don't get a chance to read it before you go, just read it along the way or at the beach. If you are looking for specific information about a particular place or activity, you can find it quicker in the subsequent chapters, which describe the major tourist attractions, beaches, activities, dining, lodging, and services in detail.

Chapter III is a guide to northern Oahu's three major tourist attractions: the Dole Pineapple Plantation, Waimea Valley Historical Nature Park, and Polynesian Cultural Center. Chapter IV describes each beach along the northern coastline, with a "short list" of great swimming beaches up front. Chapters V, VI, and VII identify the huge variety of things to do in northern Oahu, on water, on land, and in the air. Chapter V includes a detailed description of northern Oahu's surf spots.

Chapter VIII identifies places to eat, with a short list of great eateries up front. The dining guide includes restaurants, cafes, outdoor dining, fast food, and other specialties in five geographical areas: (1)

the Central Plateau, (2) Haleiwa Town, (3) the North Shore between Haleiwa and Kahuku, (4) Laie Town, and (5) the Windward Shore from Hauula to Kaaawa.

Northern Oahu is not lined with high-rise hotels, which is why we love it so. Accommodations are limited to the full-service Turtle Bay Resort, some nice condominiums, and a variety of homes, cottages, and other lodgings that are available for rent. To help you find appropriate accommodations, Chapter IX provides contact information for rental agents and internet services. These listings are for convenience only and are not an endorsement of individual accommodations or agents.

Chapter X provides a Glossary of Hawaiian Words And Phrases. Hawaiian terms are italicized and defined in parentheses the first time they are used in the text. If you forget their meaning, you can look them up in the Glossary. Chapter XI is a Directory of Services. The Index and list of maps will help you find what you want in a hurry.

Directions are given island-style: *mauka* (toward the mountains or inland) and *makai* (toward the sea). This may be confusing at first, but you will soon get used to these "island-style" directions, as the mountains and sea are natural points of reference.

Whether you spend a day, a week, or a lifetime in northern Oahu, its beauty, charm and *aloha* (love, grace, welcome) will remain with you always. So pick up some Hawaiian music, leave your troubles behind, and get ready to discover a true paradise.

THE ISLAND OF OAHU

Oahu is divided by two mountain ranges, vestiges of the two volcanoes that formed the island millions of years ago. The Koolau Range runs from south to north along the east side of the island. The Waianae Range runs from south to north along the west side of the island.

With its protected harbors, the South Shore is the seat of government and center of commercial activity, but it lacks the sandy beaches and natural beauty of the other coasts. On the Leeward Shore, arid slopes and sandy beaches bake in a dry, sunny environment. On the Windward Shore, the Koolaus are often shrouded in mist and rain as they sweep dramatically toward the sea. Northern Oahu is the best part of the island, because it enjoys a moderate climate with cooling trade winds, verdant mountains, gorgeous foliage, wide sandy beaches, and abundant sea life.

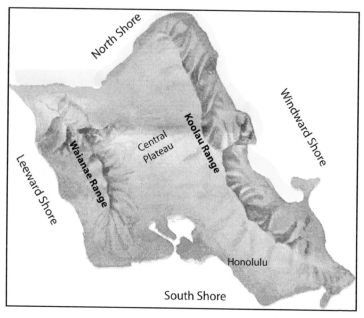

The Island of Oahu

GETTING TO NORTHERN OAHU

Getting to northern Oahu from Honolulu or the airport requires a motor vehicle. For the greatest convenience, rent a car or hire one of the airport transportation services listed in Chapter XI.

Public transportation is provided by "The Bus." Route 52, the "Wahiawa Circle Isle," runs from Honolulu to Mililani, Wahiawa, Haleiwa Beach Park, Pupukea Beach Park, Turtle Bay Resort, Laie/Polynesian Cultural Center, Hauula Elementary School, Kaaawa Beach Park, and back to Honolulu. Route 55, the "Kaneohe Circle Isle," makes the same stops in the opposite direction. Route 88, "the North Shore Express," runs between Honolulu and the Turtle Bay Resort with fewer stops. Detailed route maps and schedules are available at www.thebus.org. Fares are $2 each way for adults and $1 for youths under 17. Visitors can buy an unlimited four-day pass for $20.

If you plan to drive, take a few minutes to familiarize yourself with Oahu's highway system. There are three interstate freeways: H-1, H-2, and H-3. H-1 runs along the heavily populated South Shore, with a loop to the airport. H-2 heads north from H-1 near Pearl City and cuts through the Central Plateau. This is the most direct route to northern Oahu. A more scenic route, the old Kunia Road (Route 750), heads north from H-1 near Waipahu and runs along the eastern side of the Waianae Mountains.

North of the airport, H-3 runs north from H-1 and cuts through the Koolau Mountains to the Windward Shore. East of the airport, the Likelike Highway (Route 63) and Pali Highway (Route 61) run from H-1 through the Koolaus to the Windward Shore.

Northern Oahu has no freeways. The two-lane Kamehameha Highway, known locally as the "Kam Highway," is the main road. It connects with H-2 at Wahiawa, continues north to Haleiwa, and follows the coastline up the North Shore and down the Windward Shore, where it connects to H-3. Note that different sections of the Kam Highway bear different route numbers.

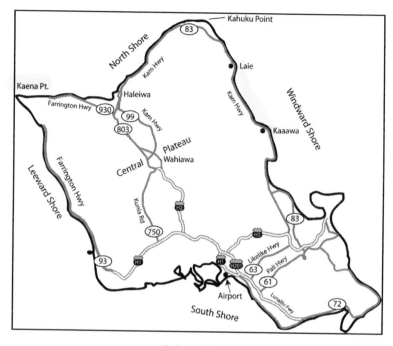

Oahu's Highways

There is no road around the whole island. The Farrington Highway runs up the Leeward Shore on the west side of the Waianae Mountains as Route 93, and along the northwestern shoreline on the north side of the Waianaes as Route 930, but it deadends on both sides. The road around Kaena Point, the northwestern corner of the island, has been closed for many years.

A QUICK OVERVIEW

The Central Plateau

Scenic plateau between Oahu's two mountain ranges, home of the Wahiawa Botanic Garden, Dole Pineapple Plantation, Kukaniloko Birthing Stones, and Schofield Army Barracks.

Haleiwa Town

Quintessential surf town on Waialua Bay, featuring quaint old buildings, surf shops, surf museums, art galleries, boutiques, restaurants, historic churches, tours and equipment rentals. Swimming, surfing, kayaking, boating and fishing charters, and other water activities are available at Alii and Haleiwa Beach Parks and Haleiwa Boat Harbor.

The Northwest Shore From Waialua To Kaena Point

Miles of secluded shoreline stretch beneath towering volcanic cliffs to Kaena Point, where the road ends at the northwestern tip of Oahu. See the old Waialua sugar mill. Enjoy polo games and horseback riding at a beachside ranch, colorful kitesurfers and windsurfers at Mokuleia, gliding and air tours at Dillingham Airfield, and hiking and mountain biking around Kaena Point and the Waianae Mountains.

The North Shore From Haleiwa To Turtle Bay	Famous shoreline boasting fabulous beaches and surf spots, with basking Hawaiian sea turtles at Laniakea; swimming and snorkeling at Waimea Bay Beach Park; Hawaiian history and beauty in Waimea Valley and Puu O Mahuka Heiau State Monument; snorkeling and diving at Pupukea Beach Park; biking, hiking and trail rides on Pupukea Ridge; world-class surfing at the Banzai Pipeline, Sunset Beach, and other famous surf spots; and top-rated golf, tennis, riding, spa treatments, restaurants, and other amenities at the Turtle Bay Resort.
The Northeast Shore From Turtle Bay To Laie	The northeastern corner of Oahu, with tree-fringed white sand beaches and two charming towns. Look for roadside stands and shrimp trucks, bird refuges, miles of pristine shoreline, swimming, bodysurfing, bodyboarding, and the Polynesian Cultural Center, where the cultures of the Polynesian islands are presented in seven villages, an authentic *luau*, and a fabulous Polynesian review.

The Windward Shore
From Laie To Kaaawa

The quiet Windward Shore, where verdant mountains descend steeply toward the sea, scenic hiking trails lead to sparkling waterfalls and cool swimming ponds, and the coastline offers magnificent views, historic fishponds, abundant fishing, and lovely, tree-fringed beaches.

TEN COMMANDMENTS

For a safe and enjoyable time in northern Oahu, follow these "Ten Commandments."

Rule Number 1:
Protect Yourself From The Tropical Sun.

Apply sunscreen liberally and often, being careful not to miss any spots. Wear a hat or visor and sunglasses. Bring beach sandals or shoes to walk on the hot sand, and tatami mats, towels or chairs to sit on. Keep sandals out of the sun so they don't heat up. Don't spend the whole day on the beach. Get out of the sun during the midday hours. If you rent a convertible, be mindful of sun exposure—especially on bald heads!

Rule Number 2:
Guard Against Theft.

Theft is a problem in paradise. Try to park your car where you can see it. Don't leave valuables in the car or be seen placing items in the trunk. Keep your driver's license, passport, credit cards, money, and other valuables on your person or in your lodging place. If you are staying in a house or condo, be sure to lock all the doors, including all sliding glass doors, when you leave.

Rule Number 3:
Stay Aware Of Water Conditions

North Shore beaches are beautiful, but large waves and strong currents can make them extremely dangerous. Be aware that wind, waves, currents, and tides are constantly changing. Check the HawaiiBeachSafety.org website for current conditions in order to choose the appropriate beach for each day's activities. Never turn your back on the ocean. Stay alert for water conditions that are beyond your ability. Don't swim alone or far from shore. Be on the lookout for jellyfish and Portuguese man-of-war, especially when swimming on the Windward Shore, and stay out of their way.

Waimea Bay on a calm summer day

Waimea Bay shorebreak on a rough day

Rule Number 4:
Pay Attention To Warnings

Trust the judgment of local authorities on dangerous conditions. On lifeguarded beaches, a three-level rating system is used: Caution, High Hazard, and Extreme Hazard. The "Caution" sign calls for normal caution—stay aware of changing conditions, such as strong shore breaks and currents, and don't swim alone or far from shore. The "High Hazard" sign means that currents and surge on the beach are quite strong and can cause injury—stay out of the water and beyond the reach of the waves as indicated by wet sand or rocks. The "Extreme Hazard" sign means shoreline activity is extremely hazardous and likely to cause injury—stay out of the water and away from the shore. Similar warning signs are used for offshore conditions, primarily for boaters and kayakers launching from the shoreline. Please take these warning signs seriously and check for small craft warnings before you go boating. In Hawaii the motto is, "When in doubt, don't go out." If you go hiking or biking in the mountains, observe warnings of falling rocks, flash floods, and other dangers.

Rule Number 5:
Don't Walk On Rocks Near The Surf

Never walk out on rocks near the surf, even if other people are out there. One large wave might drag you into dangerous surf or currents.

Rule Number 6:
Avoid Sharp Rocks And Coral

Avoid swimming or walking barefoot near sharp rocks or coral. Remember that coral is an animal. It gets hurt when people walk on it. It can also hurt you by causing scrapes, cuts, and infections. If you walk on a rocky shore, wear sandals or shoes and be aware that crevices may hide spiny sea urchins and moray eels. If you walk barefoot on rough lava, you will learn why the Hawaiians call it *aa* ("aah! aah!").

Rule Number 7:
Go Under, Not Over, Waves

If you get caught in a turbulent shore break or wave, dive under the breaking waves before they reach you. If you try to swim or jump over waves, the force of the water may push you to the bottom or drag you out in the backwash.

Rule Number 8:
Don't Fight The Current

If you feel yourself being pulled out to sea or along the shore by a current or riptide, do not try to swim directly against it. Swim diagonally across it or let it take you out and then swim back another way. Swimming against a strong current is counterproductive; it only exhausts you.

Rule Number 9:
Respect Hawaii's Treasures

The people of northern Oahu come from Hawaiian, Chinese, Japanese, Filipino, Tongan, Samoan, European, and other ancestries. Their religious beliefs, traditions, and cultures may differ dramatically from yours. Respect for these different heritages is part of the beautiful spirit of *aloha* that enriches life here. Please do not touch *heiau* (Hawaiian temples or shrines made of rocks) or the offerings left at them. Also respect Hawaii's natural treasures. Do not touch, feed, or disturb marine mammals or sea turtles. When snorkeling or diving, do not feed the fish. Many native plants and flowers are fragile. Do not break or remove coral or plant life from its natural habitat. Souvenirs are available in dozens of gift shops.

Rule Number 10:
Don't Let A Little Rain Spoil A Day In Paradise

It isn't unusual for rain to fall once or twice a day in northern Oahu. Typically, a gentle "pineapple rain" is soon followed by sunshine and a beautiful *enui nui* (rainbow). Sometimes rain will fall on one beach or valley while the next one remains dry and sunny. Don't go hiking or biking in the mountains, especially on the Windward Shore, when it is raining or rain is predicted. If it starts to rain while you are at the beach, you can still enjoy the water as long as there is no thunder or lightning, or you can find something else to do and return later. In some places, people say, "If you don't like the weather, wait five minutes." On Oahu it is more appropriate to say, "If you don't like the weather, just go down the road."

THE TOP TEN TOURIST ATTRACTIONS
In clockwise order on the Circle Tour:

1. **The Dole Pineapple Plantation**, a pleasant stop with the "Pineapple Express" Train Ride, plantation garden tour, world's largest maze, and delicious pineapple treats.

2. **Haleiwa Town**, the quintessential surf town with surf shops, surf museums, boutiques, art galleries, restaurants, shave ice, historic buildings and churches, Rainbow Bridge, Alii Beach Park, Haleiwa Beach Park, and Haleiwa Boat Harbor.

3. **Dillingham Airfield and Gliderport**, with thrilling glider rides, air tours, and skydiving over breathtaking mountain and ocean scenery.

4. **Laniakea Beach**, a popular surf spot where *honu* (Hawaiian green sea turtles) congregate and bask on the shore.

5. **Waimea Bay Beach Park**, one of the world's most beautiful beaches.

6. **Waimea Valley Historical Nature Park**, an exquisite valley filled with the history and natural beauty of Hawaii.

7. **Pupukea Beach Park**, 80 acres of scenic shoreline with fabulous snorkeling and diving along magnificent coral reefs.

8. **The Banzai Pipeline**, one of the world's great surf spots, with its iconic curl forming a tube or "pipeline" over a menacing coral bottom.

9. **Sunset Beach Park**, a two-mile horseshoe shaped beach popular for swimming and snorkeling in the summer and surfing in the winter.

10. **The Polynesian Cultural Center,** where the cultures and traditions of the Polynesian islands are presented in seven villages and the most authentic *luau* and Polynesian review on Oahu.

SHORT LISTS

For Beachgoers

Depending on conditions, the best beaches for recreational swimming are:

Alii Beach Park

Waimea Bay Beach Park

Three Tables Beach in Pupukea Beach Park

Sunset Beach Park

Hukilau Beach

Kokololio Beach Park

The only lifeguarded beaches are:

Alii Beach Park

Haleiwa Beach Park

Laniakea Beach Support Park

Chun's Reef Support Park

Waimea Bay Beach Park

Ke Waena Beach Park

Ehukai Beach Park

Sunset Beach Park

For Surfers

It all depends on conditions, but the most popular surf spots are:

Alii Beach Park

Laniakea

Chun's Reef

Ke Waena

Banzai Pipeline

Kammieland

Sunset Beach

Velzyland

For Snorkelers
The best snorkeling spots are:

Three Tables Beach

Shark's Cove

Kuilima Cove

For Families
Families with young children will enjoy:

Dole Pineapple Plantation

Basking Hawaiian sea turtles at Laniakea and Papailoa

Waimea Valley Historical Nature Park

Three Tables Beach and Waimea Beach Park in the summer

Kuilima Cove Beach and Hukilau Beach year-round

Keiki Rides at Happy Trails Hawaii and Gunstock Ranch

The Polynesian Cultural Center

Older kids and teenagers will enjoy:

Surfing lessons and competitions

Jumping off the rock at Waimea Bay Beach Park

Bodyboarding at Waimea Bay, Sunset, and Hukilau Beaches

Bodysurfing at Ehukai and Pounders Beaches

Snorkeling and scuba diving at
Three Tables Beach and Shark's Cove

Horseback riding at the Mokuleia Polo Ranch
and Happy Trails Hawaii

Mountain biking or hiking the Kaena Point,
Kaunala, and Hauula Loop Trails

Kua Aina's hamburgers

Ted's chocolate *haupia* (fresh coconut pudding) pie

For Foodies

Food freaks will not want to miss the following local specialties:

Chocolate covered pineapple at the Dole Pineapple Plantation

Shave ice at Matsumoto's or Aoki's

Huli-huli chicken fresh off the grill

Bento boxes

Hot malasadas from a Filipino lunch wagon

Cholo's Mexican food and margaritas

Ted's breakfast pastries, teriyaki beef, hot crab
and bacon sandwich, and chocolate *haupia* pie

The five-course tasting menu with
wine pairings at 21 Degrees North

Lei Lei's prime rib

Mai Tais at Tommy's Hang 10 Surf Bar on Kuilima Point at sunset

Fresh Kahuku corn, watermelon, and coconut from roadside stands

The garlic shrimp plate lunch from Giovanni's lunch wagon

The Portuguese sausage breakfast at the Hukilau Café

Poke (a raw fish dish) and sushi from Tamura's Market in Hauula
Kai Shopping Center

For Nature Lovers

The best places to enjoy northern Oahu's unique flora and fauna are:

Wahiawa Botanic Garden

Kaena Point Natural Area Refuge

Waimea Valley Historical Nature Park

Pupukea Beach Park

Kaunala Trail on Pupukea Ridge

James Campbell National Wildlife Refuge

Mokuauia Island Seabird Sanctuary (Goat Island)

Hauula Loop Trails

For History Buffs

Learn about the fascinating history of northern Oahu at:

Kukaniloko Birthing Stones

Tropic Lightning Museum at Schofield Army Barracks

Haleiwa Town

Pearl Harbor Air Tour from Dillingham Airfield and Gliderport

Hale O Lono Heiau

Waimea Valley Historical Nature Park

Puu O Mahuka Heiau State Monument

Huilua Fishpond National Historic Landmark

For Daredevils

We disclaim responsibility, but daredevils in search of thrills can:

Surf the famous "big surf" on the North Shore

Bodysurf at Pounders Beach

Kite surf and windsurf at Mokuleia

Try skydiving or acrobatic flying at Dillingham Airfield and Gliderport

Mountain bike down the Kealia Trail

Hike the Koloa Gulch Trail

Play polo with the pros at the Mokuleia Polo Club

For Lovers

Romance is sure to bloom when you

Take a sunset dinner cruise on a catamaran

Paddle a kayak for two up the Anahulu

Swim under a 45-foot waterfall in Waimea Valley or hike there under a full moon

Snorkel together at Three Tables and Shark's Cove

Watch the sun set at Sunset Beach or Kuilima Point

Share a romantic dinner at 29 Degrees North or Ola's

Beach comb along the deserted shoreline between Turtle Bay and Malaekahana

Swim or wade to Mokuauia to see the birds (and bees)

Enjoy a moonlight trail ride at the Gunstock Ranch or Turtle Bay Resort

Get married

SUGGESTED ITINERARIES

One Day

To see as much as possible in one day, take this circle tour and choose the stops you find most interesting.

- **Dole Pineapple Plantation:** Enjoy the train ride and a pineapple treat.
- **Haleiwa Town:** Browse the surf shops, art galleries and boutiques. Have a plate lunch or pick up a picnic to enjoy at Alii Beach Park, site of the first leg of the Triple Crown of Surfing. Stop at Matsumoto's or Aoki's for shave ice before crossing the Rainbow Bridge and heading up the famous North Shore.
- **Laniakea Beach:** See giant Hawaiian sea turtles basking in the afternoon sun. Remember Rule No. 9!
- **Waimea Valley Historical Nature Park:** Soak up the beauty and history of the exquisite Waimea Valley. Take the ¾ mile self-guided trail and swim under the 45-foot waterfall. Stop to see the Hale O Lono Heiau before you leave.
- **Waimea Bay Beach Park or Pupukea Beach Park:** Swim at Waimea Bay Beach Park or snorkel along the reef at Three Tables Beach or Shark's Cove. (You can rent snorkel equipment across the street).
- **The Banzai Pipeline:** Park at Ehukai Beach Park and walk down the beach to see the Banzai Pipeline, site of the Third Leg of the Triple Crown of Surfing.
- **Sunset Beach Park:** This famous two-mile long strand is the site of the Second Leg of the Triple Crown of Surfing.
- **Kahuku and Laie:**
- **Option 1-The Polynesian Cultural Center.** If time allows, stop to see Hukilau Beach and Laie Point. Arrive at the Polynesian Cultural Center by 5:30 p.m. for the Alii Luau (a *luau* is a traditional Hawaiian feast) and Polynesian Review,

"Horizons, Where The Sea Meets The Sky." If you want to see more of the Polynesian Cultural Center, buy a full-day package and return another day.

- **Option 2-Sunset And Dinner At Turtle Bay**. Make dinner reservations at 21 Degrees North, Ola's or Lei Lei's at the Turtle Bay Resort. Before dinner, explore the shoreline, browse the shops, enjoy the Hawaiian singers in the lobby, and watch the sunset from the Hang Ten Surf Bar on Kuilima Point.

- **Option 3-The Windward Shore**. Pick up a takeout dinner from Giovanni's Aloha Shrimp Truck, Laie Chop Suey, or Tamura's *poke* and sushi bar. See Hukilau Beach, Laie Point, and Pounders Beach. Picnic at Kokololio Beach Park and enjoy the scenic drive down the Windward Shore.

- **At Day's End:** Either retrace your route back along the North Shore or continue south down the Kam Highway to H-3 and return to your starting point.

One Weekend

Reserve a condo or hotel room at Turtle Bay or a beachside cottage, get tickets to the Polynesian Cultural Center for Saturday, and start out as early as possible on Friday.

Friday Afternoon-Evening

Tourist Version

- **The Dole Pineapple Plantation:** Enjoy the train ride and a pineapple treat.
- **The Kukaniloko Birthing Stones:** See the sacred stones where noble Hawaiian women gave birth to the islands' royal children. Remember Rule No. 9.
- **Haleiwa Town:** Browse the surf shops, surf museums, art galleries, and boutiques, then enjoy a leisurely dinner in Haleiwa or pick up some *huli-huli* chicken (chicken marinated and grilled in a delicious sauce made with lime juice, soy sauce, and other ingredients) and enjoy a picnic at Alii Beach Park.
- **Plans:** Get any rental gear and reservations needed for your weekend activities.
- **Sunset:** Watch the sunset from Jameson's patio or Haleiwa Beach Park.

Surf And Turf Version

- **Surf:** Head straight to Haleiwa and catch some waves at Alii Beach Park, Laniakea, or Chun's Reef.
- **Haleiwa Town:** Browse the surf shops and have dinner.
- **Plans:** Get the surf report and any rental gear you need for the weekend.
- **Sunset:** Watch the sunset from Jameson's patio or Haleiwa Beach Park.

Saturday

Tourist Version

- **Morning:**
- From April to October, enjoy swimming and snorkeling on the North Shore. Have an early breakfast at Ted's Bakery, then snorkel along the reef with schools of colorful tropical fish at Shark's Cove or Three Tables or enjoy swimming, bodyboarding, and bodysurfing at Sunset Beach.
- From October through April, the ocean is calmer on the Windward Shore. Have a local-style breakfast at the Hukilau Café, then enjoy swimming, bodyboarding, and bodysurfing at Hukilau Beach or go to Malaekahana State Recreation Area and swim or wade to Mokuauia (Goat Island) to see the birds.
- **Lunch:**
- Have a plate lunch at Ted's Bakery or Giovanni's Aloha Shrimp Truck. For an upscale lunch, try Ola's or Lei Lei's at the Turtle Bay Resort.
- **Afternoon:**
- Drive out to Laie Point for spectacular scenery and photographs. Remember Rule No. 5. Follow the Drive Guide down the Windward Shore from Laie to Kaaawa.
- **Late Afternoon And Evening:**
- **Option 1-The Polynesian Cultural Center:** Return to Laie by 2:30-3:00 p.m., tour the villages, see the IMAX movie, and enjoy the Alii Luau and Polynesian review.
- Alternative: spend more time touring, hiking, or swimming along the Windward Shore and arrive at the Polynesian Cultural Center by 5:30 p.m. for the Alii Luau and Polynesian review.
- **Option 2-Sunset And Dinner At Turtle Bay:** For a nice restaurant meal, make a reservation at 21 Degrees North, Ola's or Lei Lei's at the Turtle Bay Resort. Before dinner, explore the shoreline, browse the shops, enjoy the Hawaiian

entertainment in the lobby, and watch the sunset at the Hang Ten Surf Bar on Kuilima Point.

- **Option 3-Sunset At Pupukea:** Drive up the Pupukea Ridge, visit the Puu O Mahuka Heiau State Monument, and watch the sun set over Waimea Bay. Pick up a healthy dinner of skewers and salad at Shark's Cove Grill and walk across the street to the lawn above Pupukea Beach Park to enjoy a picnic supper with an exquisite view.
- **Option 4-Evening Trail Ride:** Take a dinner or moonlight trail ride at Gunstock Ranch or Turtle Bay Resort.
- **Nightcap:** If you are in the mood for a nightcap, stop at 21 Degrees North, Ola's, the Bay Club, or Lei Lei's on the way back to your condo, hotel or cottage.

Surf and Turf Version

- **Morning:** Surf lessons or surfing on the North Shore. If there's no surf, try bodyboarding or bodysurfing at Ehukai, Sunset or Pounders.
- **Afternoon:** Hiking or mountain biking on the Kaunala Trail or Hauula Loop Trails; golf or tennis at the Turtle Bay Resort; or horseback riding at Happy Trails Hawaii, Gunstock Ranch, or the Turtle Bay Resort.

Sunday

Tourist Version

- **Morning:**
- Attend an early church service and have breakfast at Ted's Bakery or Shark's Cove Grill. Arrive at Waimea Bay Beach Park by 9:15 a.m. for a parking space. Visit the memorial to Eddie Aikau. If the water is calm, enjoy swimming, jumping off Jumping Rock, and spotting sea turtles and spinner dolphins. If the surf is up, watch the action at Waimea, Banzai Pipeline, and Sunset, then head to Kuilima Cove or Haleiwa Beach Park for a swim.

- Alternative: sleep in and have a great Sunday brunch at the Turtle Bay Resort, Jameson's, or the Haleiwa Café.
- **Lunch:**
- Drive up Waimea Valley and have lunch at the Waimea Grill. Soak up the beauty and history of this exquisite valley. Take the self-guided trail to the 45-foot waterfall and have a swim in the pond. Stop to see the Hale O Lono Heiau.
- **Afternoon:**
- Stop at Laniakea to see the *honu* basking in the afternoon sun. Remember Rule No. 9. Get a shave ice at Matsumoto's. Follow the Drive Guide from Haleiwa to Mokuleia.
- **Option 1-Mokuleia:** Between April and October, enjoy the Sunday polo match at the Mokuleia Polo Field. From October to April, try horseback riding along the beach with Hawaii Polo Oceanfront Trail Rides at the polo club's 100-acre waterfront ranch. Watch the colorful kitesurfers and windsurfers off Mokuleia Beach Park. Take a glider ride or air tour at Dillingham Airfield and Gliderport.
- **Option 2-Waialua Bay:** Rent a kayak and paddle around Waialua Bay, or take a chartered boat trip from the Haleiwa Boat Harbor. Watch the sunset from Jameson's patio or take a sunset cruise on a catamaran.
- **Evening:**
- Have dinner in Haleiwa or Mililani Town.

Surf And Turf Version

- **Morning:** Hike or bike around Kaena Point, go surfing on the North Shore, or try kite surfing or windsurfing at Mokuleia.
- **Afternoon:** Take a snorkel, dive or fishing trip from Haleiwa Harbor. Try an acrobatic airplane ride, glider lessons, or skydiving at Dillingham Airfield and Gliderport.

One Week

Plan your time for maximum enjoyment of each area,
choosing the activities and attractions that interest you most.

Sunday

Escape the weekend crowds on the secluded Northwestern
Shore or a chartered boat.

Tourist Version

- **Haleiwa Boat Harbor:** Take a dive boat, snorkeling excursion, fishing charter, whalewatching expedition, or eco-tour from Haleiwa Boat Harbor.
- **Alii Beach Park:** Surf, take a surfing lesson, or watch the surfing action at Alii Beach Park, where the Hawaiian *alii* (persons of royal or noble ancestry) once surfed. If there's no surf, enjoy swimming and bodyboarding.
- **Waialua Bay:** Rent a kayak and paddle up the Anahulu or around Waialua Bay. If a kayak is too tame for you, rent a jet ski.
- **The Northwestern Shore:** Follow the Drive Guide from Haleiwa to Kaena.
- **Mokuleia Polo Field:** From April to Labor Day, enjoy a great lunch and polo match at the Mokuleia Polo Field. From September to March, have lunch in Haleiwa and then head to the Mokuleia Polo Field for polo or riding lessons or a trail ride along the beach.
- **Mokuleia Beach Park:** Watch the kitesurfers and windsurfers at Mokuleia.
- **Dillingham Airfield and Gliderport:** Take a thrilling glider ride or air tour.
- **Kaiaka Bay Beach Park:** Take a leisurely walk, jog, or bike ride around the loop at Kaiaka Bay Beach Park. See the balancing stone known as Pohaku Lanai and enjoy the view of

the old Waialua Sugar Mill, the shoreline curving out to Kaena Point, and Mount Kaala, the highest point on Oahu.

- Watch the sun set from Jameson's patio or Haleiwa Beach Park, and have dinner in Haleiwa Town.

Surf and Turf Version

- **Hike or bike**: The Kaena Point Trail.
- **Dive**: Kahuna Canyon.
- **Kitesurf or windsurf**: Mokuleia Beach Park.
- **Take flight**: try gliding, acrobatic air tours, or skydiving at Dillingham Airfield and Gliderport.

Note: If you are staying at Turtle Bay, another way to avoid the weekend crowds is to spend the day there. Swim and snorkel at Kuilima Cove, explore the five miles of secluded shoreline between Turtle Bay and Malaekahana, kayak or walk to Kawela Bay, golf, play tennis, go horseback riding, indulge in a spa treatment, and enjoy Hawaiian music and fine dining.

Monday

Enjoy The Dole Plantation And Haleiwa Town On Their Quietest Day

Tourist Version

- **The Dole Pineapple Plantation:** Enjoy the train ride, take the plantation garden tour, see the world's largest maze, and have a pineapple treat.
- **Wahiawa Botanic Garden:** Take a guided tour of this 27-acre collection of tropical plants that thrive in the cool, shady habitat of a tropical rain forest.
- **Kukaniloko Birthing Stones:** Stop to see the sacred stones that were the site of royal births for eight centuries. Remember Rule No. 9.
- **Old Haleiwa Town:** Follow the Drive Guide through Haleiwa Town, then browse the surf shops, surf museums, art galleries, and boutiques, and enjoy a leisurely lunch.

Visit Liliuokalani Church and stop at Matsumoto's or Aoki's for their famous shave ice.

- **Waialua Town:** Follow the Drive Guide to the old plantation town of Waialua and see the picturesque sugar mill that powered the local economy for 100 years.

- **Alii Beach Park and Haleiwa Boat Harbor:** Surf or take a surfing lesson at Alii Beach Park, or relax and swim on the shady south side of Waialua Beach.

- **Laniakea and Papailoa:** Pick up a fresh flower *lei* (a flower garland worn around the neck) at Alluvion Nursery (before 3:30 p.m.). See the basking sea turtles at Laniakea Beach. Take a walk on Papailoa Beach.

- **Waialua Bay.** Watch the sun set over Waialua Bay as the outrigger canoes return to shore, or rent a kayak and paddle up the Anahulu or around Waialua Bay as evening falls.

Surf and Turf Version

- **Surf:** Alii, Laniakea, or Chun's Reef.
- **Hike or bike:** The Kealia Trail.

Tuesday

Enjoy Hawaii's Natural Beauty At Spectacular Waimea Bay And Waimea Valley. Call the Waimea Valley Historical Nature Park in advance for the schedule of guided tours and other events.

Tourist Version

- **Waimea Bay Beach Park:** Arrive at Waimea Bay Beach Park by 9:15 a.m. for a parking space, or take The Bus. See the memorial to Eddie Aikau. If the water is calm, enjoy swimming, jumping off Jumping Rock, and spotting turtles and spinner dolphins. If the surf is up, watch the action at Waimea, Banzai Pipeline, and Sunset, then head to Kuilima Cove or Haleiwa Beach Park to swim. Remember Rule No. 1 and get out of the sun by noon.

- **Waimea Valley Historical Nature Park:** Drive or walk up Waimea Valley and have lunch at the Waimea Grill. Take a guided tour or follow the self-guided trail to the 45-foot waterfall. Bring your bathing suit and enjoy a swim in the pond.
- **Hale O Lono Heiau:** Visit the restored *heiau* at the end of the Waimea Valley parking lot.

Surf and Turf Version
- **Surf:** Board surf, bodysurf or bodyboard at Waimea, Ke Waena, Banzai Pipeline, Ehukai, or Sunset. Paddle a kayak or paddleboard from Waimea to Kuilima Point.
- **Golf:** The Fazio Course at the Turtle Bay Resort.

Wednesday
Visit The Polynesian Cultural Center Mid-Week When It Is Less Crowded.

Tourist Version
- **The Hukilau Café:** Follow the Drive Guide to Laie, enjoy a local-style breakfast at the Hukilau Café, talk story with the locals, and don't miss the photos of local heroes and *hukilaus* (traditional community net fishing).
- **Malaekahana State Recreation Area and Mokuauia Bird Sanctuary (Goat Island):** Enjoy the white sand, tree fringed beach at Malaekahana State Recreation Area, then wade or swim over to Mokuauia Island Seabird Sanctuary, commonly known as Goat Island. Take a hike around the island to see the birds. Have a swim at lovely Mokuaula Beach on the leeward side of Mokuauia before returning to Malaekahana.
- **Hukilau Beach:** With lovely white sand and a bottom as flat as a floor, this is an ideal beach for young children, especially on the southern end where the houses are.
- **Giovanni's Aloha Shrimp Truck:** Stop at Giovanni's Aloha Shrimp Truck for a plate lunch.

- **Laie Point:** Drive up to Laie Point for spectacular scenery and photographs.
- **The Polynesian Cultural Center:** Arrive by 2:00 p.m. to tour the villages and see the canoe pageant and IMAX movie. Stay for the Alii Luau and Polynesian review.
- **Option 1:** Take a dinner or moonlight trail ride at Gunstock Ranch.
- **Option 2:** Pick up takeout food in the Laie Village Shopping Center, have a picnic and swim at Hukilau Beach or Pounders Beach, and/or see a movie at the Laie Theater.

Surf and Turf Version
- **Surf:** Bodyboarding and bodysurfing at Pounders Beach
- **Golf:** Kahuku Golf Course
- **Hiking or Mountain Biking:** The Laie Trail, Koloa Gulch Trail, or Maakua Gulch Trail.

Thursday
Visit The Famous Surfing And Snorkeling Spots On The North Shore.

Tourist Version
- **Pupukea Beach Park:** Swim and snorkel along the reef at Three Tables Beach or Shark's Cove.
- **Ke Ala Pupukea Bike Path:** Rent a bike and pedal along the North Shore from Pupukea to Velzyland and back.
- **Shark's Cove Grill:** Enjoy a healthy plate lunch of teriyaki skewers and salad.
- **Sunset:** Follow the Drive Guide along the North Shore from Pupukea to Turtle Bay. Stop to see the famous surf spots along the way. In the summer, swim and snorkel at Sunset Beach Park. In the winter, see the surfing action at the Banzai Pipeline and Sunset Beach and swim at Kuilima Cove or Hukilau Beach.
- **Turtle Bay:** Park at the resort and walk along the shoreline to Malaekahana. Have a swim, and take The Bus back

to Turtle Bay. Enjoy the resort's Hawaiian entertainers and watch the sunset from Kuilima Point.

Surf and Turf Version

- **Surf:** Board surfing and bodysurfing at the Banzai Pipeline, Sunset Beach or Velzyland.
- **Golf:** The Palmer Course at the Turtle Bay Resort.
- **Biking:** Kahuku Motocross Park.

Friday

Enjoy Spectacular Mountains, Waterfalls And Beaches On The Windward Shore.

Tourist Version

- **The Hauula Loop Trails:** Follow the Drive Guide to Hauula and hike one of the beautiful Hauula Loop Trails. Bring your bathing suit and have a refreshing swim under a sparkling waterfall.
- **Hauula Seafood Restaurant and Bar or Papa Ole's:** Enjoy a local-style plate lunch.
- **Kokololio Beach Park:** Relax, sunbathe, and swim at beautiful Kokololio Beach Park.
- **The Windward Shore:** Follow the Drive Guide to Kaaawa, stopping to see the historic churches, art galleries, Kahana Bay, Huilua Fishpond, and the Koa and Kilo Loop Trail.
- **Option 1:** If your package to the Polynesian Cultural Center includes a return visit, you can see what you missed on your first trip today.
- **Option 2:** Attend the Voyages of Polynesia Luau at the Turtle Bay Resort.

Surf And Turf Version

- **Surf:** Fish and kayak along Kahana Bay and explore the Huilua Fishpond.

- **Hiking and Biking:** Take a hike or mountain bike deep into the historic Kahana Valley.

Saturday
Natural Beauty And Dramatic History Await On Pupukea Ridge. End The Week With Sweet Aloha.

Tourist Version
- **The Kaunala Trail:** Follow the Drive Guide up the Pupukea Ridge. Hike or bike the Kaunala Trail, which is only open to the public on weekends.
- **Happy Trails Hawaii:** Explore the beautiful Pupukea Ridge on horseback with Happy Trails Hawaii.
- **Puu O Mahuka Heiau State Monument:** Visit this important Hawaiian religious site. Remember Rule No. 9. Don't miss the sweeping views of Waimea Bay and the North Shore from the *heiau.*
- **Last Chance:** It's your last day in northern Oahu! This is your last chance to take that surf lesson, glider ride, or snorkeling tour you've been talking about all week. If you've been working up the courage to jump off Jumping Rock or ask your sweetheart to marry you, today's the day! Whatever you wanted to do and didn't, do it now! Or return to your favorite place—for us that means swimming across Waimea Bay or snorkeling at Three Tables or Shark's Cove.
- **Sweet *Aloha*:** Soak up the *aloha* of northern Oahu and her people and carry it home in your heart.

Surf and Turf Version
- **Surf:** Wherever the surf is up.
- **Hiking or Biking:** The Kaunala Trail

A Dozen Things To Do On A Rainy Day

1. Drive down the Windward Shore to see the waterfalls cascading off the Koolau Mountains.

2. Browse the shops at the Polynesian Cultural Center. You can stroll through the shopping area near the entrance without paying for admission to the villages. Watch local artisans practice traditional crafts. Pick up some books and videos about Polynesian cultures and enjoy them.

3. Tour the art galleries, surf museums, surf shops, and boutiques in Haleiwa.

4. Get a massage at the Kaala Healing Arts Center in Haleiwa or the Spa Luana at the Turtle Bay Resort.

5. Relax over afternoon tea or a glass of wine and enjoy the Hawaiian entertainment in the beautiful lobby of the Turtle Bay Resort.

6. Buy a twilight package to the Polynesian Cultural Center and enjoy the IMAX movie, shops, dinner, and fabulous Polynesian Review.

7. If there is no thunder or lightning, go for a swim.

8. Go to the library in Kahuku or Waialua. If you have children, take them to the story hour.

9. Visit the Waialua District Park for a workout, indoor sport, or other activity, or visit one of the local fitness facilities and get some exercise.

10. See a movie at the Laie Theater.

11. If you are up for a drive, you can find a wide selection of movies and restaurants at the Mililani Shopping Center. In Honolulu, you can tour the Bishop Museum, 1525 Bernice Street, Honolulu, telephone 847-3511, the premier institution of natural and cultural history of Hawaii. Be sure to see the show on Hawaiian star navigation techniques in the Museum's Planetarium. Or visit the Waikiki Aquarium (telephone 923-9741, open daily 9:00 a.m. to 5:00 p.m. except Christmas and

New Year's Day). Other indoor activities in Honolulu include the Contemporary Museum, telephone 526-0232; the Damien Museum and Archives, telephone 923-2690; the Iolani Palace, and shopping at Ala Moana Mall or Ward's Center.

12. Take a nap!

Dreamy Things To Do Under A Full Moon

1. Go for a moonlight sail on a catamaran.
2. Take a moonlight horseback ride at Turtle Bay Resort or Gunstock Ranch.
3. Join the guided moonlight hike in Waimea Valley on the Friday nearest the full moon.
4. Enjoy a picnic dinner and watch the sun set, the stars come out, and that big beautiful moon come up over the endless ocean.

TRAVEL TIPS

Climate

There are two seasons in northern Oahu: summer and winter. From April through October, the weather is dry and temperatures along the shore are in the 80s during the day and the 70s overnight. Trade winds blow steadily from the southeast, cooling the coast and creating clouds and occasional rain over the mountains. The ocean is generally calm.

From November through March, the weather is wetter and temperatures along the shore are in the 70s and low 80s during the day and the 60s and low 70s at night. Ocean waves roll along the reefs and beaches. The world-famous big surf arrives when storms in the Arctic produce large ocean swells that move across the Pacific with nothing to stop them until they reach the North Shore. When these deep-water swells hit the shoreline, they jump up to two or three times their size, creating spectacular breakers and tubes. Areas that are unprotected from the open ocean, such as Waimea Bay and Sunset Beach, sometimes have stupendous waves that only the most experienced and daring surfers can ride. At the same time, beaches with protective reefs or different exposures remain safe for swimming and other activities. Each day and place is unique due to the differences in wind and water conditions, the formations below the surface, and the shape and angle of the shoreline.

The weather varies with the terrain. The Windward Shore tends to be wetter and cooler than the North Shore, especially during the winter. The rain that falls in the Koolau Mountains produces lush vegetation and waterfalls that cascade down the steep slopes toward the sea. When it is rainy or cloudy on the Windward Shore, try a beach on the North Shore. If it is raining on the North Shore, go a few miles up the road.

Clothing

When packing for a vacation in northern Oahu, forget what you usually wear at home. Leave jeans, sweaters, and heavy knits behind. You will be more comfortable in cool cottons and cotton blends. Bathing suits, shorts, shirts, and sandals will be the mainstay of your wardrobe. Gentlemen do not need jackets and ties; a nice *aloha* shirt (a shirt made of cotton or other natural fibers with an island print or design, worn outside the belt) is suitable anywhere. Ladies may want to bring a few nice sundresses, with a light cotton sweater or wrap to cover your shoulders in the evening breeze. Don't forget hats, sunglasses and sunscreen for sun protection. Water shoes or reef walkers may come in handy. If you plan to spend time in the mountains, add walking shoes or hiking boots, a rain parka, and mosquito repellent. Depending on your plans, you may want to bring golf, tennis, snorkeling, diving, fishing or other sports clothing and equipment. Don't over pack—you can rent whatever equipment you need and you will certainly want to do a little shopping for some lovely island clothing.

Culture

The more you experience the unique, multiethnic culture of northern Oahu, the more you will enjoy your visit. Pick up some CDs by Hawaiian artists (for example, Amy Hanaialii Gilliom or Alfred Apaka) or tune your car radio to a station that plays Hawaiian music. Buy some beautiful *aloha* clothing and wear a flower *lei*. Instead of hamburgers, French fries, and pizza, sample Hawaiian plate lunches, teriyaki chicken, Korean barbecue, chili rice, Portuguese sausage, *haupia*, shave ice, tropical fruits, and other local specialties. Look for lunch trucks, shrimp trucks, and little markets, which go back to the days when North Shore residents bought their food from wagons and mom and pop stores near their homes. Treat yourself to a *luau*. Attend art festivals, hula contests, and other local events. Strike up conversations with local residents. Learn about Polynesian culture at the Waimea Valley Historical Nature Park and Polynesian Cultural Center. Go to a surf competition, visit the surf museums in Haleiwa, and talk to the surfers on the North Shore. Better yet, go surfing!

Activities

Northern Oahu is famous for its fabulous beaches and miles of unspoiled shoreline. All of the beaches are open to the public. Even where the shoreline has been developed, public rights of way provide access for everyone. There are endless opportunities for water sports: swimming, snorkeling, scuba diving, surfing, bodysurfing, windsurfing, kite surfing, paddle boarding, kayaking, canoeing, sailing, boating, and fishing. Surf competitions offer unique spectacles. The shoreline teems with sea life, including humpback whales, spinner dolphins, sea turtles, monk seals, and endless varieties of tropical fish. Whale watching, turtle and dolphin tours, dive boats, fishing charters, snorkeling expeditions, and eco-tours are all available at Haleiwa Boat Harbor.

Numerous land-based activities are also available. Golfers will find excellent courses where PGA and LPGA tournaments are held. Golf Channel.com filmed *The Big Break* at the Turtle Bay Resort in 2006. Seaside and mountain trails beckon hikers and bikers. Extensive equestrian facilities are located along the seashore and mountainsides, and polo matches are held every Sunday from April through October. Tennis courts dot the landscape. Gliding, skydiving, hang-gliding, and air tours in small planes and helicopters offer thrilling views of spectacular scenery. Botanical gardens hold fascinating varieties of tropical plants and birds. Many sites and traditions of ancestral Hawaiian life have been preserved. Waimea Valley Historical Nature Park and the Polynesian Cultural Center provide fabulous opportunities to learn about the cultures of Hawaii and Polynesia. The Dole

Pineapple Plantation, Tropic Lightning Museum, and other historic sites offer insights to plantation life and military history. Tourists can enjoy watching everything from humpback whales, spinner dolphins, basking sea turtles, and exotic birds to golf tournaments, surf competitions, television and movie shoots, and visiting celebrities. With its spectacular scenery, northern Oahu has been the setting for numerous television shows and movies, including *Lost, Baywatch Hawaii, North Shore, George of the Jungle,* and the classic *From Here to Eternity.*

On this side of Oahu, art galleries, surf shops, boutiques, restaurants, and *luaus* can all be enjoyed at a leisurely pace, free of the crowds and commercialism of Waikiki. The award-winning Spa Luana and other health spas offer refreshing opportunities for physical and spiritual renewal. Evenings bring spectacular sunsets, star-filled skies, moonlit walks, interesting dining experiences, Polynesian entertainment, and occasional live music at local nightspots.

HISTORY

Hawaii offers a unique glimpse of an environment that is still being formed. The islands are the peaks of huge undersea volcanoes that were fueled by primeval fires deep within the earth. Over the course of eons, the sea floor shifted to the southeast over the magma below, and the area of volcanic activity moved with it. As new volcanoes erupted, weather and waves eroded the older islands into a string of islets, atolls and rocks. Of the 132 volcanic islands in the Hawaiian archipelago, only the youngest eight are large enough to be inhabited. The youngest of the eight inhabited islands, the Big Island of Hawaii, continues to grow as the volcanic eruptions of Kilauea build new land. Southeast of the Big Island, a new island named Loihi is being formed under the sea. Today, the Hawaiian archipelago sprawls across 1,400 miles—the distance from Chicago to Miami. In addition to the islands and a string of atolls, it includes 4,500 square miles of underwater coral reef.

As millennia passed, soil slowly formed from the volcanic rock. Certain plants and animals managed to cross the vast ocean to the older islands, then made the shorter inter-island jump to Oahu. With a range of habitats stretching from tropical rain forests to sun-kissed shores, northern Oahu gradually became the home of a vast array of ferns, flowering plants, invertebrates, birds, stream life, and Hawaii's only native land mammal, the rarely seen hoary bat. Some of the species that evolved in this isolated archipelago exist nowhere else on earth.

The Polynesians

Hawaii's human history is as unique as its geological history. Approximately 2,000 years ago, Polynesians migrated to the Hawaiian Islands in double-hulled sailing canoes, probably from the Marquesas and Tahiti. To insure their survival, they brought plants and animals from their home islands. Eventually, some of these Polynesian settlers crossed the channel from Kauai to northern Oahu. These early Hawaiians did not believe in the private ownership of land. Lacking metal, they followed a cooperative subsistence lifestyle, sharing abundant harvests from the land and sea.

The Hawaiians had a highly developed, feudal type of social order. Islands were divided into districts called *moku*, which were ruled by *alii* chiefs. The *moku* were in turn divided into land divisions called *ahupuaa*, which were managed by *konohiki* (headmen appointed by the chiefs). Each *ahupuaa* was a wedge of land extending from the mountains to the sea, containing all of the resources needed for the subsistence of its inhabitants. The *alii* and *konohiki* took part of the farming and fishing harvests as tribute.

Chiefs derived their *mana* (power) from the gods and maintained the social order through the enforcement of strict *kapu* (rules establishing prohibited conduct, or taboos). *Kapu* controlled all facets of life, including politics, religion, sex, property, food, and even play. To violate a *kapu*, even accidentally, was to forfeit the right to live.. High-ranking chiefs could demand the *kapu moe,* requiring commoners to prostrate themselves in the chief's presence.

Because bloodlines determined rank, genealogy was a crucial element of wealth and power. Incest was practiced among the *alii* as a means of purifying their bloodlines and maintaining their godly status, rights over commoners, and ranking within the *alii* class. Generally, marital relationships were polygamous and sexual mores were relaxed, but chiefs could impose restrictions by placing a *kapu* on certain conduct.

During the 12th century A.D., a great spiritual leader named Paao introduced the use of stone terraces and walls for *heiau* (sacred sites used for religious ceremonies). Paao established a priesthood that endured for centuries. *Kahuna* (priests) were trained to conduct religious ceremonies as well as other important functions, such as medicine. The chief appointed a *kahuna nui* (chief priest) to take care of spiritual matters and enforce the *kapu*.

Heiau played a pivotal role in Hawaiian spiritual life. The word *hei* means to summon, to capture or ensnare. The word *au* implies a vibration, current, invisible energy, or power. A *heiau* was a place dedicated to capture spiritual power, or *mana*. Some *heiau* were elaborately constructed stone platforms enshrining *kii akua* (tiki gods or idols), while others were simple earthen terraces.

Kapu restricted the role of women of all ranks. Females were prohibited from entering the *luakini heiau*, where political and religious decisions were made, and from participating in certain activities. Only men could enjoy certain foods, and men and boys over seven years of age ate separately from the women and girls.

In the 15th century, the chief of Oahu divided the island into six *moku* (districts). Northern Oahu was divided in two: Waialua *moku* included northwestern Oahu from Kaena Point to the southern edge of Waimea Bay, and Koolauloa *moku* included northeastern Oahu from Waimea Bay to Kaaawa. These traditional boundaries and place names continue today as the Districts of Waialua and Koolauloa, with two changes: Waimea has been placed in the Waialua District, and a new Wahiawa District has been created in the central plateau south of Waialua and Koolauloa.

The Arrival Of The Haoles

When British Captain James Cook arrived on the Big Island in 1778, the Hawaiian Islands entered a period of unalterable change. Although Cook was killed in an altercation with the natives, his arrival marked the beginning of the end of the traditional Hawaiian way of life. *Haoles* (foreigners from Western countries) soon descended on the islands, bringing weapons that altered the Hawaiian form of government, diseases that decimated the Hawaiian population, and religious and commercial values that profoundly changed the Hawaiian culture.

The Hawaiian Kingdom

When the Hawaiian chiefs saw the Western weapons and other metal objects on Cook's ships, they immediately grasped their importance. Kamehameha I, chief of the Big Island, acquired *haole* firearms, ammunition, and advisors. With these military advantages, he methodically conquered the other islands, united them for the first time, and became the first "King" of the "Kingdom of Hawaii" in 1795. Kamehameha's descendants succeeded him as monarchs.

Unfortunately, the *haoles* brought more than new technology. The native population was devastated by diseases that were previously unknown in the islands: measles, mumps, influenza, smallpox, typhoid, and venereal diseases. Historians estimate that 75 per cent of the Hawaiian people died from foreign diseases in the decades following Western contact.

During this period, Western traders discovered that northern Oahu's forests contained sandalwood, a fragrant wood that was in great demand in China. King Kamehameha I and his successors granted the foreigners rights to the sandalwood in return for a portion of the proceeds. The king allowed the forests to be burned to expose the aromatic sandalwood, and required the commoners to leave their fields and fishing to harvest the precious wood. This sustained the solvency of the Kingdom at tremendous cost to the local population. Soon the forest canopy was gone, leaving the villages and farmland vulnerable to erosion and flooding.

The Hawaiian people suffered another blow when Kamehameha I died in 1819 and his son, Liholiho (Kamehameha II), became king. Under the influence of the high chiefess Kaahumanu (Kamehameha's favorite among his 21 wives), Liholiho abandoned the *kapu* system, abolished the traditional religion, and ordered all the *kii akua* destroyed. Many Hawaiians clung to their ancient beliefs, but the abolition of the *kapu* system and old religion, together with the onslaught of Western diseases and deforestation of the land, severely affected their traditional way of life.

Between 1820 and 1848, 12 companies of Calvinist missionaries came to Hawaii from Boston to convert the natives, who were literally left "godless" by Liholiho's abolition of their traditional religion.

In addition to converting many Hawaiians to Christianity, the New England missionaries and their descendants had an enormous impact on the islands. By the end of the 19th century, economic and political power over the islands was concentrated in five conglomerates known as the "Big Five," which were largely controlled by the American missionaries and their descendants.

Control over Hawaii's land changed dramatically in what is called the *Great Mahele* of 1848–1850. Breaking with tradition, Liholiho's successor, King Kamehameha III, gave up his rights to all the lands of the kingdom except for certain estates reserved as "crown lands." Chiefs were allowed to acquire fee simple titles to the lands they held in fief as retainers of the king. Commoners were allowed to purchase small lots, or *kuleanas,* in fee simple. However, both chiefs and commoners had to perfect their titles by having their lands surveyed and paying fees. Most chiefs paid their fees in land, which became government land. For the commoners, the fees, paperwork, and even the concept of private title to ancestral land were a real hurdle to acquiring ownership. In the end, only about 30,000 acres went to commoners, compared to almost a million acres for the crown, 1.5 million acres for chiefs, and 1.5 million acres for government land.

In 1850, foreigners were given the opportunity to purchase land on the same terms as natives. With the Hawaiian population decimated by Western diseases, this laid the way for huge tracts to pass into the hands of *haole* planters and developers. By 1893, *haoles* had sufficient strength to overthrow the Hawaiian monarchy and establish the "Republic of Hawaii." Five years later, this short-lived Republic was annexed as a territory of the United States. In 1959, Hawaii became the 50th state of the United States of America.

The Plantation Era

The development of northern Oahu was facilitated by the construction of a railroad system that nearly circled the island. Hawaii's seventh monarch, King David Kalakaua, was a great proponent of modernization. In 1878 he signed the Railway Act, which authorized the taking of land to create rights of way for railroads.

A *haole* entrepreneur named Benjamin Dillingham seized this opportunity. He formed the Oahu Railway and Land Company (the "OR&L"), leased large tracts of land, and sold bonds to finance the construction of a railroad. Between 1886 and 1899, the OR&L built tracks from Honolulu up the Leeward Shore, around Kaena Point, and along the northern coastline all the way to Kahuku. Before long, the OR&L was hauling sugar cane to Honolulu from nine sugar plantations—some of them Dillingham's.

Then Dillingham persuaded Castle & Cooke, a well-financed member of the "Big Five," to take over a struggling sugar plantation in Waialua. As the 19th century came to a close, Castle & Cooke formed the Waialua Agricultural Company, acquired additional land, created a reliable water supply, constructed a modern sugar mill, and started cultivating sugar on a large scale. Before long, the deforested fields of Waialua were filled with sugar cane.

At the same time James Castle, a principal of Castle and Cooke, undertook the development of the Windward Shore. Castle started the Kahuku Sugar Plantation on land he subleased from Dillingham. Little by little, he extended the Kahuku Plantation until its cane fields stretched down the Windward Shore. He also extended the island's railroad system by building the Koolau Railroad from the terminus of the OR&L in Kahuku down the Windward Shore to Kahana Bay. His goal was to extend the Koolau all the way to Honolulu so that the railroad system circled the entire island. Castle died without completing that dream, but the construction of the railroad from Honolulu to Kahana Bay opened all of northern Oahu to development as he had planned. Wealthy residents of Honolulu built second homes along the shoreline and tourists flocked to hotels and golf courses.

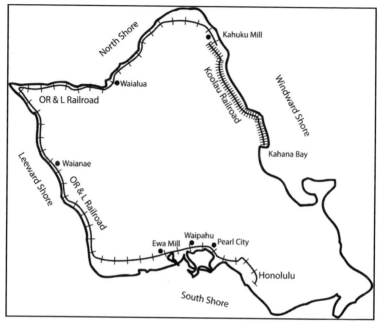

OR&L and Koolau Railroads, early 20ᵗʰ century

One resource northern Oahu lacked was an economical labor force. Foreign diseases, floods, famines, and other misfortunes had decimated the Hawaiian population. Even if the surviving Hawaiians had been willing to work under early plantation conditions, there were simply too few of them. From 1906 to 1946, agents of the Waialua and Kahuku Plantations made regular trips—first to China, then to Korea, Portugal, Japan, and the Philippines—to recruit plantation laborers. The workers were housed in camps that functioned as self-contained communities.

This immigrant pool produced a multiethnic society blending Asian and Western cultures. Each ethnic group brought its own religious and cultural traditions, which combined to produce a rich cultural broth. In northern Oahu today, no single ethnic group constitutes a majority. Everyone is a minority.

After the attack on Pearl Harbor on December 7, 1941, Oahu played a pivotal role in World War II. Hawaii was placed under martial law, and served as the headquarters for the War in the Pacific. Over 30,000 Hawaiians served in the Armed Forces, including the famous Japanese-American 100th Infantry Battalion and 442nd Regimental Combat Team. Together the 100th and 442nd won seven presidential unit citations and almost 6,000 individual awards for bravery. The role of Hawaii and her people in World War II broke down racial and social divisions in the islands and paved the way for statehood.

More changes lay in store for northern Oahu. Throughout the war, Oahu's railroads hauled passengers, freight, and war materiel around the clock. But after the war, the railroads could no longer compete with motor vehicles. The last train to northern Oahu ran in 1947.

Tourism And Surfing

For a time, northern Oahu returned to a quiet agricultural area. Then, the era of jet transportation arrived, bringing thousands of tourists and surfers to the fabulous beaches and surf of the North Shore.

The development of the Turtle Bay Resort and Polynesian Cultural Center attracted tourists. Surf contests, golf tournaments, movies and television shows revealed the beauty of northern Oahu to people all over the world. Veterans who visited the area during their military service returned to vacation or retire.

While tourism grew, the sugar industry declined. As a global economy emerged in the late 20th century, Hawaiian sugar produced under American labor laws had difficulty competing with the sugar products of underdeveloped countries. By the year 2000, all of the sugar mills on Oahu were closed and the cane fields lay fallow or were turned to other crops. The lovely hillsides that were once covered with sugar cane are being converted to coffee, papaya, mango, lichee, taro, seed corn, sweet corn, flowers, and other crops tended by northern Oahu's newest immigrants—Vietnamese and Laotians. As the 21st century unfolds, northern Oahu remains a uniquely beautiful place, graced with incredible natural beauty, a multicultural heritage, and true *aloha*.

State And County Government

Unlike other states, Hawaii has only two levels of government—state and county. There are no municipal governments. The City and County of Honolulu is a single entity that governs the entire island of Oahu as well as the northwestern Hawaiian islands. The ancient *moku,* or districts, function as judicial, tax, police, fire protection, and civil defense districts, but they do not have any employees or powers separate from those of the county. Towns like Waialua, Haleiwa, and Laie are centers of population with neighborhood councils, but they have no governmental authority of their own.

The policy of the state and county government has been to promote commercial development in Honolulu and Waikiki and keep northern Oahu primarily residential and rural. Locals and environmentalists urge government officials to "keep da country country." They seem to be listening. The State of Hawaii has recently taken steps to acquire and preserve the undeveloped shoreline around Turtle Bay. The State and County are working together to improve roads, beaches, and services. By protecting agricultural and coastal lands, exploring the potential for renewable energy projects, and using the unique natural assets of northern Oahu to promote tourism, recreation, film and television, the state and county are working hand in hand to preserve the area's economic vitality without losing its incredible natural beauty and spirit of "old Hawaii."

II. DRIVE GUIDE

HOW TO GET THERE

The Direct Route

The quickest and easiest route from Honolulu to northern Oahu is to take H-1 west to Pearl City, where it intersects with H-2, then take H-2 north to Wahiawa, where it ends. From there, you can either continue north through the Town of Wahiawa on the Kam Highway (here called Highway 80) or circumvent the town on Highway 99.

If you take Highway 99, after it passes Schofield Army Barracks there are two forks in the road. For Haleiwa and the North Shore, keep to the right and continue on Highway 99 until it merges with Kam Highway, then continue north on the merged road. If you are going to the North Shore, stay on the main road and bypass Haleiwa. If Haleiwa is your destination, continue north on the merged road 4.7 miles past the Helemano traffic light, turn left at the large sign to "Historic Haleiwa Town," stay on the right as you go around Weed Circle, and take the right exit from the circle into Haleiwa.

For Waialua Town or the northwestern coast, take the first left fork off Highway 99 after Schofield Barracks, Wilikina Drive (Highway 803). The second left fork is Kaukonahua Road (Highway 801), which joins Wilikina Drive and continues northwest to Thompson's Corner. From Thompson's Corner, the Kam Highway (here called Highway 83) runs northeast. The Farrington Highway (Highway 930) heads northwest to the shoreline and continues west until it deadends about three miles east of Kaena Point.

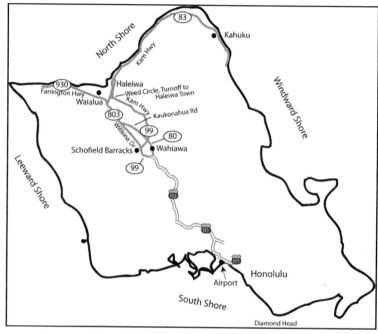

The Direct Route to Northern Oahu

The Scenic Route

Old Kunia Road (Highway 750) provides a longer but more scenic route through the Central Plateau. To take this scenic route, stay on H-1 west to Waipahu and turn north on Highway 750, which merges with Highway 99 west of Wahiawa. Continue north on Highway 99 past Schofield Barracks. For Haleiwa and the North Shore, stay right on Highway 99 to its merger with the Kam Highway and continue north on the merged road. For Waialua Town or the northwest coast, turn left on Wilikina Drive and continue northwest to Waialua and the Farrington Highway (Highway 930).

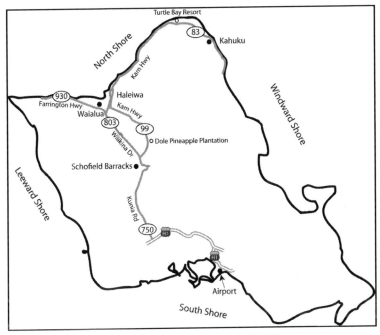

The Scenic Route to Northern Oahu

Circle Island Tour

What is commonly called the "Circle Island Tour" does not circle the entire island. At the northwestern corner of Oahu, the road around Kaena Point has been closed for many years. The "Circle Tour" runs northwest from Honolulu on H-2, continues north on Highway 99 to the Kam Highway, and stays on the Kam Highway up the North Shore and down the Windward Shore to H-3, the Likelike Highway, or the scenic Pali Highway, skipping the leeward side of the island.

This circle tour can also be made in the reverse direction, heading northeast from Honolulu to the Windward Shore, up the Windward Shore to Kahuku, down the North Shore to Haleiwa, and back to Honolulu through the Central Plateau. The problem with the counterclockwise route is that it heads into the afternoon sun. The Drive Guide follows the clockwise route. If you prefer to go counterclockwise, take H-1 west to H-3. Take H-3 east across the Koolau Mountains to the Kam Highway, and follow the Kam Highway north to Kahana Bay. From there, you can follow the Drive Guide in reverse.

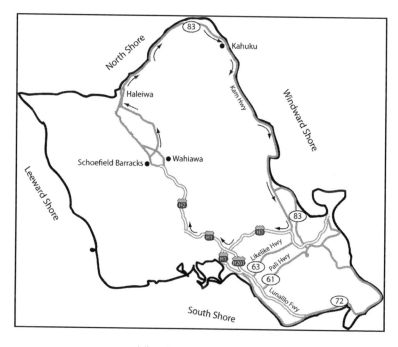

The Circle Island Tour

Watch out for confusing and overlapping highway numbers. The three freeways are clearly labeled H-1, H-2 and H-3, but other roads, such as the Kam Highway, bear different highway numbers in different places. Conversely, the same highway number may be assigned to roads with different names. When in doubt, follow the map rather than the name or number on the street sign, which may be just another interesting piece of local history. Don't worry—it's an island so it's really hard to get lost.

If you want to see the Leeward Shore, take H-1 west to Farrington Highway (here Highway 93) and follow the Farrington Highway north until it deadends south of Kaena Point. Just remember that you will have to go back the way you came.

Pitstops

If you plan to stay on the North Shore, you may want to pick up some groceries and other items at one of the large stores located along Route H-2. For **Costco**, take the Ka Uka Boulevard exit from H-2 and head west past the auto dealership to the Costco store on the south side of Ka Uka Boulevard. This is one of the most successful Costco stores in America. It carries a good selection of beach and snorkel equipment as well as groceries. It is also a good place to pick up Kona coffee, macadamia nuts, and other local goodies, and to fill your gas tank.

If you need a bite to eat, try **Zippy's** on the north side of Ka Uka Boulevard a few blocks west of Costco. Zippy's is a Hawaiian chain that offers a wide variety of local specialties and diner-type food. It is open 24 hours a day, making it a reliable stop on the way to and from the airport. A **Subway Sandwich Shop** is located on the south side of Ka Uka Boulevard just past Costco.

North of Ka Uka Boulevard, you can take the Mililani Town exit from H-2 and head west (left) to the **Mililani Town Shopping Center. A Star Market, Long's Drug Store** and **Wal-Mart** are located in the shopping center. Wal-Mart carries island clothing and Hawaiian jewelry, books, and souvenirs at reasonable prices. There are many eateries in the Mililani Shopping Center, including an excellent white tablecloth Thai restaurant called **Phuket Thai, Chili's Grill & Bar,** and **Ruby Tuesday's.** A popular Italian restaurant, **Assaggio,** is located on the south end of the Mililani Shopping Center.

In the town of **Wahiawa, Zippy's** and **Maui Mike's Fire Roasted Chicken** offer tasty alternatives to the fast food chains lining the Kam Highway. For military personnel, there is a large **PX and Commissary at the Schofield Army Barracks.**

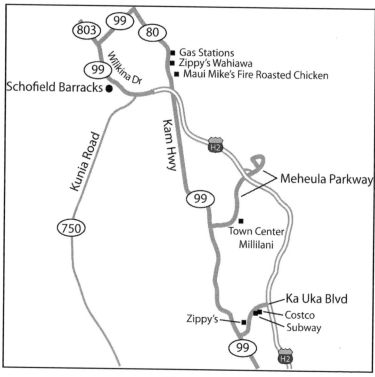

Pitstops

THE WAHIAWA DISTRICT

The Central Plateau, Gateway To Northern Oahu

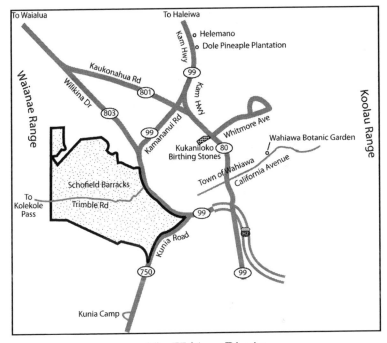

The Wahiawa District

Wahiawa's Story

The Wahiawa District of Oahu extends from the crest of the Waianae Mountains on the west to the crest of the Koolau Mountains on the east. The broad plateau between the two mountain ranges forms a natural gateway to northern Oahu.

Before the *haoles* arrived, Wahiawa was part of the *moku* of Waialua. Its slopes were heavily forested and densely populated. Terraced farms were irrigated with water from mountain streams. Women of royal lineage traveled to the sacred Kukaniloko Birthing

Stones to birth their children. Four *heiau* and other ruins in the area attest to the presence of a vibrant native community.

After Western contact, traditional life in Wahiawa was all but obliterated. The beautiful forest canopy was destroyed to harvest sandalwood for the China trade. Western diseases decimated the native population. Many of the survivors left the deforested plateau.

Wahiawa remained desolate for generations. In 1872, United States Army General John Schofield investigated the strategic potential of the area as part of a secret mission to determine the defense capabilities of the island's ports. A former Secretary of War, Schofield thought Wahiawa was a good place for an Army base. When the United States annexed Hawaii in 1998, the War Department received 14,400 acres of land near Wahiawa. Due to the lack of a reliable water supply, another ten years passed before construction began.

The lack of water also impeded private development. The Annexation Act set aside 1,320 acres of pastureland for homesteads, but few lots were taken because of the lack of irrigation water. When James Dole settled on 12 acres in 1901, he was only the 13th homesteader.

Eventually, a group of developers combined to create a dependable water supply. In 1907, the Wahiawa Water Works Company completed the construction of a large dam. The resulting Wahiawa Reservoir held 2.5 million gallons—enough water to supply a new army reservation, large agricultural plantations, and a much larger population.

As soon as water became available, Wahiawa began to boom. Construction began on the Schofield Army Barracks. James Dole leased more land, planted pineapples, built a small cannery, quickly outgrew it, and built a larger cannery in Honolulu. By 1909, the OR&L railroad had completed one spur from Honolulu to the Schofield Barracks and another from Honolulu to the Dole Pineapple Plantation.

The growth of the Wahiawa area led to the creation of a new land district—the first time in over 500 years that a new *moku* was established. In 1913, land was taken from the Waialua District to form the new District of Wahiawa. In 1932, the Wahiawa District was enlarged with small tracts of land that had been acquired by the Federal Government and included within Schofield Barracks.

Wahiawa Town

Today, Wahiawa is a bustling community of military families, agricultural workers and shopkeepers. The plateau surrounding Wahiawa holds some interesting sites, but there is nothing scenic about the little town. It has been a barracks town for almost a century, and it looks it. Beachgoers and surfers seldom bother to stop as they whiz through the main drag filled with fast food outlets or circumvent the town entirely by driving around it on Highway 99.

If you want a bite to eat in Wahiawa, **Zippy's** at 100 N. Kam Highway has both a table service restaurant and quick-service window open 24 hours a day. Across the street from McDonald's at 96 S. Kam Highway, **Maui Mike's Fire-Roasted Chicken** serves rotisserie chicken, sandwiches, and side dishes to eat in or take out.

There is a reasonably priced **Mahalo gas station** on the Kam Highway just north of Zippy's. Across the street in the southbound lane, a **Vista** station usually matches Mahalo's price.

Wahiawa Freshwater State Recreation Area

The 66-acre Wahiawa Freshwater State Recreation Area is located at 380 Walker Avenue in Wahiawa. This is the only place for bass fishing on Oahu. Situated on the wooded shore of the Wahiawa Reservoir, this state park offers shady picnic facilities and fresh water fishing from shore or by boat. The launching ramp is restricted to fishing boats. Swimming and water skiing are prohibited. The park is on the east side of the Kam Highway immediately north of its juncture with H-2. Take Kam Highway to Avocado Street. Turn

right on Avocado Street and right again on Walker Avenue. Follow
Walker Avenue to the park.

Wahiawa Botanic Garden

The 27-acre Wahiawa Botanic Garden is located at 1396
California Avenue, just east of the center of Wahiawa. If you are interested in tropical horticulture, this 40-year old collection is worth the
short detour. Located in a forested ravine, the garden nurtures native
Hawaiian plants and other tropical flora that thrive in the cooler
environment and shady habitat of a tropical rain forest. Guided tours
can be arranged. To reach the Garden, take the Kam Highway into
the center of Wahiawa and turn right (east) on California Avenue.
There is a sign before the intersection on the northbound lane of
the Kam Highway. From the Wahiawa Freshwater State Recreation
Area, take Walker Avenue north to California Avenue and turn right
on California.

Kukaniloko Birthing Stones

Kukaniloko is one of two places in the Hawaiian islands where
Hawaiian women of royal lineage came for the birth of their children. One of the most significant cultural sites on Oahu, it is listed
on the National and Hawaii Registers of Historic Places. The sacred
stones lie among coconut and eucalyptus trees in the middle of a
field with the Waianae Mountains rising in the background. Local
Hawaiians adorn them with fresh *leis*, coconuts, sweet potatoes
and yams.

To visit the Kukaniloko Birthing Stones, drive north from the
town of Wahiawa on the Kam Highway and stay in the left lane.
Where Whitmore Avenue intersects the Kam Highway on the right
(east), you will see a red dirt road on the left. Turn left (west) onto
this dirt road. In only .2 miles, you will find a convenient parking
area directly in front of the sacred stones. Please keep in mind that
this is a holy site. Remember Rule No. 9. Be respectful and do not
touch the stones or offerings.

Schofield Army Barracks

Schofield Army Barracks has been an important military base since it was built a century ago. Betweeen World War I and World War II it was the home of the U.S. Army's Hawaiian Division, which was responsible for the land defense of the islands. In 1922, the drill grounds in the southern part of Schofield were converted to an Army airfield known as Wheeler Field.

In October of 1941, the 25th Infantry Division was formed from units of the Hawaiian Division. Only ten weeks later, Japanese planes attacked Oahu on December 7, 1941. The first wave came from the north, with one group of planes circling around the Leeward Shore to attack Pearl Harbor and a second group flying down the Central Plateau to attack the fighter planes at Wheeler Field. The second wave came down the Windward Shore and attacked Wheeler again from the east. The losses were heavy: 83 of 153 aircraft at Wheeler were destroyed, the Schofield Barracks were heavily damaged, and 37 Americans were killed.

Japanese-Americans were not interned in Hawaii during the War as they were on the mainland. However, after the Japanese attack the soldiers of Japanese ancestry were withdrawn from the 25th Division and placed in the 100th Infantry Battalion. The 100th was sent to the European Theater, where the Japanese-American soldiers served with great distinction.

With its extensive training in jungle warfare, the 25th Infantry Division was dispatched to the South Pacific. It saw action at Guadalcanal, the Solomon Islands, and the Philippines, where it set a record of 165 consecutive days of active combat. After the War, the 25th was part of the Army of Occupation in Japan. Subsequently, it served in Korea from 1950 to 1953, Viet Nam from 1963 to 1970, the First Gulf War in 1991, a peacekeeping mission to Haiti in 1995, and operations in Bosnia-Herzegovina in 2002. It saw action in Iraq from 2004 to 2007, and continues to serve in Afghanistan. The 25th's

Second Brigade is preparing to serve as a Stryker Brigade Combat Team for the new Stryker armored vehicles.

The 25th became known as the "Tropic Lightning Division" because of its tropic home and its "lightning" manner of conducting operations. It proudly adheres to the motto it earned over 60 years ago: "Ready to Strike! Anytime. Anywhere." The Division's shoulder patch is a red and yellow taro leaf, incorporating the colors of the Hawaiian monarchy, the symbol of Old Hawaii, and a lightning bolt referencing the Division's splendid history and nickname. Look for the distinctive red and yellow patch when you see uniformed soldiers in northern Oahu.

When the Air Force became a separate branch of the military, Wheeler Field became Wheeler Air Force Base. In 1989, after more than 40 years as an Air Force base, the field was returned to the Army in exchange for land near Hickham Air Force Base on the South Shore.

Schofield has a well-deserved reputation as one of the most beautiful military bases in the world. Its broad, palm-lined streets and Art Deco buildings appeared in the movie *From Here To Eternity.* Above the Barracks, **Kolekole Pass** provides a lookout over the leeward side of the island. There are several sites of historical interest near Kolekole Pass. A large stone, from five to eight feet high and about eight feet across, is said to represent the traditional guardian of the pass, a woman named Kolekole. A scenic road across Kolekole Pass and wonderful hiking trails are accessible from Schofield Barracks. Unfortunately, access to the base and the mountains above it has been restricted since the tragic events of September 11, 2001.

You can, however, visit the **Tropic Lightning Museum,** which tells the history of Schofield Barracks and the 25th Infantry Division. To reach it, take Highway 99 to Kunia Road (Highway 750) and turn south on Kunia Road. Turn right onto Lyman Road, right onto Flagler Road, and left onto Waianae Avenue. The museum is located in Building 361. It is open from 10:00 a.m. to 4:00 p.m. Tuesday through Saturday. Before you go, call the museum at 655-0438 to check on access due to varying levels of security.

There are two 18-hole golf courses attached to Schofield Barracks. **Leilehua Golf Course** is the U.S. Army's premiere course on Oahu. It is located on the Leilehua Plateau overlooking the Wahiawa Reservoir, south of the Town of Wahiawa. It is primarily open to authorized military and government personnel and their guests, but *kamaaina* (Hawaiian residents) may use it on a standby basis. **Kalakaua Golf Course** is inside the gates of Schofield Barracks. The Kalakaua course is restricted to authorized military and government personnel and their guests.

Kunia

For an interesting view of Hawaiian plantation life, drive south on Highway 99 to Kunia Road (Highway 750). Turn right on Kunia Road, continue past the Schofield Barracks, and look for the sign to Kunia Drive, which loops through the old field camp of Kunia. Filipino pineapple workers have resided in Kunia for generations, but the days of pineapple growing are coming to an end. Look for the lovely old school and recreation center on the far side of the loop, and the general store where residents bought necessities and gathered to "talk story." The road loops back to Kunia Road, where you can turn left and retrace your route back to Highway 99.

Dole Pineapple Plantation

Drive north on Highway 99 to the **Dole Pineapple Plantation,** 64-1550 Kam Highway, about a mile north of Wahiawa. The Dole Plantation offers an interesting walking tour through a tropical garden, the "world's largest maze" with nearly two miles of paths lined by over 11,000 colorful Hawaiian plants, and an attractive gift shop with an incredible variety of pineapple products, souvenirs and treats. A narrated train tour called the "Pineapple Express" tells the story of James Dole and the Hawaiian pineapple industry. Outdoor kiosks sell local products, such as the luscious kukui nut body oils that are made in nearby Waialua.

Helemano

Immediately north of the Dole Plantation, handicapped persons participating in a state-run program serve hot lunches, hamburgers, and sandwiches in the **Helemano dining room**. The all you can eat lunch is reasonably priced.

As you continue north on Highway 99, you will see agricultural fields stretching from the Waianae Mountains on the west to the Koolau Mountains on the east. Beautiful *enui nui* (rainbows) often appear over the lovely peaks and valleys. You may still see pineapple workers laboring behind immense picking machines, though the fields are gradually being turned to other crops.

At the traffic light, notice the sign to the **Helemano Military Reservation** on your right. **Helemano** is remembered in Hawaiian folklore as the hideout of a cannibalistic chief from the South Seas named Ka lo aikanaka ("the chief who eats men"). Unlike the early Hawaiians, Ka lo aikanaka and his followers had no laws of *kapu* and held feasts at which human flesh was eaten. Perhaps they came from one of the Polynesian islands where cannibalism was practiced. According to Hawaiian legend, these cannibals were ejected from Kauai, came to northern Oahu, and were driven off by the Hawaiians of Mokuleia and Waialua. Ka lo aikanaka and his followers holed up on a mountain ridge between two steep gulches where they could prey on passing travelers. One by one the followers were killed, until Ka lo aikanaka remained alone at Helemano. The cannibal finally met his end when a vengeful relative of some of his victims hurled him over the cliff to his death. Like many old Hawaiian tales, it is impossible to determine if the story of Ka lo aikanaka is truth or fiction. In the mid-19th century, native Hawaiians used to take visitors to Helemano and show them the foundation of a *heiau,* a large flat rock they called the *ipukai* (platter) where victims were supposedly laid, and a hollow where an *imu* (oven) was allegedly dug to bake them. Although there are many records referring to these ruins, the legend has never been verified by scholars.

As you continue north past Helemano, the North Shore comes into view. To your left is the Waianae Range, with Mount Kaala marking the highest point on Oahu at 4,025 feet. To your right is the majestic Koolau Range. Soon you will top a rise and behold the blue Pacific spread out before you, from Kaena Point on the northwest tip of the island as far as the eye can see. You are now on the fabulous North Shore of Oahu. *Aloha*!

A Perfect Day In Wahiawa

Take a guided tour of the Wahiawa Botanic Garden. Visit the Kukaniloko Birthing Stones. Stop at Maui Mike's Chicken or Zippy's for lunch, then go to the Dole Pineapple Plantation, take a ride on the Pineapple Express, see the tropical garden and maze, and enjoy a pineapple treat. If you have time, see the Tropic Lightning Museum and take the short drive to the old Kunia camp. Take the scenic route to the North Shore in time for a refreshing swim and dinner in Haleiwa.

THE WAIALUA DISTRICT

Northwestern Oahu From Kaena To Waimea

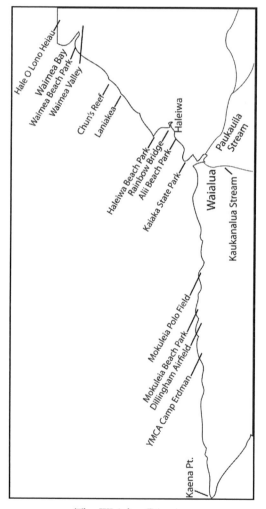

The Waialua District

WAIALUA'S STORY

The Polynesians

The name Waialua means "two waters," a reference to the two streams that run from the Waianae Mountains into the ocean. Waialua was one of the earliest Polynesian settlements on Oahu. With a coastline graced by two beautiful bays, it was a natural landing place for canoes from Kauai.

Waialua *moku* was divided into 14 *ahupuaa*. The names of those land divisions are still used today. The early Hawaiians lived in villages along the streams and valleys. Later, during plantation days, the neighboring towns of Waialua and Haleiwa developed into the principal population centers of the Waialua District.

Missionaries

The Protestant missionaries established stations in the rural areas of Oahu. The first rural station was founded in Waialua in 1832 by John and Ursula Emerson. The high chief of Waialua, Gideon Laanui, had already converted to Christianity. He welcomed the Emersons, gave them land to build a church, and ordered his subjects to worship there each Sunday.

The Emersons settled on the south bank of the Anahulu Stream near the legendary Kawaipuolo spring, which provided a steady supply of *ama ama* (mullet) and drinking water. There are many Hawaiian legends about this spring. The name Kawaipuolo means "bundled water," referring to the traditional practice of giving strangers who asked for a drink a taro leaf cup filled with water, or "bundled water." It also refers to an old Hawaiian legend holding that the Kawaipuolo spring suddenly disappeared and was found after a long search on a hilltop near Kaena Point, where the *menehune* (legendary small people) had transported it one night in bundles of ti and taro leaves—again, "bundled water."

John Emerson traveled throughout the region teaching the Hawaiians practical as well as spiritual matters. When commoners were allowed to purchase land in the Great Mahele, Emerson made sure their deeds were properly recorded. As a result of his efforts, the Hawaiian population of northern Oahu did not lose their land to the same extent as commoners in other parts of the Kingdom. Medical problems forced Emerson to retire in 1864. He died at his home on the Anahulu in 1867.

Another American missionary named Orramel Gulick was appointed to succeed Emerson. In 1865, Gulick and his wife settled on the north bank of the Anahulu, across the stream from the Emerson homestead. The Gulicks established the Waialua Female Seminary for Hawaiian girls, where classes in reading, writing, and domestic arts were taught in Hawaiian. The girls' school was called "Hale Iwa," which means "house of the *iwa.*" The *iwa* is a type of frigate bird that is native to the area. It flies over the surface of the ocean to fish during the day and returns to land at night. Since it was said that the *iwa* bird built a beautiful nest, the name was symbolic of a beautiful home. The school closed in 1881, but the name "Haleiwa" stuck to the whole area.

The Waialua Sugar Plantation

Efforts to grow sugar commercially in Waialua began in 1864 when a *haole* missionary started growing cane there. During the Civil War, there was a demand for sugar because the northern states were cut off from the sugar produced in the southern states. But after the Civil War ended, the demand for Hawaiian sugar dropped and the little sugar plantation began incurring losses. Eventually, the property was turned over to creditors and sold to Robert Halstead. For several decades, Halstead kept the little plantation going. He used oxen and mules to haul the cane to coastal steamers for shipping.

In the 1890s, Benjamin Dillingham spurred the development of northern Oahu. In an effort to make his OR&L Railway more profitable, Dillingham encouraged Castle & Cooke, a well-financed member of the "Big Five," to take over the struggling Halstead sugar plantation. At his urging, the Waialua Agricultural Company was formed. With a reliable water supply from the Wahiawa Reservoir and rail transportation on the OR&L, large-scale sugar production became feasible.

From 1898 until 1923, William W. Goodale was the manager of the Waialua Agricultural Company. Under his astute supervision, the plantation employed every available means to cut costs and increase profits. An extensive irrigation system was built to deliver the huge amounts of water required for large-scale sugar cultivation from the Wahiawa Reservoir to the cane fields. Over 20 smaller reservoirs were scattered around the plantation. A siphon piping system with five-foot diameter pipes irrigated 2,500 acres of upland fields near Wahiawa. Steam reciprocating pumps irrigated the lower fields. Later, the steam pumps were replaced with electric centrifugal pumps. Ground water was accessed by wells with high-capacity pumps. A hydroelectric plant at the Wahiawa Reservoir produced electricity to run the mill and service the camps. Notably, the power plant's generating frequency was matched to that of the commercial power grid so excess power could be sold to the grid. A plantation railroad was installed to haul the cane from the field to the mill and take the refined product to the OR&L for shipment. Later, the development of mechanical derricks to load the harvested cane onto rail cars eliminated the dangerous job of loading it by hand.

Soon the deforested slopes of Waialua were filled with endless cane fields. The Waialua Plantation became one of the largest producers in the islands. By the 1930s, it was cultivating sugarcane on 10,500 acres and milling additional cane grown by independent planters on another 500 acres.

At one time, about 1,700 plantation workers lived in camps owned by the Waialua Agricultural Company. Field workers were housed at Spanish camp, Ranch camp, Kawailoa camp, Helemano camp, Opaehula camp, Takayama camp, and Waimea camp. Mill workers lived in Mill Camps One and Two next to the mill in Waialua Town. Lunas (supervisors) lived at Skill Camp in Waialua, near the current Waialua Library. The plantation owned and operated its own stores and recreational facilities. Its dairy supplied beef and milk. Its hospital, doctors and nurses provided medical care. Three movie houses showed films in the workers' native languages on alternating nights—"Chinese night," "Japanese night," "Filipino night," and so forth.

The Haleiwa Hotel

In the meantime, Dillingham found another way to spur development and create steady fares for the OR&L. Waialua was a popular beach community replete with hotels and vacation homes. Queen Liliuokalani, Prince Kuhio, and other Hawaiian royals visited frequently, and wealthy *haoles* came up from Honolulu. Dillingham set out to create a first class resort hotel overlooking the spot where the Anahulu Stream flowed into the sea. Unfortunately, he chose the site of the Kamani *heiau*, which was destroyed when the hotel was built. Many Hawaiians believed that the destruction of the *heiau* was an omen of doom for the new hotel.

The Haleiwa Hotel opened its doors to the public in 1899. It was an immediate success. Designed by architect Oliver G. Traphagen, the elegant, two-story Victorian building had a rounded portico entry, broad lanai, and 40 well-appointed guest rooms. It was impeccably furnished and managed by a distinguished Hawaiian diplomat, Colonel Curtis Peahu Iaukea, who had served as the Secretary of Foreign Affairs for both King Kalakaua and Queen Liliuokalani and royal chamberlain to King Kalakaua.

The new hotel had all the latest amenities, including electric lights and a telephone in every room. It was supplied with the famously pure water from the Kawaipuolo spring. Guests could rent canoes and rowboats and take horseback tours from the hotel's stable. Men could play billiards and shoot at a rustic "men's lodge" five miles away. By the 1940s, a nine-hole golf course extended from the hotel along Waialua Bay, where Haleiwa Alii Beach Park now stands. Horse races were held every Sunday on the dirt road between the hotel and Fresh Air Camp, which is now the site of Kaiaka Bay Beach Park. Sunday excursion trains from Honolulu to Haleiwa were filled to capacity.

The Haleiwa Hotel catered to the wealthy. A weekend excursion from Honolulu, including a round-trip on the OR&L and one night's stay, cost $10.00—a considerable sum in those days.

The 20th Century

In the early 20th century, the area around the Haleiwa Hotel became a thoroughfare for tourists arriving on the railway and plantation workers traveling between the mill camp and fields. In 1921, the old wooden bridge across the Anahulu was replaced with the double-arched Anahulu Bridge so that cars could cross the stream there. The new structure quickly became known as the "Rainbow Bridge."

Some of the plantation workers saw an opportunity in this traffic—particularly the Japanese. When their work contracts expired, they opened shops in Haleiwa. Today, Haleiwa's main street is still lined with quaint storefronts erected in the 1920s and 1930s by Japanese families who ran their shops and lived behind them or on the second story.

World War II brought tremendous activity to the Waialua District. The Army installed numerous defenses to guard against a Japanese invasion of the island. Airfields in Mokuleia and Kawailoa were in constant use. As the young men went off to battle, the merchants' trade grew, the sugar plantation thrived, and the OR&L hit new peaks of profitability hauling sugar, military personnel, and war materiel among the many military bases and fortifications on Oahu.

When the War ended, the railroad fell into decline. It couldn't compete commercially with the heavy-duty, diesel-powered trucks developed after the War. Nor could it dissuade passengers from preferring the speed and convenience of cars. On April 1, 1946, a tsunami destroyed several sections of the OR&L tracks at Mokuleia. By 1947, the OR&L was out of business.

The days of the lovely old Haleiwa Hotel also came to an end. As tourists started flocking to new hotels in Waikiki, the elegant hotel in the country started losing money. It was converted to a private beach club. Then, during World War II, it was used as a recreation center for Army officers. Termites and structural problems beset the building, and it was finally torn down in 1952. Many old-time Hawaiians attributed the hotel's demise to the destruction of the Kamani *heiau* when it was built. Although nothing remains of the *heiau*, some Hawaiians maintain that on certain nights the beating of drums and notes of flutes can still be heard on the wind.

Although the military continued to maintain a strong presence in northern Oahu, the Haleiwa airstrip and shoreline defenses were abandoned after the War. The Waialua District was a quiet agricultural area when tourists and surfers discovered it in the 1970s.

As tourism grew, sugar declined. Despite having the world's most productive cane fields and an extremely efficient mill, the Waialua Sugar Plantation found it more and more difficult to compete against sugar from underdeveloped countries. In 1996, the Waialua Sugar Mill closed. Retired field workers, who had been guaranteed lifetime housing as a condition of their employment, were moved to vacant houses in the Waialua mill camp. Other employees lost their jobs and homes. When the last retiree passes on, the mill camp will also pass into history. The fields that were once covered with sugar cane are now planted with other crops.

HALEIWA TOWN

Old Haleiwa Town is the heart of the North Shore. Steeped in Hawaiian history, it has become the quintessential surf town. This charming community hosts the Reef Hawaiian Pro surf competition, the first leg of the Triple Crown of Surfing, at Alii Beach Park each November. The famous surf beach is named for the Hawaiian *alii* who surfed there centuries ago.

The early Hawaiians invented surfing. Skilled in making large outrigger canoes and handling them in ocean swells and surf, they crafted their surfboards from the same *koa* (an indigenous tree with beautiful, hard wood) and *wiliwili* (a tree with light wood) they used for their canoes and outriggers. The Hawaiian word for surfing is *he enaluor*, which means "wave sliding." Historians believe that Hawaiians were sliding down the waves of Haleiwa on finely crafted wood surfboards as early as the 15th century. Take some time to explore the surf shops and surf museums in Haleiwa to learn how this exciting sport has developed over six centuries.

In addition to surfing competitions, Haleiwa also hosts the Hanapaa Deep Sea Fishing Tournament at Haleiwa Harbor in June, the Haleiwa Arts Festival at Haleiwa Beach Park on the third weekend in July, a *luau* at the historic Queen Liliuokalani Church on the first weekend in August, and numerous other festivals and activities throughout the year. The Chamber of Commerce recently initiated a "Haleiwa Art Walk" from 6:00 to 9:00 p.m. on the last Saturday of every month.

Haleiwa has been designated a special historic and cultural district of the City and County of Honolulu. *Paniolo* (Hawaiian cowboy) style buildings give the town a quaint appearance. Many of the old structures are on the State Register of Historic Sites. Among them, you will find a wide diversity of dining, shopping, activities, and services. It is impossible to mention all of the surf shops, boutiques, eateries, and other attractions of Haleiwa. Instead, this Guide provides highlights from which you can venture out on your own in "Surf City, USA."

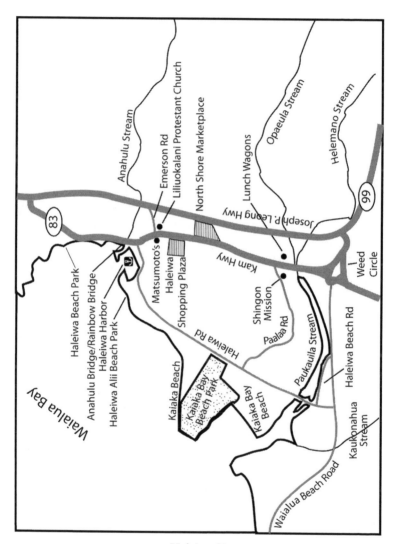

Haleiwa Town

Driving Through Old Haleiwa Town

As you drive north on the Kam Highway, 4.7 miles past the Helemano traffic light you will see a large sign to "Historic Haleiwa Town." Turn left at the sign, stay on the right as you go around Weed Circle, and take the right exit from the circle into Haleiwa.

This section accompanies you on a drive through Haleiwa Town, pointing out the places of interest as you pass them. If you have a specific purpose, such as finding a place to swim or feed hungry children, refer to the subsequent chapters and return to this Drive Guide when you are ready for a leisurely tour.

The South End of Town

As you enter Haleiwa Town from Weed Circle, you will find clusters of businesses on both sides of the road. **Macky's Shrimp Truck, 7-11, X-Cel surf shop, a chiropractor, an acupuncturist,** and a **tattoo shop** appear on the east side of the highway. The next building is occupied by **Killer Tacos, Wiki Wiki tanning salon,** and another chiropractor. A local family has operated the **K Bros. auto repair** business for decades. A **fishing supply store, Hawaiian Isle surf shop, and another shrimp stand** are located on the west side of Kam Highway.

Just past this first group of businesses, the Kam Highway crosses **Paukauila Stream.** As you cross the bridge, look for **lunch wagons** in the shady grove on the north side of the stream. After ten years in Kahuku and recognition by Travelocity as one of Hawaii's "best finds," **Giovanni's Aloha Shrimp** installed a second lunch wagon here. It has been joined by at least three other lunch wagons—a veritable food court with shady picnic tables. On the north side of this grove, you can pick up dessert at the **Chocolate Gecko. A smoke shop** and **Ken's Hair Studio** share the building. Across the street is a new business that specializes in **Wave Riding Vehicles.**

Don't miss **Café Haleiwa,** at 66-460 Kam Highway. This long-time cafe has been serving breakfast and lunch to surfers and tourists from all over the world for more than 20 years. It is a comfortable place to enjoy traditional or Mexican fare with vintage surf pictures and an assortment of surfers, old and young. There is an espresso bar, and the morning newspaper is always available. Café Haleiwa's neighbor is a surf and dive shop called **North Shore Diving and Deep Ecology,** which conducts whale-watching, turtle and dolphin tours, boat dives, shore dives, introductory dives, snorkeling excursions, and eco-tours.

On the west side of Kam Highway after the senior citizens' housing, **McDonald's** now occupies the site where the Haleiwa Theater once stood at the intersection of Kam Highway and Paalaa Road. This road provides an interesting glimpse of old Haleiwa. The picturesque **Haleiwa Shingon Mission** on the south side of Paalaa Road is one of two Shingon churches on Oahu. Built by Japanese sugar workers in 1925, it is meticulously maintained by their descendants. Over the entrance, an engraved pinewood sign is decorated in gilded English and Kanji characters, with a cloud design designating it a holy place. The altar is made of gold-plated brass. The mission bell came from Japan. After the Shingon Mission, Paalaa Road passes through a quaint but dilapidated residential neighborhood until it intersects with Haleiwa Road.

Continuing north on the Kam Highway past Paalaa Road, the building that houses Billy's Barber Shop and Celestial Natural Foods has a colorful history. It once was the Fujita Hotel and Coffee Shop, the closest thing in Haleiwa to a Wild West saloon. On the second floor, girls, liquor, and opium were readily available. Chinese men sat on the balcony smoking their long opium pipes. **Billy's Barber Shop** may be tame by comparison to the old opium den, but it's a good place to go if you need a haircut. Billy visited Haleiwa several years ago, realized it had no barber, and never returned to Chicago. The Windy City's loss was Haleiwa's gain.

Celestial Natural Foods has an impressive inventory of natural foods, fresh organic produce, health supplements, bulk foods, cosmetics, and other items. Tucked in a corner of Celestial Natural Foods, the charming little **Paradise Found Cafe** serves a vegetarian menu that includes smoothies, organic soups, fresh-pressed vegetable juices, sandwiches, and healthy plate lunches.The old Haleiwa Garage was torn down to make room for the **Haleiwa Post Office,** next door to the **Subway sandwich shop** and **Christian bookstore.** Across the driveway from the post office is **Hawaiian Moon gift shop. A Pizza Hut** is located behind Hawaiian Moon. There is additional parking behind these businesses.

Directly north of Café Haleiwa is the **Waialua Community Association Building,** which was built as a gymnasium in 1937. The Waialua District had the first community association on Oahu. Founded to make rural life more attractive, the Waialua Community Association was responsible for bringing dial telephones, streetlights, street names, and other community services to the area. Today, it offers a wide range of social service programs. The building is used for community affairs ranging from hula lessons to town meetings. It is also the home of the Haleiwa Chamber of Commerce.

Continuing north, the Kam Highway passes through fields punctuated by the only stop light in Haleiwa, at the intersection of Cane Haul Road. If this seems like an odd place for a traffic signal, it was installed when all of this area was part of the Waialua Sugar Plantation so that big turn haulers (trucks used to haul cane) could make their way from the cane fields to the mill in Waialua Town.

The North Shore Marketplace

The North Shore Marketplace is very popular with tourists, because it provides a concentration of shops and eateries with convenient parking. In the southwest corner of the center, a large building houses several excellent shops. **The North Shore Quicksilver Board Riders Club** carries top-of-the-line surfboards crafted by legendary North Shore shapers like Barry Kanaiaupuni, John Carper, Jeff Bushman, and Pat Rawson, as well as the latest surf wear by Quicksilver. **Silver Moon Emporium** carries fashionable women's apparel ranging from casual wear to evening gowns, as well as shoes and accessories. **Polynesian Treasures** specializes in island crafts, while the **Pearl Shop** offers jewelry. The **Aloha General Store** serves shave ice and smoothies. Two restaurants—**Kono's** and **Breakers**—are located on the Kam Highway side of the building. Public restrooms are on the east end. The two-story building across the parking lot from Silver Moon Emporium holds a number of services, including several surfing schools.

Along the east side of the Marketplace, stop in at the **Coffee Gallery** for a coffee or mocha treat to sustain you as you browse through the shops. The **Britton Gallery** is part gift shop, part art gallery. **Jungle Gems** carries gemstones, crystals, silver, and beadwork. **Cholo's Homestyle Mexican Restaurant & Margarita Bar** serves the best margaritas and Mexican food on the North Shore, and also sells interesting Mexican artwork. **North Shore Swimwear** allows you to create your own bathing suit by choosing the top, bottom, and fabric that are most complimentary to your individual figure. If your top and bottom are not the same size, this is the place! Public restrooms are located on the north end of this building, around the corner from North Shore Swimwear.

The next building to the north houses **Barnfield's Raging Isle Surf & Cycle**. Raging Isle carries surfboards, surf gear, clothing, and a large inventory of mountain bikes for sale and rent. The adjacent surfboard factory produces custom-built boards. Next to Raging Isle, **12 Tribes International Imports** carries an eclectic assortment of imported clothing and curios. **Banzai Sushi Bar** occupies a shady site on the north end of the Marketplace.

On the northwest end of the complex, the **North Shore Surf and Cultural Museum** contains a treasure trove of surfing memorabilia, including surfboards, posters, photos, and videos. **Oceans In Glass** sells charming handmade glass sculptures of dolphins, turtles, and other sea creatures that can be shipped to your home with a guaranty against breakage.

On the south side of **Oceans in Glass,** walk through the corridor to the **Haleiwa Art Gallery.** This is the most interesting art gallery in Haleiwa, with a diverse selection of originals and reproductions by many Hawaiian artists. A well-stocked **Napa Auto Parts** store is located between the art gallery and Oceans in Glass.

South of Oceans in Glass, a broad porch welcomes you to **Patagonia,** which carries a wide range of surfing and casual apparel. Next to Patagonia, **Wyland's Art Gallery** offers the sea life paintings of James Wyland and works by other artists. Wyland created the turtle logo for the Turtle Bay Resort and the charming sea turtle poster for the 2000 Haleiwa Arts Festival.

There are four restaurants in the North Shore Marketplace. The most popular is **Cholo's. Breakers Restaurant & Bar** is open for lunch, dinner, and late-night snacks, with live entertainment on weekends. Next door to Breakers, **Kono's** serves breakfast and lunch, with limited seating. The **Banzai Sushi Bar** is open only for dinner from Tuesday through Sunday.

The North End Of Town

As you leave the North Shore Marketplace, you will see the tiny **Haleiwa Florist** across the street. The attractive boutique next door, **Oogenesis,** carries a wide range of colorful fashions. Oogenesis has been popular with locals for decades.

On the east side of the highway, an outdoor vendor sells shell products. Continuing north, you will pass **Dawn's, Hawaiian Island Creations, Black Pearl Source, Grass Skirt Grill, Strong Current Surf Design, Bali Moon,** and **Del's Photo Lab.** The **Grass Skirt Grill** offers delicious food at reasonable prices, with seating inside and outside. **Strong Current Surf Design** carries nostalgic surf memorabilia and Hawaiiana. It also features top-quality longboards shaped by famous North Board shapers like Dick Brewer and Mike Diffenderfer. Its store has expanded into the old gas station next door. Across the street from the Grass Skirt Grill is **Aikane Kai Surf Company** and **Storto's Deli and Sandwich Shop.**

The **Waialua District Courthouse** was built in 1912 on the site of the Puupilo *heiau*. It held the district court, police substation, and holding cells where lawbreakers were kept until they could be transported to Honolulu. The building was restored in 1997. It is used for local and civic functions under the management of the Office of Hawaiian Affairs.

Haleiwa Shopping Plaza is the home of several popular eateries. **Pizza Bob's** offers pizza, pasta, sandwiches, salads, and a full bar. Local specialties like chili rice and teriyaki chicken are the mainstay of **L & L Hawaiian Barbecue**, a Hawaiian fast food chain. **Kainoa's Sports Bar & Restaurant** is in transition from a local bar to an outdoor restaurant serving seafood and barbecue. **Rosie's Cantina** features Mexican food but is most popular for its Margarita specials. **North Shore Country Okazu & Bento** prepares bento boxes and other Japanese specialties for takeout only. A **lunch wagon serving hot malasadas** (a Filipino treat) operates in front of the Haleiwa Super Market. **Flavormania ice cream parlor** is located next to Pizza Bob's. Other shops in this plaza include **Bali Moon's new home and décor shop, Haleiwa Beach Treasures, Sand Castle, Shore Around Surf Shop, Radio Shack, Curves,** and the **Atlantis Salon. Crank and Carve** focuses on two under-represented board sports on the North Shore: skateboarding and body boarding. **Haleiwa Family Health**, with several doctors and dentists in residence, is located in the rear of the shopping plaza. **Haleiwa Super Market** is older than Malama's across the street, but has a loyal following.

Across the highway from the shopping plaza, **Malama's** has replaced the old Fujioka grocery store. The new store is clean and attractive, with fresh produce and grilled meals available for take out. A street vendor sometimes sells **huli-huli chicken** fresh off the grill in the parking lot. **Spaghettini's** serves New York-style pizza, pasta, salads, and sandwiches for take-out or casual outdoor dining. **Waialua Bakery** is a good place to pick up breakfast rolls or sandwiches to take to the beach; it also offers ice cream and a juice bar.

A few doors north of Malama's grocery is **Kua Aina Sandwich Shop**, which claims to serve the greatest hamburgers in the world, and possibly the entire solar system. Kua Aina started in Haleiwa, and now has locations in Honolulu, Tokyo, and Santa Monica. In addition to burgers, Kua Aina offers a variety of sandwiches, salads, vegan specials, homemade French fries, and various accompaniments. Tables are available inside and outside on a pleasant patio. **Hawaii Surf & Sail** next door provides ambience and something to do while you wait for your order. The dramatic island scenes of Ron Tabora, as well as works by other artists, are featured at the adjacent **Tabora Galleries**. **Planet Surf** occupies the north end of the building.

The **Ace Hardware Store** is a good place to pick up an ice chest, thermos, missing kitchen accessory, or a flashlight for the moonlight walk at Waimea Valley. **Haleiwa Pharmacy** is immediately south of Ace Hardware.

The charming little **Iwa Gallery** is across the street. This gallery operates like a guild for local artists. If the door is open, you will usually find a local artist working on a new creation while tending the shop. Feel free to go in, introduce yourself, and browse around. The Akiyama family constructed this pretty building in 1920. They ran a photo shop in front and lived in the back. It became Ikuta's Watchmaker before its current incarnation as an art gallery.

It is almost mandatory to stop for a shave ice as you are passing through Haleiwa. Japanese immigrants brought shave ice with them to the island. Don't mistake shave ice for a sno-cone or slushie—it is much finer ice powder shaved from a rotating ice block by a fixed knife blade, formed into a ball, and covered with a home-made syrup.

Matsumoto's Shave Ice occupies a building that was erected in 1920 as a post office, then became a dry goods store, and was turned into a grocery store by Mamoru and Helen Matsumoto. Mamoru traveled from one plantation camp to another selling groceries to the workers from a bicycle, and later a truck, while Helen manned the little grocery store and took in sewing to make ends meet. In 1951, they added shave ice to generate extra income. Today, their son operates the famous shave ice emporium. Long lines form outside, especially on weekends. Take a snapshot sitting on the bench out front while you enjoy this famous local treat.

If Matsumoto's line is too long, try Aoki's next door. Sumie Aoki ran a sewing school there from 1946 until 1981, when she and her three sons opened **Aoki's Shave Ice**. They started with hand-powered machines from Japan, jury-rigging them with electric motors. The old machines still hang from the walls of the store, which is run by Sumie's son and granddaughter.

Across the street from Aoki's and Matsumoto's is the historic **Liliuokalani Protestant Church**. The Emersons founded this church in 1832. Chief Laanui donated the land for the original church building where Haleiwa Joe's Restaurant now stands. It was a *pili*-grass hut with no walls, allowing the trade winds to cool the congregation. When that building was destroyed by fire, the Emersons built a larger grass church that could accommodate 1,500 worshippers. In 1840, they built an adobe church on the present location. A 400-pound bronze bell was hauled overland from Honolulu to replace the traditional conch-shell call to worship. In 1890, the adobe church was replaced by a wooden structure. Queen Liliuokalani walked to services at the wooden church from her summer home on nearby Lokoea Pond. The congregation proudly called it the "Queen's Church" for generations before the name was changed officially to Liliuokalani Protestant Church in 1975.

When the wooden church succumbed to termites, the existing cinderblock church was built in 1961. At the top of the New England-style steeple, a copper *iwa*, Haleiwa's namesake, sits holding a fish in its mouth. The beautiful stone archway, a natural arch with no mortar, was built in 1912 in honor of the Emersons. A spectacular night-blooming syrius grows along the wall. For a touch of local history, walk through the church graveyard where the Emersons, three of their children, Chief Laanui, and generations of Hawaiians, plantation workers, and other members of this historic church are buried.

If the church is open, be sure to step inside. The stained glass windows are the work of artist Erica Karawina. The pews are made of koa wood. On the rear wall, next to a portrait of Liliuokalani, there is a wonderful handcrafted wooden clock that England's Queen Victoria presented to Liliuokalani when she attended Victoria's Golden Jubilee. Liliuokalani gave the clock to the Church on New Year's Day of 1892, the year before she was forced to abdicate. The wooden gears drive seven dials that tell the time, days of the week and month, phases of the moon, and other information. The twelve letters of the Queen's name mark the hours.

On the north side of the Church, Emerson Road leads to the Emersons' home site, which lies hidden behind a grove of Pride of India trees. When the Emersons lived here, the entire area was filled with fragrant lilacs and beautiful trees, including mango, mulberry, fig, Pride of India, and other varieties. Picture the area then, so full of life with the missionaries, their children, and the Hawaiians coming from their villages and fishing shacks to worship at the church.

Colorful tourist shops now line the street north of the shave ice stands and Liliuokalani Church. Across the street from the **Mata Hari** store, the old Yoshida building houses **Global Creations Interiors,** which carries a nice assortment of local artwork, island décor, quilts, clothing, jewelry, toiletries, and batik imports. **Haleiwa Eats Thai** serves delicious Thai food in a funky North Shore environment. **The Growing Keiki** carries adorable, but pricey island wear for tots.

At the north end of town, past the gas station and **Wiki Wiki Coffee Shop,** Haleiwa Road turns off to the left (southwest) while the Kam Highway bends to the right and crosses the Rainbow Bridge. This three-prong intersection is known as **Three Corners.** Bear right on the Kam Highway for now; we will return to explore Haleiwa Road later.

The Mouth Of The Anahulu

Makai of Three Corners, **Haleiwa Joe's Seafood Grille** is a steak and seafood restaurant with a casual atmosphere, nice views of the boat harbor, and a lively bar that is a favorite of the local lifeguards and surf crowd. The old **Bishop Bank building** sits *mauka* of Three Corners. Built in 1927, it is one of the oldest bank buildings on the island. Once a gallery for local artist Evelyn Fettig, it currently houses a realty firm.

Continue on Kam Highway across the **Rainbow Bridge**. The double-arched bridge is on the National Register of Historic Places. It has become an iconic symbol of the North Shore. Traffic sometimes backs up on each side, especially on weekends. The bridge has been repaired, but not widened. If there is a serious bottleneck, the only alternative route is to turn back and take the bypass road around Haleiwa. The bypass merges with the Kam Highway a short distance past the bridge.

Two great surf shops are located on the north side of Rainbow Bridge. *Mauka* of Kam Highway, **Tropical Rush** carries a big inventory of surf and swim equipment, surfboards, skateboards, clothing and other gear. The building dates back to the late 1920s, when it was a Filipino Pancipanci general store with the family living in back. You can rent equipment and arrange surf lessons here. Tropical Rush maintains a surf report line giving current information on the day's surf and weather details for all of Oahu; the number is 638-7874.

Makai of Kam Highway, **Surf 'n' Sea** occupies a building constructed in 1921. Originally a general store, it subsequently housed a lunch counter and sweet shop, dry goods and tailor shop, retail clothing store, hardware store, and gun store before Surf 'n' Sea took it over.

Surf 'n' Sea carries a good selection of surfboards for collectors and active surfers, including new and used boards by Dick Brewer, Barry Kanaiaupuni, and other North Shore shapers. There is a substantial inventory of longboards, short boards, and bodyboards, as well as clothing, accessories, beachwear, and other equipment. Surf 'n' Sea also rents surfboards, bodyboards, windsurfers, kayaks, jet skis, scuba gear, snorkeling equipment, and other water toys. It offers surfing, bodyboarding, and windsurfing lessons, snorkel tours, dive tours, and three-day scuba diving certifications for those who want a "deeper" look at the North Shore. Repairs, air fills, and other services, including packing surfboards for shipping back to the mainland, are available. Behind the Surf 'n' Sea parking lot (across the street from the Chevron station), there is a little picnic area with several tables and a great view of Haleiwa Harbor.

Surf 'n' Sea

The Manu O Ke Kai Canoe Club of Haleiwa practices behind Surf 'n' Sea. You may see them paddling out to practice on a Saturday morning or weekday afternoon. The broad lanai and open dining room of **Jameson's By The Sea** are a popular place to relax and watch the daily activities and sunset on the water. There is a **fudge works and gift shop** in the back of the restaurant.

Haleiwa Beach Park

Haleiwa Beach Park occupies the northern end of Waialua Bay. Built in 1939, the park stretches from the harbor breakwall across a narrow sand beach and large lawn, with picnic facilities, parking, restrooms, showers, a playground, lighted basketball and volleyball courts, and baseball and softball fields. The picnic and sports facilities are well used, especially on weekends. The pretty white pavilion along the shore was designed to welcome passengers of the OR&L Railway when the train stopped here. There are fabulous sunset views from the breakwall. The shallow, rocky bottom and narrow beach do not attract many recreational swimmers. However, the calm water and hard sand are ideal for launching canoes and kayaks. Outrigger and sailing canoe races often start here on weekend mornings.

Sailing canoes race off Haleiwa Beach Park

A war memorial stands at the entrance to the beach park. The Waialua Lion's Club erected the monument in 1947 to honor the

North Shore heroes who died during World War II. Today the memorial honors all North Shore residents who lost their lives in the service of their country. The Lion's Club holds a memorial ceremony at the monument on Memorial Day.

On the third weekend of July, Haleiwa Beach Park is the scene of the **Haleiwa Arts Festival,** where over 100 artists exhibit their work. Visual artists in all media are selected through a jury process. Live entertainment and activities for *keiki* (children) continue throughout the weekend. Knowledgeable local residents narrate historic trolley tours, pointing out the area's landmarks and sharing their own memories. The "Cool Stuff to Buy Booth" sells shirts, hats, and posters featuring images created by local artists. Half a dozen vendors sell food and beverages.

Haleiwa Boat Harbor

To continue your tour of Haleiwa Town, retrace your route across the Rainbow Bridge, pass Haleiwa Joe's, turn right (west) on Haleiwa Road, and take the first right turn into the **Haleiwa Boat Harbor**. At one time, a large boulder known as the **Akua Stone** blocked the entrance to the Anahulu here. It was removed so a glass-bottomed boat and sampans could use the river during the heyday of the Haleiwa Hotel.

The harbor is the hub of the North Shore fishing industry. The **Hanapaa Deep Sea Fishing Tournament** is held here each June. Sport fishing is available through **Chupu Charters, Kuuloa Kai Big Game Fishing Charters,** and **Go Fishing Hawaii. North Shore Catamaran Charters** offers whale watching, sunset, snorkel, and picnic cruises along the North Shore on a sailing catamaran. **North Shore Diving and Deep Ecology** has whale watching, turtle and dolphin tours, boat dives, snorkeling trips, and eco-tours.

Alii Beach Park

Alii Beach Park occupies 20 acres on the northern end of Waialua Beach, which extends from Kaiaka Bay to Kupaoa Point. The beach park has lifeguards, restrooms, showers, picnic facilities, a large lawn, boat launch, and parking.

The area near **Kupaoa Point** is one of the North Shore's most popular surf spots. There are two breaks. Near the point, the **Haleiwa surf break** is the site of the **Reef Hawaiian Pro, the first leg of the Triple Crown of Surfing,** each November. The Haleiwa break is popular for short boarding, long boarding, and bodysurfing, and a good place for surf lessons when the surf is small. South of the Haleiwa break, huge sets sometimes come in at **Avalanche.** When Avalanche breaks big, it is the site of tow-in surfing.

The best place for recreational swimming is inshore of the surf breaks. On the western end of the beach, a reef protects the water. On the eastern end, a small, protected area is tucked inside the break-wall. The long rocky outcropping and rip currents on the west side of the breakwall can be dangerous.

You may recognize the **John Kahili Surf Center,** which was used as a set for *Baywatch Hawaii*. The first floor is used for community meetings and activities. The Kahili Center was named in honor of a local man whose five sons served in the military during World War II. Throughout the War, the Kahilis entertained countless servicemen with dinners and *luaus* in their gracious home on Haleiwa Road, hoping that their sons would receive similar treatment elsewhere.

As you leave Alii Beach Park, turn right on Haleiwa Road to Walikanahele Road. Turn right on Walikanahele into a parking lot with restrooms. Here, on the southern side of Waialua Beach, you will find a nice shady beach, a gently sloping bottom, and a great view of the shoreline stretching toward Kaena Point. Straight out from the Haleiwa surf condos is the surf spot called **Walls.**

Historic Churches

West of Alii Beach Park on Haleiwa Road, notice the **Haleiwa Jo-do Buddhist Mission.** Buddhist missionaries founded the Mission in 1912 for the Chinese and Japanese sugar workers. The original building was severely damaged by the 1946 tsunami. The new temple serves the Buddhist community with weekly services and annual **O-Bon dances.** Held each year on the last weekend of July, the Bon festival includes a beautiful ceremony in which hundreds of tiny boats carry lighted candles out to sea in honor of deceased ancestors. The Mission also conducts classes in Japanese, hula, and other subjects. Kamehameha Schools runs a day care center in the building.

At the corner of Haleiwa Road and Keahipaka Lane, you will see the **Kealiiokamalu (The Prince of Peace) Protestant Church.** Built in 1898, the quaint red church building is typical of the wooden churches that once dotted the islands. Directly ahead on the *makai* side of Haleiwa Road is the **First Baptist Church of Haleiwa.** Next come old **Chun's Market** and the **Waialua Fire Station,** built in 1932 and listed on the historic registry. The green and white home on the *mauka* side of Haleiwa Road is the Kahili home. If you look up at the foothills of the Waianae Range from here, you can see the **Benedictine Monastery** overlooking Waialua.

Kaiaka Bay

Haleiwa Road continues along the waterfront to **Kaiaka Bay Beach Park,** a 53-acre park occupying the peninsula on the north side of Kaiaka Bay. Locals often refer to this site as "Fresh Air," because it was the site of the "Fresh Air Camp" for underprivileged children. During plantation days, the athletic field served as the home field of the Waialua Sugar Company's baseball team. Horse races were held every Sunday from Three Corners down the dirt Haleiwa Road to the Fresh Air Camp.

This is a great place for a family picnic, a game of Frisbee, some kite flying, or a quiet stroll when you have had enough salt water and sand for the day. There are picnic facilities and restrooms. Drive around the loop and take in the fabulous views of the Waianae Mountains and Mount Kaala, the highest point on Oahu, the shoreline curving out to Kaena Point on the northwestern tip of the island, and the old Waialua Sugar Mill. Or enjoy a leisurely walk, jog, or bike ride around the loop—the distance from the entrance, around the loop and back to the entrance is one mile.

Notice the large oval-shaped stone about 18 feet in diameter that is balanced on a smaller base on the western point of land, **Kalaeoiupaoa Point**. There are many Hawaiian folk tales about how this balancing stone, known as **Pohaku o Lanai**, arrived at this location. The ancestral Hawaiians used it as a *kilo* (lookout) for shoal fish. A *kiloia* (spotter) stood on top searching for a school of fish entering the bay. When the fish arrived, he alerted the fishermen of the village to assemble with their nets and canoes. A fishing *heiau* was located near the *kilo*. Most fishing *heiau* were small in size, just a circle of stones with a small altar where a pig was roasted. After a prayer the pig was eaten and the *imu* in which it was roasted was covered with dirt. Roast pigs were still being offered to fishing gods here in the late 19th century to ensure a plentiful supply of fish. Salt beds provided salt to preserve and season the catch.

The **Kapukapuakea *heiau*** once stood in this area. An important *heiau* dating from the 13th century, Kapukapuakea served as the state temple for Oahu. In the mid 1700s, the *kahuna* crowned high chief Mailikukahi to reign as the chief of Oahu. Nothing remains of the *heiau* now.

Kaiaka means "shadowy sea." The "Two Waters" of Waialua, **Kaukonahua and Paukauila Streams**, both empty into Kaiaka Bay. The wave action is gentle, allowing silt carried by the streams to accumulate near the shoreline. When heavy rains fall, the entire bay becomes muddy. For this reason, the beach fronting the bay is used mostly by fishermen and local children. Most swimmers favor the sandy beach on the north side of the peninsula.

Offshore of Kaiaka Bay, a surf spot known as **Hammerheads** produces challenging left tubes in the winter. However, it is a breeding area for hammerhead sharks, which causes most surfers to look elsewhere for waves.

"Two Waters"

As you leave Kaiaka Bay Beach Park, turn right (west) on Haleiwa Road to **Haleiwa Elementary School.** Recently restored, this pretty old school building is on the National Register of Historic Places. Notice the A-frame building next to the school. It was built for the construction of a large Polynesian canoe. The funding for that project did not come through, so the A-frame is being used for smaller outrigger canoes.

Haleiwa Elementary originated in 1871 as the Waialua English School, an independent school with no government funding. In 1880, it became a public school. This "New Waialua School" served the entire Waialua District until Waialua Elementary was built in 1965. In 1911, the school was moved to wooden buildings at this location. In 1921, the lovely building you see today was erected along with seven teachers' cottages across the street. In plantation days, there was no high school in the area and most local children went no further than the eighth grade.

Continue west on Haleiwa Road as it meanders through old cane fields and crosses **Paukauila Stream**, one of the "two waters" that gave Waialua its name. The area *makai* of the bridge is a popular spot for crabbing and fishing and a good place to see wetland birds.

Haleiwa Road ends at **Waialua Beach Road.** In plantation days, there were a number of mom and pop stores at this T intersection. Turn right (west) onto Waialua Beach Road and look for **Koukonahua Stream,** the second of Waialua's "Two Waters." Taro and water lilies grow in this well-irrigated neighborhood. The entire area is crisscrossed with turn haul roads once used to haul cane. Today these dirt roads offer great potential for bike trails.

Continuing west on Waialua Beach Road, you will see the **Waialua Elementary School**. Here you can continue west on Waialua Beach Road toward Kaena Point, or turn around, take Waialua Beach Road to Weed Circle, and return to Haleiwa Town.

Despite its name, **Weed Circle** is carefully maintained. It was named for a family that donated the land to enhance the entrance to Haleiwa Town. Follow the signs at Weed Circle to return to Haleiwa, take the Kam Highway northeast along the North Shore, or take Farrington Highway west toward Kaena Point.

A Perfect Day in Haleiwa

Take a whale-watching, turtle or dolphin tour, boat dive, snorkeling excursion, fishing expedition, or eco-tour from Haleiwa Boat Harbor. Then enjoy lunch and browse art galleries, surf museums, surf shops, and boutiques in Old Haleiwa Town. End the day with a swim at Alii Beach Park and a walk around the loop in Kaiaka Bay Beach Park.

Alternative: Watch a surf competition or go surfing at Alii Beach Park.

THE NORTHWEST SHORE

The remote shoreline between Waialua Town and Kaena Point beckons everyone who appreciates natural beauty and solitude. Volcanic cliffs descend to incredible beaches and reefs, providing a spectacular playground for polo players, riders, kite surfers, windsurfers, anglers, snorkelers, swimmers, picnickers, mountain bikers, gliders, skydivers, and lovers. Miles of deserted beaches and sand dunes where turquoise blue water tops endless purple reefs delight the eye and soothe the spirit.

Exploring this little-known part of the island warrants at least a full day. Except for the Farmers Market in Waialua on Saturday and the concessions at the weekly polo games in Mokuleia on Sunday, there are no restaurants. If you can't make the Farmers Market or polo game part of your itinerary, have a bite to eat or pick up a picnic lunch in Haleiwa Town before setting out.

The Drive Guide to this area is divided into two sections: (1) a circle tour of the old plantation town of Waialua; and (2) a drive along the spectacular northwest coast of Oahu from Waialua to Kaena Point. Both loops begin at Weed Circle.

The Old Plantation Town Of Waialua

To see the old plantation town of Waialua, start at Weed Circle, take Waialua Beach Road northwest past the Waialua Elementary School to Goodale Avenue, and turn left on Goodale to Waialua District Park.

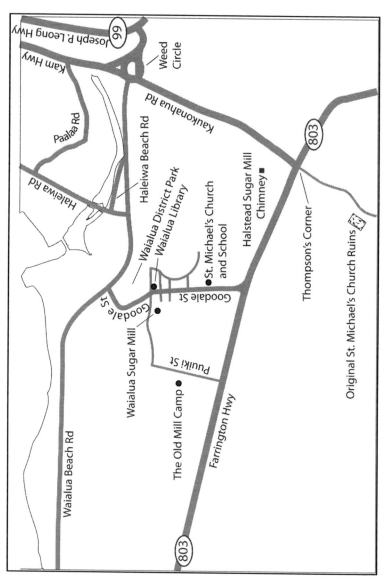

Waialua Town

Waialua District Park has the only public swimming pool in northern Oahu. The hours are irregular, so call ahead if you want to swim there. In addition to outdoor facilities for football, baseball, soccer, and picnics, this large public facility has badminton and volleyball courts, lighted basketball and tennis courts, a gym, weight room, playground, and facilities for crafts, meetings, and other activities.

Continue on Goodale Avenue approximately .3 miles to the stop sign at Kealohanui Street. To your right is the **Waialua Sugar Mill**, which was the heart of the local economy from 1898 until 1996. Locals remember how their days were punctuated by the sound of the mill's whistle marking the beginning and end of the workday and the 8:00 p.m. curfew. The people of Waialua want to preserve this iconic landmark.

A number of small businesses now operate in and around the old mill. On Saturday morning, a Farmers Market is held here and food stands sell *huli-huli* chicken and other local specialties. Try some *huli-huli* chicken and Waialua pineapple soda.

Waialua Bandstand on the corner of Goodale and Kealoha Nui is a replica of the gazebo that was built for boxing matches during plantation days. Monthly concerts are held here now, with programs ranging from military bands to Hawaiian and Filipino music and dance.

Diagonally across the intersection from the bandstand is the **Waialua Library**. Built in 1930, it has been named one of the best small libraries in the United States.

To your left is a white building that once housed the Bank of Hawaii. After the bank moved to Haleiwa Town, the building became the site of a legendary tavern called the **Sugar Bar**, where mill workers, bikers, surfers, tourists, and other characters gathered to "talk story," play darts, and imbibe.

St. Michael's Catholic Church and School

Continue on Goodale to **St. Michael's Catholic Church and School.** The Catholic Church in northern Oahu is as old as Liliuokalani Church, but its early years were much more difficult. The French Congregation of the Sacred Hearts of Jesus and Mary were the first Catholic missionaries on Oahu. When they arrived in Honolulu in 1827, the Protestant missionaries from America branded them "idolators." The priests were banished from the islands and their native converts were persecuted. Natives caught favoring Catholicism (for example, attending Catholic services or instruction, refusing to help build a Protestant church, or refusing to tear down a Catholic chapel) were jailed, put in irons, forced to cut and carry stones, and made to carry excrement by hand.

In 1831, a native convert named Luika Kaumaka moved to Waialua and started instructing her fellow Hawaiians in the Catholic faith. When the Hawaiian monarchy recognized religious freedom in 1839, Catholic priests were able to come to northern Oahu for the first time. They founded St. Michael's Parish in a thatched hut. In 1853, a large church with a three-story steeple was built on land donated by King Kamehameha IV. The Catholic community grew as sugar workers were recruited from Portugal, the Azores, the Madeira Islands, the Philippines, and other Catholic countries. In 1912, a new church with twin steeples was built near the sugar mill. After a kerosene stove explosion destroyed that church, a third church was constructed. Built in 1923, the current church is a replica of the San Gabriel Mission in southern California. St. Michael's School was established in 1944, and now serves youngsters from pre-school through eighth grade. In 1953, St. Michael's Parish added a second church—Sts. Peter and Paul Mission in Waimea.

The Waialua Mill Camp

To see what remains of the **old Waialua mill camp**, continue on Goodale Avenue until it dead ends at Farrington Highway, turn right on Farrington, continue past Waialua High and Intermediate School, and turn right again on Puuiki Street. Along Puuiki Street are the surviving homes and gardens of the old mill camp. What was once a bustling community for thousands of workers and their families now houses a few dozen retirees, most of them now in their 80s or 90s.

Turn left on Kealohanui Street to the **Waialua Hongwanji Buddhist Mission**. The temple is said to occupy the site of an ancient *heiau* that served as a place of refuge for those who broke *kapu*. Across the street from the temple is the old **Fujioka general store**, where generations of plantation workers gathered to "talk story." Fujioka's closed in July of 1997. From Fujioka's, return down Puuiki Street to the Farrington Highway and turn left on Farrington Highway to Thompson's Corner. On the south side of Farrington Highway between Goodale Avenue and Thompson's Corner, the **Kaala Healing Arts Center** offers healthy food, holistic remedies, and massages.

Thompson's Corner

The Farrington Highway intersects with Kaukonahoka Road at Thompson's Corner. As you approach the intersection, notice a dirt sugar cane road to the south where a gate holds a sign indicating there are "goats for sale." Down this road lie the **ruins of the original St. Michael's Catholic Church,** built in 1853. The adjacent cemetery is carefully maintained. Please remember Rule No. 9.

Before the arrival of the *haoles,* a beautiful grove of trees stood near this area. Known as the Paloa Grove, it was considered sacred to the Hawaiian goddess Pele. The trees were all cut down and the stones were moved during plantation days. Four *heiau* in this area were also destroyed when the land was used for agriculture.

Continue south on Farrington Highway for a few miles. At the top of the slope, turn around at the entrance to the housing development and take in the sweeping views of Waialua Valley and the

Pacific. Not long ago, all of these slopes sweeping down to the sea were filled with sugar cane. With King Sugar gone, the fields are slowly being converted to other crops. After stopping to enjoy the beautiful vistas, turn back on Farrington Highway past Thompson's Corner to Kauukonajuua Road, turn right, and look for a tall brick chimney standing in the fields on the west side of the road. This is the chimney of the **Halstead sugar mill**.

Continue on Kaukonahua Road toward Weed Circle. On the left is an old theater building from plantation days. Now it houses the **Oils of Aloha** factory. This thriving local business produces lovely oils, skin creams and lotions made with kukui nut oil. The products are available at local gift shops; there is no retail outlet at the factory.

At one time there were three movie theaters in the Waialua-Haleiwa area. On alternating nights, films were shown to the plantation workers in their native languages. The Haleiwa Mc Donald's replaced one theater, the Oils of Aloha factory took over this one, and the third no longer exists.

THE COASTLINE FROM WAIALUA TOWN
TO KAENA POINT

The drive along the beautiful northwest shore begins on Waialua Beach Road. From Weed Circle, drive west on Haleiwa Beach Road, which becomes Waialua Beach Road. From Thompson's Corner, drive west on Farrington Highway, turn right on Goodale Avenue to Waialua Beach Road, and turn left on Waialua Beach Road.

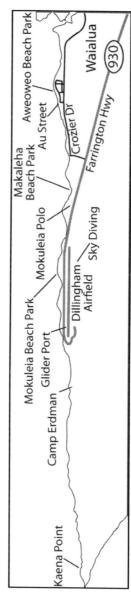

Northwest Shore from Waialua Town to Kaena Point

Aweoweo Beach Park

Take Waialua Beach Road to Apuhihi Street. Turn right on Apuhihi and drive several blocks to the T intersection. Straight ahead between two tall residential buildings, there is a public right of access to the beach. Turn left on Au Street and continue west to little Aweoweo Beach Park. Here you will find a sandy beach and wonderful views of the shoreline curving toward Haleiwa on one side and Kaena Point on the other, with restrooms and showers. This is a nice beach for sunbathing and wading, but not the best place for recreational swimming. Depending on conditions, the offshore reef, seawall, and beachrock can be hazardous.

The Quaint Beach Colony Of Crozier Drive

From Aweoweo Beach Park, drive west on Au Street to Waialua Beach Road, which becomes Crozier Drive. Turn right into the residential beach colony and continue west on Crozier Drive past Olohilo Street and the Salvation Army Camp. About .2 miles west of Olohilo Street, there is a public right of way to the beach. Park *mauka* and walk through the right of way to enjoy the views of the quaint beach colony and the northwest shoreline of Oahu. Past the public right of way, Crozier Drive dead ends at a gated housing compound. At the T intersection, turn left and drive by the Mokuleia Landscape and Nursery Company and Hibiscus Lady hibiscus farm to the Farrington Highway. Turn right (west) on Farrington Highway past the lovely **Crowbar Ranch** into the *ahupuaa* of Mokuleia.

Mokuleia

Mokuleia means the "district of abundance." In ancestral days, there was a large settlement here. The Hawaiians cultivated many terraced crops, including taro, sweet potatoes, bananas, and *awa* (a plant whose root was mashed into a medicine or drink used in ceremonies). Seafood was also abundant.

The Mokuleia shoreline was the first and largest residential area along the coast of Waialua to be developed by *haoles*. Most of the shoreline is private property.

Makaleha Beach Park

Makaleha Beach Park is a somewhat misleading name. Right now, it is still an undeveloped, 28-acre pasture where Makaleha Stream runs into **Kaiahulu Bay**. A public right-of-way through the pasture at 68-539 Farrington Highway (about .6 miles west of Mahinaai Street) leads to a wide, sandy beach. Kaiahulu means "foamy sea," a condition caused by the two streams (Makaleha and Kapalaau) that run into the bay. A surf spot on the reef, **Sylva's Channel**, was named for Edward Sylva, who lived in the area. At present, the beach is used mostly by local fishermen and surfers heading for Sylva Channel. A private beach retreat for employees of Castle and Cooke is on the east side of the pasture.

A Hawaiian legend about Makaleha tells of an enchantress named Kalamainuu. The legend was used to teach young Hawaiians the proper way to weave fishing baskets. Kalamainuu was an *e'epa*, born as a lizard and able to transform herself into different beings. One day a prince of Kauai named Puniaikoae was surfing off Kauai when Kalamainuu, in search of a husband, appeared as a beautiful woman on a longboard. The enchantress enticed Puniaikoae to leave his surfboard, jump on hers, and make love to her. Then she carried him out to sea and took him to her home in Makaleha Valley. There they feasted on the abundant fish and vegetables of Mokuleia and made love day and night. Eventually, Puniaikoae grew pale and sickly from his confinement. Gazing out at the sea, he begged Kalamainuu to let him go surfing. She gave him permission but commanded him not to speak to anyone along the way. Unfortunately, he did talk to two men who told him his lover was an *e'epa* and the surfboard was her tongue. Being an *e'epa*, Kalamainuu was aware of this betrayal. She let her young prince return to Kauai and carried out her revenge on the informers by weaving a basket in which she trapped them, killed them, and tore them to pieces. The pieces into which she tore them became hinalea fish. For generations, Hawaiians who followed the legendary directions for weaving the basket caught abundant supplies of hinalea fish.

Mokuleia Polo Field

Continue west on the Farrington Highway and follow the signs to the Mokuleia Polo Field. Polo has been played in Hawaii for more than a century. The Hawaii Polo and Racing Association began in the late 19th century at Kapiolani Park in Honolulu. In 1964, the **Hawaii Polo Club** acquired this 100-acre oceanfront ranch for a polo field and training facility. This is the only polo field in the world that is located on a beach. Polo matches are held here every Sunday from April through Labor Day. For a very enjoyable Sunday afternoon, drive out to watch a polo match, meet interesting people, have a dip in the ocean, and enjoy a delicious lunch or your own picnic. In addition to the Sunday matches, the Mokuleia polo team offers polo lessons and horseback riding on their thoroughbred polo horses through **Hawaii Polo Oceanfront Trail Rides**. The riding trails extend along the beautiful shoreline. The rock island offshore from the polo field is **Devil's Rock,** the only rock island on the Mokuleia shoreline.

Mokuleia Beach Park

Almost five miles of unspoiled beaches lie between Mokuleia and Kaena Point. Purplish reefs and aquamarine water color the shoreline. About a mile west of the polo field, 38-acre **Mokuleia Beach Park** has a paved parking lot, restrooms, showers, picnic facilities, and a playground and lawn area. Keep a close eye on children, as the water is easily accessible from the picnic and parking areas but hidden from view by sand dunes. The beach is long and sandy. The bottom is rocky, but there are sandy openings. When the water is calm, the shallow reef is popular for snorkeling and spear fishing. Wherever you see bright green *limu* (seaweed) clinging to the rocks, look for *honu* (Hawaiian green sea turtles).

Colorful kitesurfers and windsurfers zoom through the surf making jumps and turns. Further offshore, there are two surf breaks suitable for short boards. **Park Rights** is directly offshore and **Day Star** or **The Boat** lies about 200 yards west of the beach park. Offshore from Mokuleia, an undersea formation called **Kahuna Canyon** is a favorite location for scuba divers. The walls of the canyon rise steeply from the ocean floor, creating the illusion of a subterranean Grand Canyon.

Dillingham Airfield and Gliderport

Dillingham Airfield and Gliderport lies directly across the Farrington Highway from Mokuleia Beach Park. It was built in 1943 as an Army Air Corps Base for bombers and fighters. When the Air Force was created after World War II, it became an Air Force Base. Deactivated in the late 1960s, it was turned over to the Army and then leased to the State of Hawaii.

Dillingham has become a busy hub for glider rides, air tours, hang gliding, and skydiving. A glider ride is a memorable experience. A tow plane takes the glider to an altitude of about 5,000 feet. When the plane releases the glider, it floats silently with the uplifts off the Waianae Range. The view is unbelievable, with average visibility of 30 to 40 miles over a breathtaking panorama. Piloted glider tours float over ancient volcanic cliffs, lush valleys, brilliant coral pools, vividly colored windsurfing sails in the turquoise water, and the U.S. Air Force Satellite Tracking Station at Kaena Point. Occasionally, they even yield sightings of humpback whales, dolphins and sea turtles.

Bill Star ("Mr. Bill") and Sam Bleadon introduced gliding in northern Oahu in 1970, when they arrived fresh out of college and formed the Honolulu Soaring Club. Today, their Glider Ride Hawaii and several other glider operations offer scenic and acrobatic rides at the Dillingham Airfield. Airplane tours are also available. In addition to scenic tours of the North Shore and the entire island of Oahu, you can take an historic "Pearl Harbor tour" that retraces the Japanese bombing route on December 7, 1941 in a World War II airplane. For those seeking more adventure, there are acrobatic flying, hang gliding, ultralighting, and skydiving lessons and high altitude jumps.

The Forests Above Mokuleia

The Waianae Mountains rise high above Mokuleia to the summit of Mount Kaala, the highest point on Oahu. There are wonderful hiking and biking trails in these mountains. State or military permits are required for some areas, but there are two routes you can take without a permit.

About two miles west of Waialua High School, the **Mokuleia Access Road** winds 2.8 miles up a steep bluff to the **Peacock Flats Campground**, where a jeep trail leads another half mile to the boundary of the **Pahole Natural Area Reserve**. A hiking path takes you through the reserve to a lookout over the **Makua Valley** and Leeward Shore. The paved road continues west to the Kealia Trail.

The **Kealia Trail** begins on the west side of Dillingham Airfield and zigzags up the escarpment to the Mokuleia Forest Reserve. The arduous climb has an elevation gain of 2,000 feet. The reward is a magnificent view of the North Shore, the Waianae Range, and the Makua Valley leading down to the Leeward Shore. As you descend the Kealia Trail, gliders, biplanes, and skydivers from Dillingham Airfield may float past you while colorful kitesurfers and windsurfers skim along the turquoise waters below. During the winter, humpback whales can sometimes be spotted from the trail. Mountain bikers beware: The Kealia Trail is too steep for biking uphill and the downhill is strictly for experts.

Kealia Beach, Mokuleia Army Beach, and Camp Erdman

West of the Dillingham Airfield, the Farrington Highway passes **Kealia Beach** and **Mokuleia Army Beach**. With no offshore reef, the water here can be dangerous during winter or stormy conditions.

West of the Army beach, the YMCA operates **Camp Harold Erdman** as a summer camp for children and a year-round center for family camps, resident camps, leadership programs, conferences, and retreats. Josh Heimowitz runs the camp with help from his personable wife Courtney and their two darling children. The area west of the YMCA camp is a popular fishing area.

During the summer of 2004, my husband and I were driving along this shoreline on a quiet afternoon when we came upon a horrific sight. The beach was strewn with large pieces of wreckage of a jumbo jet! We were thrown into confusion, as there was no smoke, fire, or other evidence of a recent plane crash except the plane itself. Then we realized that this must be the set of a movie or television show. Suddenly people materialized on the road with fingers to their lips urging quiet as the miniseries *Lost* began shooting its first season. In the summer of 2005, we saw the same wreckage in a hangar at the Dillingham Airfield, ready for the next season's episodes. Keep your eyes open throughout northern Oahu for filming on *Lost* and other television shows and movies.

Kawaihapai, Kealia, Kaena, And Kuaokala

As you drive past Mokuleia toward Kaena Point, you will pass through four of the 14 *ahupuaa* of Waialua: Kawaihapai, Kealia, Kaena and Kuaokala. This region is steeped in legend.

Kawaihapai's fertile terraces are watered by Kawaihapai Stream. The name Kawaihapai, meaning "lifted water," comes from a Hawaiian legend about a long drought that was broken when water was carried in a cloud from Kahuku to Kawaihapai and came out in a spring from a rock. A large *heiau* was located at the base of the hill. Several fishing shrines were near the shore. Nothing remains of the *heiau* or shrines, but according to Hawaiian lore the *menehune* still fish off Kawaihapai at night. From the north side of Waialua Bay, when the night is dark, rows of twinkling lights can be seen on the water off Kawaihapai. Scientists say the lights are phosphorescent glow, but Hawaiian folklore maintains they are the *menehune* at their fishing, working fast against the coming of the dawn.

The *ahupuaa* of **Kealia** is not as fertile as neighboring Kawaihapai. Except for the lowland terraces between the cliff and the coral, Kealia was only suitable for growing sweet potatoes.

West of Kealia, the *ahupuaa* of **Kaena** stretches along the shore to the northwestern tip of the island, with **Kuaokala** in the mountainous area to the south. Except for a few dozen taro patches that were irrigated by springs, Kaena and Kuaokala were too arid to cultivate anything but sweet potatoes. However, Kaena was an excellent fishing ground. The Hauone fishing shrine was located near the edge of the water near Kaena Point. A small fishing village called Nenelea sat on the nearby sea cliffs. The reefs teemed with fish, and crabs were dug out of the sand. Squid were speared and eaten stewed or salted, sun-dried and roasted on coals. The salt likely came from salt-water evaporation in the holes of rocks along Kaena Point or from the salt pans near Paukauwila Stream. A salt industry continued on a small scale in Kaena into the 20th century.

There were numerous *heiau* in Kaena and Kuaokala. Some of the early Polynesian settlers were sun worshippers. A temple dedicated to the sun and restricted to the *alii* was located in Kuaokala, on the Waianae side of Kaena Point. None of these shrines has survived.

During World War II, the Army took over this area and erected defenses to guard the island against a Japanese invasion. Later the Kaena Point Satellite Tracking Station was erected in the Waianae Mountains above Kaena. Access to military land in this area remains restricted.

Lava and reefs border the entire Kaena shoreline. The waters are turbulent and the currents are extremely powerful. There are a few small coves, but no place that is safe for swimming. When big swells come in from the north during the winter months, enormous waves crash along the shore. Many believe that the mammoth waves that thunder against Kaena Point in the winter are the largest in the world. No one has ever ridden them successfully.

Kaena Point

Kaena Point lies about 2.5 miles from the end of the Farrington Highway. The views from the point stretch forever along the Leeward and North Shores and out to sea. From this northwestern extremity of Oahu, the island of Kauai is visible on a clear day.

Kaena Point State Park includes 778 acres on the scenic point. You can hike or bike around Kaena Point on a rutted jeep road that runs along the former roadway of the OR&L Railroad. If you go, be sure to stay on the main trail—it is unsafe to descend toward the ocean. The round-trip from the parking lot to Kaena Point and back is about five miles. The trail continues around Kaena Point to Yokohama Beach on the Leeward Shore, a round trip of approximately ten miles. The Sierra Club and Hawaiian Trail and Mountain Club conduct organized hiking and biking trips.

The **Kaena Point Natural Area Refuge** is a short detour from the main trail. The refuge was created in 1983 to preserve the coastal lowland dune ecosystem, which had been severely damaged by the railway and all-terrain vehicles. Many native Hawaiian plants and animals depend on this fragile ecosystem. In November the *moli* (Laysan Albatross) breeds here, and the sandy areas in the refuge serve as potential breeding sites. Seabirds, including red-footed and brown boobies, the wedge-tailed shearwater, and the brown noddy, are common. The rare Hawaiian monk seal favors the area, along with dolphins and *honu*. Humpback whales are seen breaching offshore during the winter breeding season.

For the early Hawaiians, Kaena Point was the main place on Oahu where the souls of the dead departed this earth. When a person lay on his deathbed, the soul left the body and wandered about. If all earthly commitments had been fulfilled, the newly released soul came to Kaena Point, where it was met by the souls of ancestors or friends who had preceded it. If the person's time had not come, the ancestral spirits would return the soul to the body. But if death had come, the spirits would lead the soul to **Ka Leina a ka Uhane**, "the soul's leap," where it would make its plunge into the sea on its way to eternity.

There are many Hawaiian folk tales about Kaena Point. According to one, it was here that the ancient god Maui attempted to unite Kauai and Oahu by casting his hook far out into the ocean to catch Kauai and drag it to Oahu. When Maui gave a mighty tug on the line, a huge boulder, the **Pohaku o Kauai**, fell at his feet. The boulder can still be seen off the north side of Kaena Point.

A Perfect Sunday on the Northwest Shore

Take an early morning hike or bike ride to Kaena Point. Then head for the Mokuleia Polo Field, have lunch, enjoy the polo match, and wade or swim in the ocean. Afterwards, take a glider ride or air tour at Dillingham Airfield and watch the kitesurfers and windsurfers cavort off Mokuleia Beach.

Alternative: Go on a weekday with a picnic lunch and reservations for a polo lesson or oceanfront trail ride at the polo field or a kitesurfing or windsurfing lesson at Mokuleia Beach. End the day with a glider ride or air tour at Dillingham Airfield.

KAWAILOA

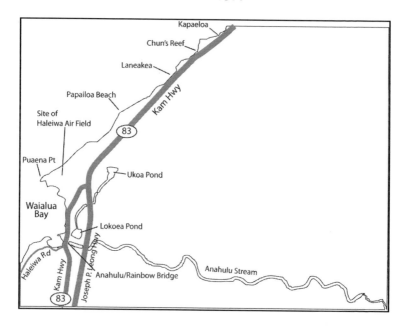

Kawailoa

Fishponds

To begin your drive along the famous North Shore, take the Kam Highway across the **Anahulu Bridge** into the *ahupuaa* of Kawailoa. The name Kawailoa means "long waters." The eastern border of Kawailoa is the Anahulu Stream, the longest streambed on Oahu. Over 20 miles long, the Anahulu and its tributaries run from the peaks of the Koolau Mountains all the way to Waialua Bay. Anahulu means "ten days"—the time it took to travel the length of these "long waters" on foot.

There were many Hawaiian villages along the Anahulu in ancestral days. Skilled in agriculture, the natives grew taro along the streams and other crops on the upland terraces. Irrigation was provided by a system of ditches that carried water from natural springs as well as the Anahulu and its tributaries.

The early Hawaiians were also skilled in aquaculture. They used fishponds not only to hold catches for future consumption, but also to cultivate food fish. The fishponds had wooden gates with slats spaced close enough to keep the fish in, but far enough apart to let water flow in and out. There were two types of ponds. *Puone* (inland ponds) formed naturally as brackish groundwater flowed through porous *aa* (lava rock) and filled depressions in the rock. *Kuapa* (open-sea ponds) were constructed by enclosing part of a bay with rock walls. On the North Shore, only *puone* could be used because *kuapa* could not survive the big winter surf. During the days when the fishponds were controlled by the *alii*, most of the fish was reserved for their consumption. If a chief's land had ample fishponds, it was known as *aina momona,* meaning a sweet or fruitful land.

As you pass the Chevron gas station, look *mauka* for lovely **Lokoea Pond.** Lokoea is a very old *puone*, possibly dating to the 17th century. Fresh water from the Anahulu Stream flows through Lokoea Pond into the ocean. According to Hawaiian folklore, King Kamehameha I pulled fish from Lokoea Pond himself. Locals say it is still full of mullet.

Queen Liliuokalani's summer home was on the southern shore of Lokoea Pond, just behind the Chevron station. The Queen liked to bathe in the fresh water.

Today, the pond is owned by the Kamehameha Schools' Trust, which was established by the Hawaiian royalty to educate children of Hawaiian ancestry. Local residents have leased fishing rights from the trust since the early 20th century. The Kamehameha Trust also owns agricultural land on the inland slopes and a substantial part of Haleiwa Town—a total of 25,000 acres on the North Shore.

Continue north on Kam Highway to the intersection with the bypass road, and turn left. Hidden in the wetlands above the merged road is mile-long **Ukoa Pond,** a *puone* that was used for aquaculture into the 20th century. Ukoa Pond was the subject of many Hawaiian legends. The pond's guardian was the goddess Laniwahine, who lived in a circular hole at its head. The Hawaiians said that when Laniwahine wanted to bathe in the ocean, she traveled through a tunnel from the pond to the sea, roiling the pond's placid water as she came and went. Modern scientists say that there was a subterranean connection between Ukoa Pond and the sea, causing the pond water to be disturbed when the ocean was rough.

Puaena Point

Turn *makai* (left) at the north end of Haleiwa Beach Park and follow the road until it dead ends near the water. Park there and walk along the dirt path to **Puaena Point,** which marks the northeastern tip of Waialua Bay. Once native Hawaiians came from all parts of Oahu to visit an oval-shaped stone near the point that was believed to have curative powers. The Puupea *heiau* was located near the ocean, and *kahunas* resided in a sort of college or monastery on a series of terraces above it. Today, surfing is the main attraction. The point is too dangerous for swimming.

The offshore waters teem with sea life. A red channel buoy off Puaena Point marks an area where *honu* congregate to have their shells cleaned by symbiotic fish. About a mile down the beach, there is a World War II blockhouse that marks the spot where local fishermen dive for lobster.

Haleiwa Air Field

As you drive back to the Kam Highway from Puaena Point, notice the woods on the north side of the road. What remains of the **Kawailoa Army Air Field, commonly known as Haleiwa Field,** lies beneath the underbrush. During the 1930s and 1940s, three auxiliary runways on the North Shore were used to disperse aircraft around the island. Haleiwa Field and another short airstrip in Kahuku were used for fighters; the longer runway at Mokuleia (now Dillingham Air Field) could handle both fighters and bombers.

A few days before the attack on Pearl Harbor, pilots George Welch (heir to the grape juice fortune) and Kenneth Taylor moved their P-40 fighters from Wheeler Field to Haleiwa Field for gunnery practice. The young lieutenants were emerging from an all-night poker game at Wheeler when the Japanese attacked on December 7, 1941. In the ensuing chaos, they telephoned Haleiwa Field, learned it had not been attacked, and told their ground crews to fuel and arm their planes. Racing from Wheeler to Haleiwa in record time, they took off without waiting for orders. Under intense fire, they shot down seven Japanese planes. The two young pilots were awarded the Distinguished Service Cross for their bravery. A fictionalized version of their performance on that momentous day was included in the movie "Pearl Harbor." Fighter planes continued to use the Haleiwa Air Strip throughout World War II, but today it lies unmarked and hidden beside the Kam Highway.

Farming and Ranching

Continuing north on the Kam Highway past the bypass intersection, look for the **Alluvion Nursery and Florist** behind the white picket fence. Alluvion Nursery grows over 500 varieties of plants in the pre-fertilized meadowland where the Meadow Gold Dairy used to graze milk cows—cows that were known to all the island's school children as "Lani Moo." The Alluvion florist shop makes and ships floral arrangements, gift baskets, and *leis* in large and small quantities. Visitors are welcome on weekdays from 7:00 a.m. to 3:30 p.m. and Saturday from 7:00 a.m. to 12:30 p.m.

Adjacent to the Alluvion Nursery, **Kawailoa Ranch** has extensive equestrian facilities for boarding, riding, and training horses. Managed by Uncle George Ai, it is the home base of many local equestrian groups and holds many riding events, including rodeos. In the uplands above the ranch, the **North Shore Cattle Company** grows organic beef.

As you continue north past Kawailoa Ranch, notice the road to the Kawailoa Refuse Station and the hills above it. Until 1996, this area was covered with cane fields that Waialua Sugar leased from the Estate of Princess Bernice Pauahi Bishop. The field workers lived in a camp above the current location of the refuse station. The Kawailoa field camp was a busy place, with homes, recreational facilities, a meetinghouse, and a plantation railroad line carrying passengers and sugar cane to and from the OR&L. A company nurse made weekly visits.

During World War II, the Army placed large guns at strategic locations near the Kawailoa camp to ward off a Japanese invasion. A four-gun battery of 155-millimeter guns was placed about a mile northeast of the camp, and a four-gun battery of 8-inch caliber railroad guns was placed on a special railroad spur about a mile southwest of it. A four-story tower was built about 1/4 mile from the camp to serve as a fire control station and command post for the soldiers manning the guns. Searchlights were mounted on towers along the shoreline. The only thing left of these defenses is the tower, which still bears the remains of its World War II camouflage paint.

Nothing remains of the Kawailoa field camp. When Waialua Sugar closed down in 1996, the retired field workers were moved to homes in the Waialua mill camp. Younger workers had to find other employment and housing.

The Kawailoa Shoreline

Papailoa Beach

The shorefront between Puaena Point and Waimea Bay is known as Kawailoa Beach. There are three pretty beaches along the Kawailoa shore: Papailoa Beach, Laniakea, and Chun's Reef. Until recently, these beaches were only considered suitable for surfing and fishing because of the rocky bottom. But the beauty of this shoreline and an influx of *honu* have made them popular spots for picnicking, turtle watching, and swimming in the sand pockets between the reefs.

Honu abound in the shallow coastal waters all along the North Shore. They come close to shore to feed on *limu* (seaweed). Sometimes they crawl out on the beach to bask in the afternoon sun. When you see these gentle creatures, please remember that they are a threatened species protected by federal and state law. It is illegal to disturb them in or out of the water, and fines are imposed for violations. Moreover, as beautiful as *honu* are, they are reptiles that can carry diseases and bite. Do not touch them and instruct your children not to touch them.

Honu basking on Papailoa Beach

Papailoa Beach fronts the lovely residential loop of Papailoa Road. Unseen from the Kam Highway, this wide beach has deep white sand and wonderful views of the coastline from Kaena Point to Waimea Bay. Giant *honu* often bask in the sun. A spit of land that collects sand in the summer months creates a surf spot called **the Point**. The bottom is too rocky for swimming, but there are pockets where you can wade or take a quick dip. To reach Papailoa Beach, turn *makai* from the Kam Highway into Papailoa Road, park, and walk through the public right of way near 61-785 Papailoa.

Laniakea

Back on the Kam Highway, as you pass the Kawailoa Ranch, the road opens to a picturesque, rocky beach called **Laniakea**. The name comes from a fresh water spring that comes up in the rocky shore under the beachfront homes on the Haleiwa side. This is not a good place to swim. The shoreline is rocky, and there is a strong rip current through the channel on the Haleiwa side when the surf is running.

Laniakea is popular for two activities: turtle watching and surfing. Basking Hawaiian sea turtles have caused such a sensation here that tour guides have started calling it Turtle Beach. Dozens of *honu* congregate to enjoy the *limu* growing on the rocks. The sandy beach on the north side provides access for tourists to wade and snorkel among them. We have an old friend who wears a tag bearing the Number 113. If you see him, tell him hello for me—but please don't touch him!

There are several popular surf breaks off Laniakea: **Himilayas** on the south end, **Laniakea** off the outside reef, and **Hulton's or Off the Rocks** offshore from Pohaku Loa Way. As you continue northeast from Laniakea on the Kam Highway, **Jocko's** breaks where beachfront parking opens up again.

The City and County of Honolulu owns three acres of undeveloped land on the *mauka* side of Kam Highway across from Laniakea, which it has designated as the **Laniakea Beach Support Park**. Park on the *mauka* side of the road and be extremely careful crossing to the *maikai* side. There are no improvements at Laniakea, but a lifeguard tower has been installed and lifeguards are on duty.

Chun's Reef and Kawailoa Beach Park

Continuing north on the Kam Highway from Laniakea, the next beach you can see from the road is **Chun's Reef,** where four surf breaks attract short boarders, longboarders, and bodyboarders. The surf spot is named for John Chun, a Kawailoa resident whose children loved to surf there.

The City and County of Honolulu owns several undeveloped beachfront lots along the wide sandy beach inshore of Chun's Reef.

Designated as **Kawailoa Beach Park,** it has become a popular spot for swimming, snorkeling and picnicking. There is a lifeguard station, but no amenities. There is, however, a fresh water spring in the large rocks on the Haleiwa end of Chun's Reef. If you dig down in the sand, you will find a nice way to rinse off after swimming in the ocean.

Chun's Reef Support Park is a small, undeveloped parcel of land on the *mauka* side of the Kam Highway. Be extremely careful crossing the Kam Highway to the beach.

Kapaeloa

The last section of the Kawailoa shorefront is **Kapaeloa.** Hidden from the highway, it stretches in front of the private homes between Chun's Reef and the Wananapaoa Islands at the entrance to Waimea Bay. Alligator Rock forms a landmark in the middle. The entire shoreline is rocky and generally unsuitable for swimming. When the surf is up, there are powerful rip currents.

Half a dozen surf breaks lie offshore from Kapaeloa: **Pidley's, Right Overs, Left Overs, Baby Sunset** off Alligator Rock, **Marijuana's,** and **Elephants** (also called **Uppers**). Access is provided through **Leftovers Beach Access Park.** As the highway begins to descend toward the Waimea Valley, the rocky little Wananopaoa Islets offshore mark the entrance to Waimea Bay, with its famous shorebreak and huge winter swells.

A Perfect Day in Kawailoa

Rent a sea kayak at Surf'n'Sea, paddle up the Anahulu Stream and along the Kawailoa shoreline, do a little snorkeling and watch for turtles. Afterward, have lunch on Jameson's patio, take a walk on Papailoa Beach, see the turtles at Laniakea, and finish the day with a swim at Chun's Reef.

Alternative: Take a surfing lesson or go surfing at Laniakea or Chun's Reef.

WAIMEA

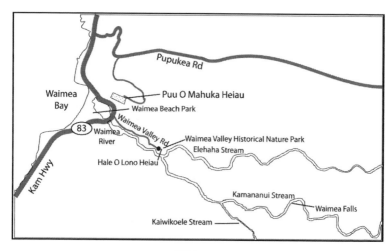

Waimea

Heading north past Kapaeloa, the Kam Highway begins to climb. As you top the rise, the road turns to reveal magnificent, horseshoe-shaped **Waimea Bay** stretching from the **Wananapaoa Islets** to the white tower of **Sts. Peter and Paul Catholic Mission**. To the south is majestic **Waimea Valley**, filled with natural beauty and the history of the Hawaiian people.

The rocky bluff on the southwest side of Waimea Bay is called **Keahu O Hapuu**. A small *heiau* encircling a stone figure of a fishing god once stood on this overlook. Another small fishing shrine was situated on the opposite bluff. The early Hawaiians watched for fish from the two *kilo* (lookouts) and signaled to fishermen below when schools of fish entered the bay. An ancient chant described the two stone sentinels as "patrons of the local fishermen."

The bluff is still used as a lookout, not so much for fishing as for taking photos, spotting humpback whales in the winter, and watching the action when the big surf arrives. When the beach park's parking lot is full (and it usually is), beachgoers often park along the road and hike down the rough paths to the bay. If you do that, be careful to observe the signs as parking is only allowed in a limited area.

Waimea Bay Beach Park

Waimea Bay is the crown jewel of North Shore beaches. The entrance to the beach park is on the north side of the bay. Slow down as you descend into the valley and make a sharp left into the parking lot. To get a parking space, you must either arrive early (usually by 9:30 a.m.) or wait for someone to leave. Otherwise, you can search for a roadside spot on the bluff above the bay, or continue north up the hill to the parking lot of Sts. Peter and Paul Catholic Mission and walk down to the beach. The beach park has restrooms, showers, lifeguard service, beach volleyball nets, and a shady lawn with picnic facilities.

Waimea's White Sands

Waimea is a world-class beach by any measure. The winter surf on the unprotected shore has produced a deep, mile-wide stretch of fine white sand. Sand so lovely, Waikiki Beach was created with sand mined from Waimea.

During the summer, the bay is so calm that sailboats anchor there. The translucent water is turquoise blue, deepening to royal blue as it stretches toward the horizon. The bottom is sandy and swimming conditions are excellent. Swimming across the bay from one side to the other is a great workout. Stay close to shore, as currents can make it difficult to swim in. Spinner dolphins frequently perform to the delight of spectators on the beach, and *honu* swim along the shoreline. If a little rain falls while you are at Waimea Bay, look for the *enui nui* (rainbows) over Waimea Valley. There are few sights more beautiful.

During the winter, Waimea is a different place. The water is rough and the currents are strong. Be sure to pay attention to all signs and warnings and obey them.

Jumping Rock

On the south end of Waimea Bay, a large rock rises from the water. Despite signs forbidding it, endless crowds of daring youngsters climb up the back of **Jumping Rock** and hurl themselves from the top into the water below. Old photos show that Jumping Rock was surrounded by beach until Waimea's sand was mined to fill in Waikiki.

Jumping Rock

The Waimea Shorebreak

The **Waimea Shorebreak** is a famous wave in its own right; it is the photogenic curl seen at the beginning of each episode of *Hawaii Five-0* as the theme song played and the opening credits rolled. Although locals enjoy bodyboarding and bodysurfing in the shore break, novices should exercise caution, particularly during the winter. Remember Rules 3 and 7.

The Big Surf

Waimea is most famous for the big surf that occurs during the winter months. There is some evidence that early Hawaiians once surfed there, riding the big surf all the way into the stream on their wooden longboards. But from the time Westerners arrived on Oahu until 1957, Waimea was considered too deadly to surf. One surfer lost his life there in 1943. Some locals believed the bay was haunted by the ancient *heiau* on the cliffs above it and the bones of the lost surfer in the water below. In 1957, a group of daring surfers finally rode the massive waves at Waimea and lived to tell the tale. After that, the evolution of short boards, skegs, leashes, and new materials combined with the rise of surfing as an international sport opened surfing up all along the North Shore.

On the north side of the bay near the cliffs, the inside break named **Pinballs** is surfable in smaller swells. The outside break is one of the world's most famous big-wave surf spots, the break called **Waimea Bay.** Several times a year, mammoth swells produce giant, bowl-shaped waves when they hit the reef and rocks along the cliffs. The park fills with spectators and photographers watching surfers challenge these monumental waves. Occasionally the huge waves close out the entire width of the bay, threatening surfers with the peril of being trapped inside. Daring rescues have been made by lifeguards and by helicopters flying under enormous waves to pull trapped surfers from their grip.

Waimea Bay attracts short boarders, longboarders, bodyboarders and bodysurfers, but only experts should attempt it in the big surf.

A dangerous riptide lurks only a few feet from shore, making it unsafe for amateurs to go near the water then.

Waimea Stream

Waimea Stream flows through Waimea Canyon from the Koolau Mountains toward the sea, but a barrier beach on the east side of Waimea Bay keeps the stream from reaching the ocean. When a strong rain causes the river to break through the barrier, the water creates a stationary wave. The name "Waimea" means "reddish brown water," no doubt referring to the color produced when the river breaks through the barrier beach. During the summer this can be a good spot for bodyboarding, although the runoff muddies the water for a few days. During winter storm conditions, big surf, or a rough shore break, the outflow can become a raging river.

Eddie Aikau Memorial

At the end of the parking lot closest to the beach, you will see **a memorial to a local hero named Eddie Aikau**. As you travel along the North Shore, you will see signs and decals bearing the legend, "Eddie Would Go." They refer to Eddie Aikau. A popular surfer, Eddie was one of the first lifeguards on the North Shore. As the head lifeguard at Waimea Bay, he was credited with making thousands of heroic rescues. In 1978, he joined the crew of the Polynesian Voyaging Society's double-hulled canoe, **Hokulea**, which set out on a voyage to prove that Hawaii's original settlers sailed similar canoes from Tahiti. The Hokulea began to break up in rough seas about 20 miles off the shore of Molokai. Eddie launched his surfboard to go for help while the remainder of the crew stayed with the Hokulea. He never made it. The remainder of the crew was rescued, but Eddie was lost at sea. Subsequent journeys proved that ancient Polynesians could travel from Tahiti to Hawaii by canoe.

Eddie Aikau's courageous spirit will be honored forever on the North Shore. His memorial reads, in part:

> Eddie Aikau is gone, but his name will live in the annals of heroism of Hawaii. His spirit will live, too, wherever the Hokulea sails and on the beach at Waimea Bay where, as a city and county lifeguard, he saved thousands of lives from the dangerous waters. This was a great man, a great Hawaiian, and he will live in our hearts forever.

A unique surfing contest, the "Quicksilver in Memory of Eddie Aikau Big Wave International," is held at Waimea when the surf consistently reaches 20 feet or higher. Participation is by invitation only.

Pupukea Marine Life Conservation District

The entire shoreline from the Wananapaoa Islets at the entrance to Waimea Bay to Kulalua Point on the north side of Shark's Cove has been designated as the Pupukea Marine Life Conservation District (MLCD). To preserve the reefs and sea life, fishing within the conservation district is strictly limited. In Waimea Bay, MLCD rules only allow hook and line fishing from the shore.

Waimea Valley

Waimea's Story

Waimea was the major political and religious center of Northern Oahu. Beautiful Waimea Valley offered cool forests, abundant water, and fertile land for agriculture. At least four streams of fresh water cascaded down the mountainsides into Waimea Stream and then the ocean. With a sophisticated agricultural system using terraces and irrigation ditches, the early Hawaiians grew taro, sweet potatoes, and bananas. Pigs, chickens and dogs were raised. Fishing in the streams and ocean was abundant, and the coastline offered good surfing and canoe landing sites.

Considered a sacred place, Waimea Valley was an important center of religion and spirituality. In the 11ᵗʰ or 12ᵗʰ century A.D., the entire *ahupuaa* of Waimea was given to the island's *kahuna nui* in perpetuity. With the assistance of fierce tattooed warriors, the *kahuna nui* enforced the traditional law of *kapu*. Three large *heiau* survive here: **Kupopolo,** on the ridge to the south; **Hale O Lono,** on the valley floor; and **Puu O Mahuka,** on the ridge to the north. There is no access to Kupopolo, but Hale O Lono and Puu O Mahuka are open to the public.

Waimea is the place where Westerners first arrived on Oahu. After Captain Cook's death on the Big Island of Hawaii in 1779, his ships continued their explorations. Heading for Kauai to pick up provisions, they sailed along the North Shore of Oahu and anchored off Waimea. Despite their disastrous experience on the Big Island, where Captain Cook was killed in a fracas with the natives, the new captain, Charles Clerke, went ashore with several men to explore Waimea. Their records reflect that they found the valley heavily populated and cultivated, and admired its beauty and natural resources.

In 1791, another British expedition under the command of George Vancouver set out to explore the islands. Vancouver's supply ship, the *Daedalus,* met the two advance ships and then set out without an escort. In 1792, the *Daedalus* dropped anchor in Waimea Bay. The captain took one of the ship's boats onto the beach and left an armed party to guard it while he went into the valley with his astronomer and two seamen. They never returned. Kahekili, the chief of Maui, had just conquered Oahu. He was soon to face attack by the chief of Hawaii, Kamehameha, who had *haole* muskets and gunpowder. Kahekili's warriors killed the captain and his companions. Then they attacked the men guarding the boat, seized their muskets, and forced them to return to the *Daedalus.* Scholars believe that the bodies of the captain, astronomer, and two seamen were offered as a sacrifice at the Puu O Mahuka Heiau on the bluff overlooking Waimea Bay.

When he learned of the murder at Waimea, Captain Vancouver demanded that the perpetrators be punished. Kahekili, the Maui chief who had conquered Oahu, seized several natives, tried them, found them guilty, and had them executed with a pistol shot to the head in a canoe alongside Vancouver's ship off Waikiki. Few believed that the men who were executed were the ones who committed the crime.

Waimea Valley continued to be heavily occupied and cultivated into the 19th century. After Kamehameha conquered Oahu, his *kahuna nui,* Hewahewa, resided there until his death in 1838. When the Europeans arrived, they introduced new crops and orchards. Unfortunately, the denuding of the forests in the upper valley to harvest sandalwood led to devastating floods. By the 1860s, the population of Waimea had been decimated by a deadly combination of floods, famine, and disease. A disastrous flood in 1894 marked the end of traditional Hawaiian life in the valley.

Waimea Valley is the site of numerous ruins and artifacts. Remnants of agricultural terraces remain on both sides of Waimea Stream for a distance of several miles. Some of these terraces appear to have been irrigated. Many old breadfruit trees are found far up the gulch. Remains of houses, other structures and burial caves have also been found.

In 1969, the Bishop Museum acquired Waimea Valley with the intention of restoring its ruins and artifacts and preserving its history. It established Waimea Valley Park to protect and maintain the archaeological treasures, provide authentic Hawaiian entertainment and recreation, and maintain a botanical garden to showcase and preserve the native plants, many of which were endangered. However, the valley did not remain under the Bishop Museum's control. It went through a series of incarnations as an arboretum, adventure park, movie set, and backdrop for weddings and other events before a coalition of community organizations took steps to protect it. Eventually, the Office of Hawaiian Affairs ("OHA") acquired Waimea Valley. For a time the National Audubon Society managed its priceless cultural, botanical, and ecological resources under a contract with OHA. In 2008, management was turned over to Hiipaka, LLC, a non-profit corporation established by OHA for that purpose.

Hale O Lono Heiau

Hale O Lono means "house of Lono." This *heiau* was built in the 15th or 16th century and dedicated to the Hawaiian god Lono. One of the four principal gods of the early Hawaiians, Lono ruled agriculture, harvests, weather, and sports. Archaeologists from the Bishop Museum have been restoring the *heiau* since it was discovered in 1974. Visitors can see its original configuration, including the thatched housing for sacred drums, an oracle tower, a storage tower for sacrificial objects, a replica of a typical carved wooden statue, and the refuse pit in which human remains were disposed.

To visit the Hale O Lono Heiau, drive north on Kam Highway past the parking lot for Waimea Bay Beach Park, cross the Waimea Stream bridge, and turn *mauka* at the sign for the Waimea Valley Historical Nature Park. As you drive down the entrance road, take in the exquisite beauty of the Waimea Valley. Continue along the Waimea Stream to the parking lot and find a shady spot. The *heiau* is located at the north end of the parking lot.

Waimea Valley Historical Nature Park

The 1,875-acre Waimea Valley Historical Nature Park, 59-864 Kam Highway, provides a delightful introduction to the natural beauty and history of Hawaii. The valley is a rich repository of pre-contact Hawaiian artifacts. Hawaiian living and games sites help visitors understand how the early Hawaiians lived. It is also a fabulous place to see native flora and fauna. The garden now contains 35 distinct collections with over 5,000 taxa of tropical plants, all carefully documented and labeled. It has one of the finest collections of

Polynesian plants in existence, as well as excellent collections of rare Hawaiian plants. Native Hawaiian animals also make their home in the park. Various species of migratory birds, including plovers and turnstones, winter here. Many introduced species, including peacocks and the ubiquitous Indian mongoose, also inhabit the valley.

Guests are given a map of the park, including information on the history and cultural importance of the land and the native wildlife. The ¾-mile self-guided trail through the garden valley leads to 45-foot **Waimea Falls** (also known as **Waihee Falls**). Wear your bathing suit and enjoy a refreshing swim. There are changing rooms and lifeguards at the pond. The park hosts daily programs and activities. It is open daily from 9:30 a.m. to 5:00 p.m. Wheelchair access is provided. An attractive grill serves sandwiches, salads, plate lunches, and drinks on a pleasant deck near the entrance and gift shop. Another snack bar near the waterfall offers snacks and drinks. Check the bulletin board outside the gift shop or call 638-7766 in advance for the schedule of guided tours and other events.

A Perfect Day in Waimea

Spend the morning swimming, bodyboarding, and watching the spinner dolphins play at Waimea Beach Park. Then visit the Hale O Lono Heiau, have lunch, and enjoy the afternoon at the Waimea Valley Historical Nature Park. Finish the day with a refreshing swim under the 45-foot waterfall.

THE KOOLAULOA DISTRICT

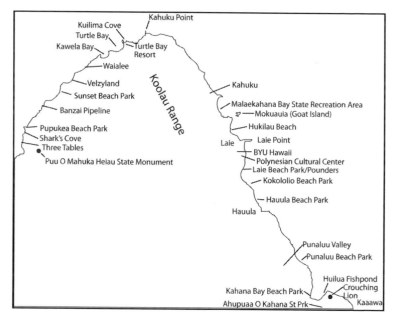

The Koolauloa District

Koolauloa's Story

Koolauloa embraces all of northeastern Oahu, including the North Shore from Pupukea to Kahuku Point and the Windward Shore from Kahuku Point to Kaaawa. In ancestral days, when Waimea was part of the Koolauloa *moku,* the great *heiau* in Waimea and Pupukea were the center of spiritual power on Oahu. Along the Windward Shore, the early Hawaiians farmed the lush mountainsides and harvested abundant seafood with nets and fishponds. Tragically, after Western contact the native population of Koolauloa was devastated by disease. Eventually, Kahuku and Laie were repopulated with imported sugar workers and Mormon settlers. Then surfers and tourists discovered the extraordinary attributes of the North Shore. As King Sugar declined, Del Webb's development of the Turtle

Bay Resort brought new visitors to Koolauloa. Fortunately, Hawaii has protected the natural beauty of this area, and created Hawaiian homesteads to preserve the traditional way of life that once flourished on the Windward Shore. Driving through Koolauloa on the Kam Highway is, in some ways, a trip back in time to "Old Hawaii."

PUPUKEA

As you leave the Waimea Valley and continue north on the Kam Highway, you will enter the *ahupuaa* of Pupukea, which means "white shell." Beautiful Pupukea extends from a magnificent shoreline with gorgeous coral reefs and tidal pools teeming with sea life to lush forests on the ridge overlooking Waimea Valley and the ocean.

Sts. Peter and Paul Catholic Mission

From Waimea Valley, turn north (right) on Kam Highway and drive up the hill to **Sts. Peter and Paul Catholic Mission.** This quaint little structure, a beloved landmark of Waimea Bay, was not originally intended to be a church. It was the site of the rock quarry that produced the gravel to build the Kam Highway from Waimea to Kahuku between 1929 and 1932. In 1953, the Catholic mission transformed the rockpit into a church. The machine sheds were converted to a patio and chapel. The rock crushing tower was converted to a belfry with the bell from the OR&L's Engine Number 6.

Priests from St. Michael's and the Benedictine Monastery in Waialua say Mass at Sts. Peter and Paul at 7:30 and 9:30 a.m. every Sunday. The congregation is a mixture of tourists and locals. The statues of the two patron saints in front of the church are often adorned with fresh *leis*.

Continuing uphill from Sts. Peter and Paul Church, there is a traffic light at the intersection of Pupukea Road and Kam Highway, just south of the **Pupukea Foodland grocery store.** Here you can either turn *mauka* on Pupukea Road to reach the Puu O Mahuka Heiau and other sites on the ridge, or turn *makai* into the 80-acre Pupukea Beach Park.

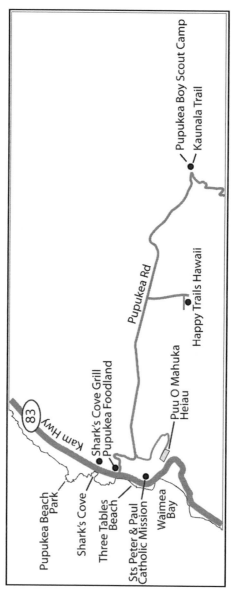

Pupukea

Pupukea Foodland is a well-stocked grocery store with lots of take-out foods at the deli counter as well as fresh fish, meats, produce and other items. It also carries a good inventory of beach supplies—sandals, hats, sunscreen, tatami mats, towels, beach chairs, snorkels and masks, and beach toys for the kids. Souvenir items are available at reasonable prices. Be sure to ask for Foodland's "Maikai card" to get the discounts afforded to regular customers. The **Starbucks Coffee shop** inside Foodland opens at 5:00 a.m.

Puu O Mahuka Heiau State Monument

Turn right off the Kam Highway at the traffic light and follow Pupukea Road to the top of the bluff, where a sign directs you to the Puu O Mahuka Heiau State Monument. A National Historic Landmark and State Historic Site, Puu O Mahuka is the largest *heiau* on Oahu. In these stone ruins, you can feel the presence of the ancient Hawaiians who worshipped and prepared for battle in sacred ceremonies centuries ago. Notice the stones wrapped in ti leaves and the offerings of flowers and fruit that have been left here by local Hawaiians, and remember Rule No. 9. The rocks are unstable, so stay on the paths as you explore the *heiau*.

Scholars believe that Puu O Mahuka was the scene of human sacrifices through the late 18th century, when the unfortunate captain and crewmen from the *Daedalus* met their end here. The *kahuna* of Puu O Mahuka maintained close ties with a *heiau* on the island of Kauai through visual communications with signal fires. Walk around to the west side of the bluff for an amazing view of Waimea Bay, Waimea Valley, and the ocean reaching toward Kauai. Imagine the *kahuna* who stood on this ridge signaling to the *heiau* on Kauai. It is especially beautiful here at sunset.

The Pupukea Ridge

To resume your tour of Pupukea, return to Pupukea Road, turn *mauka* (right), and continue uphill. Near the top of Pupukea Road, the neighborhood becomes more rural, with some properties supporting livestock and the left side of the road becoming forested. Notice how the trees support giant climbing philodendron. The paved road ends at the **Camp Pupukea Boy Scout Camp**. The **Camp Paumalu Girl Scout Camp** is nearby.

On weekends and holidays, you can take an interesting hike on the **Kaunala Trail,** a 2.5-mile loop through the **Pupukea Forest Reserve** that begins at the end of the road, about ½ mile past the Boy Scout camp. The trail is wide and well graded, with only a 500-foot gain in elevation. Native birds and vegetation delight observant hikers, and the clearings provide excellent views of the North Shore.

If you enjoy horseback riding, you will be interested in **Happy Trails Hawaii**, which has operated for over a decade on a hilltop overlooking Waimea Valley. Guided trail rides traverse cool, sun-filtered forests, lush ranch land, and wild tropical orchards with panoramic ocean and mountain views.

From Pupukea, return partway down Pupukea Road and turn right on Alapio Road. This is the exclusive Sunset Hills area, the site of Elvis Presley's Hawaiian retreat, known locally as "The Mansion." James Michener lived in one of the homes overhanging the hillside while he was writing his epic *Hawaii*. Return to the Kam Highway the same way you came. As you drive down Pupukea Road, **Pupukea Beach Park** lies directly in front of you.

Pupukea Beach Park

Spectacular 80-acre Pupukea Beach Park offers the best snorkeling and diving on the North Shore, with large protected tide pools and coves surrounding incredible coral reefs teeming with sea life. At the intersection of Pupukea Road and Kam Highway, the Honolulu Fire Department's Sunset Beach Fire Station sits where the OR&L used to pick up passengers at the Maunawai train stop. It may look like a dream workplace, but the firefighters at this station are constantly on call for dangerous ocean rescues and other emergencies.

The shoreline is rocky, with a pocket beach on each side of the Fire Station—Three Tables Beach on the south and Shark's Cove on the north. There is a lawn area in the middle, with showers, restrooms, lighted basketball and volleyball courts, and shady spots for picnicking and relaxing. From the lawn, there are great views of the shallow tidal pools and all the action below.

This shoreline is part of the **Pupukea Marine Life Conservation District**. Unlike Waimea Bay, where limited line fishing is allowed, fishing is completely prohibited in Pupukea. The only thing that can be taken is a small amount of *limu*, with the holdfast left in place.

Three Tables Beach

Three Tables Beach takes its name from the three flat sections of reef that are visible here at low tide. The pretty cove is bordered by a rock outcropping on one side and shallow tidal pools on the other. This beach is very popular with families in the summer. The sea floor is sandy and the reef protects the cove from the open sea. Little tots can play in the sand and frolic in the shallow water. Older kids can snorkel and bodyboard. It is easy to keep an eye on them within the circumference defined by the rocks, tidal pool, and reef. Snorkeling is excellent around the tables, where the water is about 15 feet deep. The area outside the tables is ideal for scuba diving, with lava tubes and arches. Many visitors like to wade in the shallow lagoon on the north side of Three Tables. If you do so, be sure to wear water shoes and avoid stepping on the delicate coral.

During the winter, Three Tables is often too rough for swimming. Waves sometimes flood the walls of the lagoon. As the water level rises, a current drains into Shark's Cove. Be sure to stay out of the water and lagoon if waves are washing over the outer wall, as the current can sweep you off your feet and drag you across the coral.

Shark's Cove

Shark's Cove is the **premier snorkeling and diving area** of northern Oahu. Don't let the name throw you—it refers to the shape of a reef outside the cove, not to denizens below. Once you are in the water, it is sheer magic. Schools of colorful tropical fish drift by you.

Large sea turtles often graze along the rocks. The water is approximately 20 feet deep inside the cove, and 45 feet deep outside the cove. There are sea caves outside the northeastern corner.

In the winter, Shark's Cove can become hazardous as rough seas wash over the sharp coral. When the water is too rough at Pupukea, good snorkeling can usually be found in the reef-protected waters of Kuilima Cove next to the Turtle Bay Resort.

Remember that Pupukea is just around the point from Waimea. During the summer, strong swimmers enjoy making their way between the two beach parks. For a great outing during the summer, paddle a kayak past Waimea and around the point to Shark's Cove. Bring your mask and snorkel and enjoy snorkeling in Shark's Cove or along the reef. As you paddle along outside the reef, sea turtles and dolphins may join you.

The Ke Ala Pupukea Bike Path

The Ke Ala Pupukea Bike Path begins at the Pupukea Beach Park and continues northward along the coast to Velzyland. This is the only paved bike path along the North Shore.

Equipment Rentals

Planet Surf, on the corner of Pupukea Road and Kam Highway (across the street from the Fire Station), offers surf lessons and rents surfboards, snorkel gear, and bicycles. **Shark's Cove Surf Shop**, on Kam Highway across the street from Shark's Cove, also rents snorkel equipment. **Country Cycles,** across Pupukea Road from Foodland, and **Barnfield's** in Haleiwa rent bikes.

Shark's Cove Grill

Across Kam Highway from Shark's Cove is a terrific lunch wagon called the **Shark's Cove Grill**. This isn't just another lunch wagon. The Shark's Cove Grill serves delicious meals, such as shrimp and teriyaki skewers with rice and salad, at reasonable prices. It is open for breakfast, lunch, and early dinners.

A Perfect Day in Pupukea

Snorkel or dive at Shark's Cove, then swim and relax at Three Tables Beach. After lunch at the Shark's Cove Grill, drive up Pupukea Road for a trail ride at Happy Trails Hawaii or (only on weekends and holidays) hiking or mountain biking on the Kaunala Trail. Visit the Puu O Mahuka State Monument and watch the sun set over Waimea Bay.

Alternative: Walk, run, or bicycle along the Ke Ala Pupukea Bike Path from Pupukea to Velzyland and back.

SUNSET

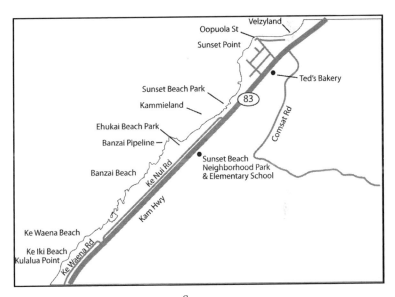

Sunset

Ke Iki, Ke Waena, Banzai, Ehukai, and Kammieland

The shoreline between Pupukea Beach Park and Sunset Beach is a surfer's paradise called "Sunset." As you head north on the Kam Highway from Pupukea, you cannot see the shore from the road. Just past Shark's Cove, a surf break known as **Pele's Followers** lies off the rocky south side of Kulalua Point. On the north side of Kulalua

Point, **Kahawai Beach Support Park** provides access to **Ke Iki Beach.** The soft sand is lovely, but remember that it is the product of a rough shorebreak and huge winter surf. Even in the summer months, the steep dropoff, sharp rocks, and strong rip currents make swimming at Ke Iki hazardous.

Continuing north from Ke Iki, take Ke Waena Road, a narrow residential loop that runs parallel to the Kam Highway. To reach **Ke Waena Beach**, use the public right of way near the lifeguard tower. **Banzai Rock Support Park**, an undeveloped 2.3-acre parcel between Ke Waena Road and Ke Nui Road, also provides access to the beach. If you can't find a parking spot on Ke Waena Road, park at Ehukai Beach Park, on the Kam Highway, or at Sunset Beach Neighborhood Park and Elementary School on the *mauka* side of Kam Highway, and walk back. Observe parking restrictions, watch out for children if school is in session, and be careful crossing the Kam Highway. Also remember Rule No. 2.

Ke Waena

With a deep beach and sandy bottom, **Ke Waena Beach** attracts strong swimmers and bodyboarders in the summer and expert surfers in the winter. Even in the summer, this is not a good beach for children or inexperienced swimmers. The winter surf carves steep dropoffs in the beach and ocean bottom. Strong currents and rough water can be dangerous. Still, it's a spectacular place to walk and watch the surfing. Before everyone had digital cameras, locals used to call it **Kodak Beach** because of all the film wrappers left there.

To find the famous surf breaks, stand in front of the Ke Waena lifeguard tower facing the ocean. On the far left you can see **Outer Log Cabins** on a deepwater reef far offshore, and **Log Cabins** closer to shore. These breaks are the product of an extremely uneven sea bottom. Flat lava tables alternate with sand and dangerous rock spikes, making the wave action extremely challenging. Swells hit these breaks from all directions. The offshore reef pushes western swells toward the Banzai Pipeline, but northern swells produce a huge outside break at Outer Log Cabins. Some of the largest waves in history were ridden there in January of 1998. Outer Log Cabins is used for tow-in surfing when it breaks big.

The large lava rocks on the south end of Ke Waena Beach are called **Rock Pile** or **Banzai Rocks**. About 250 yards offshore, the **Rock Pile** reef sometimes produces challenging waves in a northern swell. The shoreline north of Banzai Rocks is called **Banzai Beach.**

Directly in front of the Ke Waena lifeguard tower, **Off the Wall** offers fast shallow rights and occasional lefts over a bottom of reef and sand. It was known as **Kodak Reef** until the owners of the beach-front home facing the break built a stone wall that provides an easy landmark for the lineup.

Backdoor is a right break from the Banzai Pipeline. In a northwest swell, Backdoor can sometimes produce a deep right barrel that is longer and faster than the Pipeline itself, but it does not have a channel back out like the Pipeline has.

This world-famous surf beach is best left to expert long boarders, short boarders, and bodysurfers. Turbulence and strong currents make it unsuitable for recreational swimming.

The Banzai Pipeline

With its iconic curl over a menacing coral bottom, the Banzai Pipeline is one of the most famous surf spots in the world. The famous left break only occurs under certain conditions. A shallow coral shelf extends about 50 yards into the ocean. Winter swells jump to tremendous heights when they hit this coral shelf from the west or northwest. The incoming surf is so powerful that the crest of each wave is thrown forward as it breaks, forming a hollow left tube resembling a pipeline. The waves power down the line with immense force. Surfers try to crouch down inside the tube and emerge from it just before it collapses. Due to the sharp coral, rough water, and strong currents, there have been many injuries, and even a few fatalities, at the Pipeline. It is unsafe for swimming and novice surfers at any time of the year.

The first recorded attempt to surf the Pipeline was in 1957, when Bob Shepard and Bill Coleman each caught one wave before being wiped out and cut up on the coral reef. In the early 1960s, Phil Edwards rode the Pipeline successfully. Since then, the Pipeline has been surfed regularly by longboarders, short boarders, and bodysurfers, and Phil Edwards has had an illustrious career as a surfboard shaper. The Pipeline is the site of several major surf competitions, including the **Billabong Pipeline, Third Leg of the Triple Crown of Surfing**; the **Pipeline Masters**, and the **Monster Energy Pipeline Pro**, which is held on the four best wave days in late January and early February.

The Pipeline lies between Banzai Beach and Ehukai Beach Park off Ke Nui Road. The easiest way to reach it is to park at Ehukai Beach Park and either walk along the beach or walk down Ke Nui Road to the public right of way. If you can't find a parking space at Ehukai, you can park on the Kam Highway or at Sunset Beach Neighborhood Park and Elementary School and walk back. Observe parking restrictions, watch out for children if school is in session, and be careful crossing the Kam Highway.

Ehukai Beach Park

The Hawaiian word *ehukai* means "reddish-tinged water." The Hawaiians called sea spray *ehukai* because the spray of the breaking waves has a reddish or rainbow color when the sun shines through it.

Ehukai Beach Park is a tiny 1.2-acre beach park at 59-337 Ke Nui Road, across the street from Sunset Beach Neighborhood Park and Elementary School. The little park has restrooms, showers, and a small lawn with picnic tables. The lifeguard tower is visible from the Kam Highway. With a shallow reef and sandy bottom, Ehukai is popular with bodysurfers as well as boardsurfers. Strong swimmers may enjoy swimming over the sandbar when the waves are under three feet, but the water is always lively. Even in the summer, strong currents, backwash, and turbulence make Ehukai too rough for most swimmers. The breaking waves often cause severe erosion, leaving steep drop-offs and large boulders exposed. Look for warning signs and talk to the lifeguard before entering the water.

Sunset Beach Neighborhood Park

The **Sunset Beach Neighborhood Park** at 59-360 Kam Highway has lighted basketball, tennis, and volleyball courts, a soccer field, and play equipment. A **Farmers' Market** is held in the parking lot on Saturday mornings. It is a great place to pick up fresh fruits, vegetables, flowers, and local handicrafts.

More Surf Spots

More surf spots line the shoreline north of Ehukai. **Pupukea** has a sandy bottom. **Gas Chambers** has a coral bottom and breaks into a rocky point. The right break off Gas Chambers is known as **Turkey Bay**. For access, drive north on Kam Highway to the large wooden tiki with beach towels and sarongs on display. Turn *makai* into the small road across from the tiki, then turn left, park roadside, and take the right of way between the houses to the beach. Remember Rule No. 2! If you can't find parking near the right-of-way, park at Ehukai Beach Park or Sunset Beach Neighborhood Park and walk north along the beach from Ehukai. This area is not suitable for swimming.

Continuing north on Kam Highway, watch for the Chevron service station. South of the station is a shallow reef called **Rocky Point**. Despite its name and the sharp rocks on the bottom, this is a popular spot for short boarders and bodyboarders. To the north of Rocky Point is a similar reef section called **Arma Hut**.

Kammieland

As you continue north toward Sunset Beach, there is a public right of way to the **Kammieland surf spot**. The right of way is directly across the highway from the former site of "Kammie's Market," a ramshackle old store that was recently torn down to make way for a new surf shop. A single cinderblock wall now stands on the site. You can watch the action at Kammieland from the south end of Sunset Beach.

Sunset Beach Park

Sunset Beach Park is located in the *ahupuaa* of Paumalu, which means "taken by surprise." The name refers to a Hawaiian legend about a woman who was punished by the gods for exceeding the limit on octopus. Most of the Paumalu shoreline was developed with private homes in the 1920s, but a great stretch of beach remains open to the road. The beautiful, two-mile long crescent of fine deep sand is stunning.

During the summer, Sunset is a great place for swimming, snorkeling, bodyboarding and bodysurfing close to shore. Be aware that the bottom drops off quickly and there is a strong current flowing toward Kammieland and then out to sea. Keep a close eye on children, pets, plastic floats, and other objects that might sail off to Kauai. The best spot for bodyboarding and bodysurfing is on the north end of the beach *makai* of the curved coconut tree. Stay close to the shoreline—further out the coral reef makes it unsuitable for amateur boarders.

Locals sometimes ride horses along Sunset Beach, and many like to take their dogs there. It is always fun to watch the show as horses, dogs, and tourists released from tour buses cavort on the beach, and bikers, skaters, and joggers zoom by on the Ke Ala bike trail. Buddy Bigelow, the Rescue Dog, comes down late in the afternoon with his rescue bodyboard. At a signal from his master, Buddy swims out and pulls you in, turning and checking to be sure you are O.K. before he drops the leash, sits down, and waits for the next rescue. A beautiful 150-pound Newfoundland, Buddy does this instinctively. If this isn't enough entertainment, take a walk or jog along the sand to Sunset Point and pick out the beachfront home you like the best. As the name indicates, Sunset is also a nice place to watch the sun set over the Pacific.

During the winter, turbulent water and the infamous "Sunset rip" make this lovely beach too dangerous for recreational swimming. A channel runs out to sea where the Paumalu Stream once flowed into the Pacific. The shorebreak and rip currents in the Paumalu channel are extremely powerful when a big swell is running. The "Sunset rip" has necessitated many rescues and caused some fatalities. When a winter swell is running, warnings are posted, or the water is turbulent, do not even go near the water at Sunset. Remember that the Hawaiian place name means "taken by surprise."

The **Sunset Beach surf break** off the east end of the beach is legendary. In winter swells, it has some of the heaviest and longest waves in the world. Sunset is the site of major professional surf contests, including **the Roxy Pro Sunset, second leg of the Triple Crown of Surfing,** and **the O'Neill World Cup**. Spectacular peaks over 20 feet high ride atop powerful waves of water. Large waves can appear suddenly and break right on top of the surfers, throwing them into a whirlpool of whitewater and sometimes pressing them against the jagged coral reef and underwater caves below. At times Sunset Point closes out completely and the surfers have to battle their way into shore or let the westerly current take them out and hope for a helicopter rescue.

Sunset Beach Park is the narrow 18-acre tract between the Kam Highway and the beach with roadside parking on the *makai* side. To add improvements, the City and County of Honolulu built the two-acre **Sunset Beach Support Park** across the street. The support park contains restrooms, showers, and additional parking.

Sunset Point

The sandy beach continues northeast around **Sunset Point,** which provides a great view of the entire two-mile curve of Sunset Beach. The best view is from the north end of Sunset Point, known as **Velzyland Sunset Point**. This is a great place to watch and photograph the winter surfing action.

On the shallow, offshore reef off Sunset Point, a break called **Backyards** is popular with short boarders and windsurfers. During winter swells, only experts should attempt it.

There are several public rights of way among the beachfront homes on Sunset Point, but parking is virtually impossible. One right of way is **Sunset Point Beach Park**, a one-acre parcel of undeveloped land on Makanale Street. There is another right of way on

Kahauola Street, which runs *makai* of Kam Highway. Usually the easiest way to reach Sunset Point is to park at Sunset Beach Park or the support park and walk north along the beach.

Ted's Bakery

To continue your tour, return to the Kam Highway and head north again. If you are hungry, you are in the right spot! Between Sunset Beach and Velzyland is an institution beloved by locals—**Ted's Bakery**. Look *mauka* for a nondescript white building that has a deck with tables in the front and a surf mural on the side. The old name, "Sunset Beach Store," is painted over the door. A white sign in the parking lot identifies it as "Ted's Bakery." Ted lives in the white and blue house on the hill and keeps a close eye on the operation. His parents started the Sunset Beach Store many years ago. Their pictures still hang inside and Ted's Mom still comes by to arrange flowers and be sure everything is shipshape. Today, Ted's Bakery provides delicious pies, cakes and pastries to the finest restaurants on Oahu. Besides the amazing chocolate *haupia* pie that Ted invented, haupia, pineapple macadamia, guava, and other fruit pies, pineapple macadamia cheesecake, and other confections can be purchased whole or by the slice. Ted's also serves breakfast and lunch, which can be taken out or eaten on the comfortable deck. The breakfast pastries are to die for. At lunchtime, try the beef teriyaki or hot crab and bacon sandwich with a delicious smoothie. Special cakes for birthdays and other occasions must be ordered in advance. Ted's is open from 7:00 a.m. until 4:00 p.m. Monday through Thursday and 5:00 p.m. Friday through Sunday.

A Perfect Day at Sunset

Go bodyboarding or surfing at Sunset Beach Park, have lunch at Ted's bakery, walk along the beach from Ke Waena to Velzyland to watch the surfing, and walk back along the Ke Ala bike path. Take a swim at Sunset Beach if conditions allow, or at Kawela Bay or Kuilima Cove during winter surf. Watch the sun set from Sunset Beach.

Alternative: See a surf contest at the Banzai Pipeline or Sunset Beach, and walk along the shoreline to Sunset Point.

SUNSET POINT TO TURTLE BAY

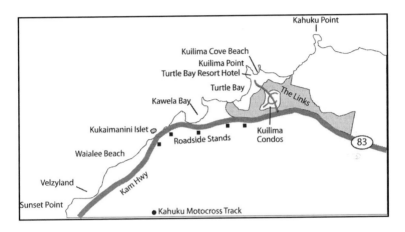

Sunset Point to Turtle Bay

Waialee

As you continue north on the Kam Highway, you will enter a beautiful agricultural area called **Waialee**, where the green fields of the **University of Hawaii Waialee Livestock Research Farm** lie between the highway and the ocean.

North of Ted's Bakery, Comsat Road runs *mauka* toward a bluff where a military communications installation is located. History might have been changed if the new technology being tested on this bluff on the morning of December 7, 1941 had been given more credence. At 7:02 a.m. on that fateful morning, two young privates operating a brand new mobile radar system picked up signals of a massive air force approaching Oahu from the north. They called in the alarm, but were told not to worry about it because a squadron of American B-17s was expected from that direction. The young privates tracked the incoming planes until 7:39 a.m., when they disappeared from the oscilloscope. The new radar system had been tracking 175 Japanese planes, which entered a "dead zone" screened by the hills between the North Shore radar station and their targets at Pearl Harbor and Wheeler Field. The **Opana Radar Station** can be seen from viewing scopes near the swimming pool at the Turtle Bay Resort. A historic marker is located on the Sunset side of the hotel (on the left if you are facing the ocean) on a little strip of sand next to Turtle Bay. The Opana Radar Station is a National Historic Landmark listed on both the National and State Registers of Historic Places. It is not open to the public because the current military installation there is secret.

Velzyland

Continuing north on the Kam Highway past Comsat Road, look *makai* for a gated development of luxury homes called **Sunset Bay Colony**. There is a private right of access through this development to the popular **Velzyland** surf spot. Walk to the right of the car gate into the Sunset Bay Colony and the beach access will be straight in front of you.

In front of the Sunset Bay Colony, **Kaunala Beach** is long, curving, and sandy but is lined with sections of coral reef and rocks. There is a small pocket at the mouth of **Kaunala Stream** where it is feasible to swim in the summer. The rest of the bottom is too rocky. The currents are strong when the surf is big. Three surf breaks— **Freddyland, Velzyland**, and **Phantoms**—lie offshore.

Mauka of Velzyland, the **Kahuku Motocross Track** is located on state land leased by the Hawaii Motorsports Association. Used mostly for motorcycle racing, the park contains miles of excellent mountain bike roads and trails.

Waialee and Pahipahialua Beaches

A little further on, the Kam Highway opens to a rocky shoreline called **Waialee Beach**. The name Waialee means "rippling or stirring water," a reference to an upwelling of fresh water that used to bubble up in small fountains above the offshore reef. **Waialee Beach Park** is an undeveloped 26-acre parcel between Kam Highway and the ocean. Coral reef and rocks extend along the entire shoreline and ocean bottom, with only a few sandy pockets where swimming is feasible in the summer. There are strong, dangerous currents when the winter surf comes in. A little surf break named **Bong's** is on the offshore reef.

A small limestone island named **Kukaimanini Islet** lies between the reef and the shore. It is possible to wade to Kukaimanini at low tide during the summer months, but the island is completely rocky with sparse vegetation and no beach. Locals sometimes wade out to fish there, and no wonder since the name Kakaimanini means "*manini* fish procession" (*manini* is a small, striped reef fish). Many passersby stop to watch the sun set, with the ironwood trees along the shoreline framing the ocean view.

Immediately north of Waialee Beach and its little islet lies **Pahipahialua Beach,** named for a fishing shrine that once stood there. Locals sometimes call it West Kawela. Puhipahialua is as rocky as Waialee Beach, without the parking. The shoreline is dotted with private homes and there is no convenient public access.

As the road bends eastward, agricultural fields stretch between the mountains and the Kam Highway. Watch for **roadside stands** selling local produce. From here to Kahuku, corn, papayas, and watermelons are grown in the old sugar cane fields, making them famously sweet and delicious. Kahuku corn is white, with small kernels, and so sweet that butter is unnecessary. The papayas are dark orange and amazingly juicy. Fresh mangoes, bananas, and ice-cold coconuts can also be purchased at these roadside stands. We like to stop at the coconut stand just north of the Crawford Rest Home for an ice-cold coconut with a straw. The rest home is located on the site of the former state insane asylum.

Don't be afraid to bargain with the roadside vendors. Kahuku corn and watermelon are sometimes sold in the stalls of Honolulu's Chinatown for less than the prices quoted to tourists at the roadside stands adjoining the fields!

Kawela Bay

Kawela Bay is an idyllic, horseshoe-shaped bay protected by an outer reef. The water is calm, current-free, and safe for swimming year-round. The sandy beach is lined with a tropical forest of ironwood, with lovely coconut palms along the shore. The bay bottom is sandy, with outgrowths of coral. The best place to swim is the middle and western part of the bay, where there is less coral.

A gated residential community was built around Kawela Bay in the early 20th century. In 1986, the residents on the Turtle Bay side were evicted to make way for a resort that was never built. Although this side of the bay is now called "**Kawela Bay Beach Park**," there are no improvements. Public access is limited to trails from the Turtle Bay Resort, a short hike with a big reward.

Because it cannot be seen from the Kam Highway and has no direct access or improvements, Kawela Bay remains wonderfully quiet and secluded. It is a lovely place for a romantic picnic or for small children to wade, build sand castles, and chase sand crabs. The calm bay waters are ideal for kayaking and snorkeling. To reach Kawela, park in the Turtle Bay Resort parking lot and follow the trail along Turtle Bay and around the point. The 25-minute walk is mostly on paved trails and perfectly flat. You can also get to Kawela Bay on horseback. The Turtle Bay Resort offers a three-mile trail ride that leads through an ironwood forest, past a World War II bunker, and along the white sandy beach of Kawela Bay.

As you continue on the Kam Highway past the white gate to the Kawela Bay residential area, a manicured hibiscus hedge signals that you have arrived at the Turtle Bay Resort. Turn *makai* (left) off the Kam Highway at the entrance and drive past the Kuilima condominiums and golf courses to the parking lot.

Turtle Bay

Turtle Bay extends from the northern point of Kawela Bay to **Kalaeokaunu Point** (also known as **Kuilima Point**), where the hotel and wedding chapel are located. The Hawaiian name "Kalaeokaunu" means point of the altar, a reference to a small altar to the fish gods that stood on the point before the hotel was built. The remains of this fishing shrine are now in the Bishop Museum in Honolulu.

The resort's pretty cabanas line the rocky shore of Turtle Bay. *Honu* can be seen in the sparkling water, but this is no swimming beach. The shoreline and sea bottom are covered with *aa* and coral (remember Rule Number 6), and there are dangerous currents. During the winter, large waves cross the bay in irregular patterns. Still, the **Turtle Bay surf spot** off Kuilima Point has been gaining popularity, with the resort sponsoring several surf contests. The poolside Hang Ten Surf Bar overlooking the bay is a great place to watch the sunset. Spotlights illuminate the surf as the surfers show off for the crowd. The resort also offers horseback riding, including moonlight rides, on trails along the shoreline.

On the Sunset side of the hotel next to Turtle Bay, look for the historic marker indicating the location of the Opana Point Radar Station on the bluff above Waialee. Use the resort's viewfinders to find the radar station and other places you've enjoyed on your drive up the North Shore.

Kuilima Cove Beach

On the north side of Kuilima Point, Kuilima Cove offers safe swimming and snorkeling year-round. This pretty beach was a favorite swimming place of the old Hawaiian community in Kahuku, who called it Kalokoiki ("the little pool"). An outer reef insulates the cove from the surf that rolls into Turtle Bay. With its tranquil water, this is a good beach for little tots. The bottom is a bit rocky close to shore, but sandy at the water's edge. Swimmers have to avoid coral outcroppings, but it is possible to find a route to the reef and back on the breakwater side of the cove. The best snorkeling is along the breakwater, where a current runs out to sea. The resort rents lounge chairs and other equipment. Tell the attendant at the gate that you want "beach access" and park in the "beach access" area of the parking lot.

The Turtle Bay Resort

Turtle Bay is the only full-service resort hotel in northern Oahu. With 880 acres of gorgeous oceanfront, it offers a unique opportunity to swim, snorkel, kayak, surf, play 36 holes of golf, go horseback riding, play tennis, take a helicopter tour, walk, hike, get married, enjoy fine dining, get in shape, and have luxurious spa treatments without leaving the property.

All of the 375 guest rooms and 26 suites have ocean views and balconies. In addition, there are waterfront beach cabanas along Turtle Bay, villas overlooking Kuilima Cove, and conference and catering facilities. A swimming pool with an 80-foot water slide, two hot tubs, and beverage and food service overlooks Turtle Bay. A lovely glass walled chapel on Kuilima Point provides a romantic setting for weddings and other special events.

The resort has two championship18-hole golf courses known as "The Links." There are ten plexi-pave tennis courts and a stable of quarterhorses. Twelve miles of hiking trails follow the pristine shoreline. The Spa Luana is considered one of the best resort spas in Hawaii. Traditional Hawaiian music is provided with afternoon tea and wine service in the lobby. The *keiki* (children's) program introduces young guests to Hawaiian culture.

Turtle Bay offers a range of dining experiences. Frommer's reports that the premiere restaurant, **21 Degrees North**, is so fabulous people are driving from all over the island to eat there. Located on the beach lawn with tiki torches aglow, **Ola's** combines the ambience of old Waikiki with a diverse menu. The **Palm Terrace** has a display kitchen where you can watch the chefs prepare elaborate buffets and island favorites for breakfast, lunch and dinner. A terrific **Sunday brunch** with live entertainment is served in the Sunset Room. The poolside grill serves lunch and *pupus* (hors d'oeuvres) until 5:00 p.m. Next to the golf shop, **Lei Lei's Bar & Grill** offers consistently good surf and turf fare in a casual, friendly atmosphere. The **Bay Club** offers cocktails, snacks, and weekend entertainment. On Friday evenings, the resort hosts a **Legends of the North Shore Luau** with a *lei* greeting, cocktails, traditional Hawaiian food, and Polynesian review.

There are **attractive shops** on both levels of the resort. On the main floor, **Jeanie's Jewelry** specializes in coral and pearls and **Kohala Bay Collections** offers a nice selection of tropical clothing and accessories. On the lower level, **Octopus Ink** carries aloha wear and beach towels; **Treasures of Polynesia** sells handicrafts, including colorful handmade neckties; and **Lamont's Gift Shop** carries a typical assortment of gift items. The flower shop, **Island Impressions,** makes everything from *leis* to traditional floral arrangements. The **golf shop** (next to Lei Lei's) and **tennis shop** (*mauka* of the cabanas) carry logo wear and accessories.

The Kuilima Condominiums

Within the gates of the Turtle Bay Resort, twin condominium communities known as **Kuilima Estates West** and **Kuilima Estates East** border the Fazio golf course. Built by Del Webb in the early 1970s, these condos range from studios to three-bedroom homes. They are privately owned and not part of the resort. With mature landscaping, golf course and mountain views, and a prime location, these condos are highly desirable vacation rentals. Cooling trade winds make air conditioning unnecessary, although some owners have installed it to meet the expectations of visitors from the mainland. Swimming pools, tennis courts, and barbecue and picnic facilities are located within each community. A condo at Kuilima Estates makes a great base of operations for a family vacation on the North Shore. Rentals are available from individual owners and rental agents.

A Perfect Day between Sunset Point and Turtle Bay

Play golf or tennis or go horseback riding at the Turtle Bay Resort. Surf Velzyland. Enjoy lunch at Lei Lei's or Ola's. Then swim, snorkel and nap at Kawela Bay or Kuilima Cove. Browse the resort's shops, enjoy the Hawaiian music in the lobby and toast the end of a perfect day with a tropical drink as you watch the sun set from Kuilima Point.

Alternative: Relax at Kuilima Cove Beach and indulge yourself with an oceanside massage at Spa Luana.

TURTLE BAY TO MALAEKAHANA

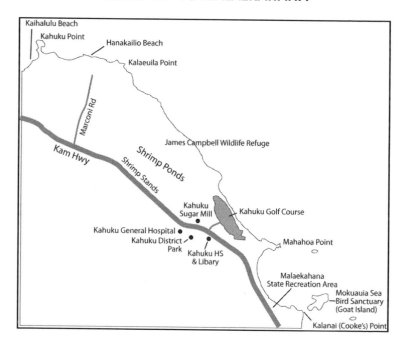

Turtle Bay to Malaekahana

Kahuku's Story

The *ahupuaa* of Kahuku occupies the northern tip of Oahu. This area was not heavily populated by the early Hawaiians, because it lacked the natural resources to support a large subsistence community. *Haole* entrepreneurs developed Kahuku during the 20th century. Today, it is the site of ranches, farms, aquaculture, roadside stands, bird refuges, and a charming little plantation town.

The first *haole* to settle in Kahuku was Charles Gordon-Hopkins, who acquired the Kahuku Ranch. The ranch changed hands several times before James Campbell bought it for $63,500. In 1889, Campbell leased the property to Benjamin Dillingham, who subleased part of it to James Castle for the Kahuku Sugar Plantation.

The plantation began as a small operation, with less than 4,000 acres under cultivation and a mill in Kahuku. But in 1896, Castle took over milling the sugar cane grown on the Laie plantation of the Church of Jesus Christ of Latter Day Saints ("the LDS Church," commonly known as the "Mormon Church"). Eventually, he also leased the Church's fields. He built the Koolau Railroad, which ran from the end of the OR&L tracks in Kahuku down the Windward Shore to Kahana Bay, and kept buying more land, planting more sugar cane, and using the Koolau to haul the cane to the Kahuku mill. Eventually, the Kahuku plantation controlled thousands of acres stretching all the way down the Windward Shore.

During the 1930s, the Kahuku plantation housed 1,100 workers and their families in seven camps. Only 30 percent of those workers were American citizens. The rest were brought to Kahuku on work contracts, mostly from Japan and the Philippines. Each camp had its own recreational facilities.

Kahuku was the only plantation served by three railroads. The OR&L ran from Honolulu up the Leeward Coast, around Kaena Point, and up the North Shore to Kahuku. Castle's Koolau Railway ran from Kahuku down the Windward Coast to Kahana Bay. The plantation's own railway operated over its cane fields.

Castle planned to continue the Koolau line through tunnels to Honolulu, creating a railway system that completely circumnavigated the island, but he died before he was able to complete it. Nevertheless, the completion of the railroad as far as Kahana Bay made it possible to travel from Honolulu to Kahuku on the OR&L and continue from Kahuku down the Windward Shore on the Koolau. This prompted the construction of weekend homes on the Windward Shore by prominent Honolulu residents. The Koolau stopped passenger service in 1933 and closed down completely in 1952. By that time, the shoreline south of Kahuku was filled with the vacation homes of prosperous *haoles*.

During World War II, the Army installed a battery of four eight-inch cannons and concrete bunkers between the Kahuku mill and the shoreline as a defense against invasion. Southwest of Kahuku Point, an airstrip for fighter planes was built next to Hanakailio Beach. Those defenses were abandoned after the War.

In 1971, the Kahuku Plantation shut down. Older workers who were guaranteed lifetime housing retired in the main village. Younger workers lost both their jobs and their homes. Fortunately, Del Webb had started construction on the hotel and condominiums at Turtle Bay, which provided temporary employment for some of the displaced plantation workers. The site of the Kahuku sugar mill was developed into shops and restaurants, with the mill machinery preserved as a tourist attraction. After dominating the economy of Kahuku and the Windward Shore for decades, the Kahuku mill was torn down. Nothing remains of it now except a few brightly painted pieces of equipment on display in the little shopping area. An assortment of small businesses, restaurants and shrimp trucks remain in the "Kahuku Sugar Mill Center."

Driving From Turtle Bay To Kahuku

As you leave the Turtle Bay Resort, turn left (east) on the Kam Highway. From here to Kahuku, the highway runs inland several miles from the ocean. The resort's manicured hibiscus hedge continues to the end of the Palmer Golf Course. Watch *maikai* for Marconi Road. This area is called **Marconi**, because in the early 20th century the American Marconi Company built a receiving unit on the sand dunes here. RCA bought the American Marconi Company in the 1920s and used the receiving unit at Kahuku for ship-to-shore communications with civilian vessels for many years. The abandoned

Kahuku Airfield from World War II lies parallel to the shoreline off Hanakailio Beach.

Soon you will see shrimp farms *makai* (on the left) and cornfields and papaya trees *mauka* (on the right). **Tanaka's Shrimp Village** houses an assortment of shrimp wagons. A little further down the road, Romy Aguinaldo operates a red shrimp stand called **Romy's Kahuku Prawns & Shrimp.** In the fields behind Romy's stand, the Aguinaldo family runs a 40-acre shrimp farm with 31 ponds of prawns and 13 acres of hatcheries.

James Campbell National Wildlife Refuge

Watch *makai* for the sign to the **James Campbell National Wildlife Refuge**, a bird watcher's delight complete with a visitor kiosk, interpretive signs, and guided and self-interpretive tours. The refuge occupies over 160 acres of wetlands, including a natural, spring-fed marsh and man-made ponds and impoundments. Its primary mission is the recovery of Hawaii's four endangered water birds—the Hawaiian stilt, moorhen, coot, and duck—but many wintering migrants are also found here. The refuge is open to the public for scheduled tours from the third Saturday in October through the third Saturday in February.

Kahuku General Hospital

As you pass the sign to the Wildlife Refuge and enter the little town of Kahuku, look *mauka* for a large brick building on a hill above the highway. This is **Kahuku General Hospital,** the only 24-hour, full service medical facility on the North Shore. Kahuku General is part of the State of Hawaii's hospital system.

Kahuku District Park

Past the hospital, turn right on Pualalea Street to the **Kahuku District Park**, which offers lighted baseball and softball fields, a soccer field, two basketball courts, picnic facilities, and a multipurpose room.

Kahuku Sugar Mill Shopping Center

Look *maikai* for the **Kahuku Sugar Mill Center.** This little shopping center was planned as a tourist attraction that would boost the local economy when the mill shut down. It has seen better days, but still contains a few unique assets. The **Phillips 66 station** has **a coin-operated car vacuum** you can use to remove the sand from your rental car before returning it. The **Kahuku Barber and Hair Salon** is tucked into the southwest corner. In the back of the center you will find the offices of **The Estates at Turtle Bay,** the most prominent agent for vacation rentals in the area. The Kahuku **Post Office** and **Curves** exercise studio are in the same building. **Sally's Feed & Country Store** carries a full line of animal feed and pet supplies.

The white wagon of **Giovanni's Aloha Shrimp** sits off the road east of the Kahuku shopping center. Giovanni's lunch wagon has been serving delicious lemon butter, garlic, and spicy shrimp in this location for more than ten years. Rated as a "find" by Travelocity, it has a loyal following of locals and tourists. Believe them when they tell you how hot the hot and spicy shrimp are (really hot), and don't forget to sign the truck. Locals stop at the **Kahuku Superette** for *poke.*

Kahuku Golf Course

Continue past the Superette, turn *makai* (left) from the Kam Highway onto Puuluana Street, and continue on Puuluana past the Kahuku Elderly Hauoli Hale (senior citizen housing) to the ocean-front **Kahuku Golf Course.** The Kahuku Sugar Plantation built this nine-hole course for its workers in 1937. If it is still operating when you visit, be sure to stop. It is truly one of a kind. What it lacks in grooming (and that's quite a bit), it makes up in novelty and fun. It features the longest hole in Hawaii, a tee on top of an old pillbox from World War II, a green where a miss puts the ball on the beach 60 feet below, and amazing views of unpopulated beaches stretching for miles in each direction. With flat, sandy terrain and strong ocean winds, it is a true Scottish links course. Unfortunately, its days are numbered. For many years, the Campbell Estate leased the land to the City and County of Honolulu for $1.00 per year. In the course of liquidating its assets, the Campbell Trust sold the land to a developer and the golf course is now operating on a month-to-month lease. Call the Golf Course at 293-5842 or 296-2000 for current information.

Red Raiders

Retrace your route to the Kam Highway and turn left (east), watching *mauka* for the **Kahuku High and Intermediate School**. Kahuku High is the home of the **Red Raiders**, a formidable football power. Frequently reigning as state champions, the Red Raiders are regularly scouted by college coaches from the mainland. The fabulous marching band, led by long-time director Michael Payton, is just as formidable. Its unique combination of excellent music and choreography with colorful Hawaiian themes and costumes makes it extremely popular on the mainland as well as Oahu. The band has received coveted invitations to participate in the Rose Parade, presidential inaugural parade, and numerous other events. If you happen to be on the North Shore when the Red Raiders have a home game or band concert, buy a ticket and join the team spirit of this charming Hawaiian community.

Library and Churches

The **Kahuku Library** is on the same street as the high school. Kahuku is also home to many churches. Continuing along the Kam Highway, you will pass the **Kahuku United Methodist Church, St. Roch's Catholic Church, Hope Chapel of Holau Loa, and Kahuku Episcopal Church**. As you reach the northeastern corner of the island, the Kam Highway rejoins the shore.

Five Miles Of Secluded Shoreline

Five miles of unspoiled, isolated shoreline lie between Turtle Bay and Kahuku, where Oahu's coastline reaches its northernmost tip at Kahuku Point and turns southeast while the Kam Highway cuts inland. Few visitors see this pristine coastline. The five-mile walk is most enjoyable in the early morning or evening hours, when you can enjoy the sunrise or sunset.

Kaihalulu Beach

Begin at the Turtle Bay Resort and walk along the trail past Kuilima Cove to **Kalaeokamanu Point**, where a breakwater juts out into the ocean. On the other side of the breakwater, **Kaihalulu Beach** stretches for a mile to **Kahuku Point**, the northernmost point on Oahu. Kaihalulu ("roaring sea") takes its name from the thundering surf that breaks on the outside reef during the winter months. The reef is broken, affording little protection from dangerous currents. The beach is sandy, but the sea bottom is rocky. Kaihalulu is unsafe for swimming, except for a protected little cove in the middle known as **Keiki Cove.**

In 2006, a Hawaiian monk seal used Keiki Cove as a nursery for her newborn pup. For 50 days, NOAA specialists, volunteers, and delighted tourists watched as the mother nursed and cared for her baby. On the 50th day, Mom left and the pup was on its own.

Kahuku Point is a good place to watch both the sunrise and the sunset. Be sure to wear shoes to protect your feet from the mollusks that attach themselves to the rocks here, or stay off the rocks. (Remember Rule No. Six!)

Beyond Kahuku Point the shoreline turns southeast down the Windward Shore. In contrast to the North Shore's deep sand beaches and big winter surf, the Windward Shore is characterized by narrow beaches with fringing reefs and small waves lapping at the shore.

Hanakailio Beach

Hanakailio Beach extends from Kahuku Point to Kalaeuila Point. There is a small cove near Kahuku Point, but the fringing reef is so broken and irregular that it is too turbulent for swimming. East of the cove, a sandy beach with a few outcroppings of rock and coral extends for about half a mile adjacent to the World War II airfield.

Here the sand is deep enough to give your legs a serious workout, but the rocky bottom and strong currents make the water unsafe for swimming.

As you continue around **Kalaeuila Point** past the **James Campbell National Wildlife Refuge,** the shoreline becomes straighter, with reaches of sand interrupted by coral and rock outcroppings. There was a nudist colony here for many years. Local fishermen still frequent the traditional fishing grounds along this shoreline.

Kahuku Golf Course Beach

Continue past the **Kahuku Golf Course Beach** toward **Makahoa Point**, where beachfront homes dot the shore. The golf course beach is a wide strip of sand and bedrock bordered by picturesque sand dunes. The **Seventh Hole surf spot** lies off the seventh hole. This is not a good place to swim. In the middle of the beach, a large channel cuts through the offshore reef and comes all the way into the shore. The backwash often creates a strong rip current out to sea.

Continue south to **Malaekahana State Recreation Area**. Here you can enjoy a well-earned swim before walking out to the Kam Highway to catch The Bus back to the Turtle Bay Resort for your car.

You can also take this hike in the opposite direction, leaving your car at the Malaekahana parking area and hiking back to the Turtle Bay Resort. You might prefer the direction that puts the sun at your back. Whichever route you choose, be sure to wear a hat and bring plenty of sunscreen and water.

Malaekahana Bay

Malaekahana Bay stretches along the northeastern corner of Oahu from **Makahoa Point to Kalanai Point**. Kalanai Point is sometimes called Cooke's Point—not for Captain Cook but for the prominent Cooke family of Castle & Cooke, who built a large country home there in the early 1900s. Many affluent residents of Honolulu built country homes that still stand along the shoreline near the state park.

Malaekahana State Recreation Area

In ancient times, Malaekahana was a *puuhonua,* a place of refuge for commoners who broke *kapu.* Today it is a place of refuge from the stresses and strains of modern living. Few tourists visit Malaekahana State Recreation Area, perhaps because the lovely beach cannot be seen from the highway. Deep white sand piles up along the mile-long shore, which is shaded by a diverse forest. The bottom is sandy, with a gradual descent. The water is sometimes choppy off Kalanai Point, but it is safe for swimming and bodyboarding near the shore.

The park is divided into two sections. The Kahuku side is a gated, 37-acre camping area with accommodations ranging from bare tentsites to furnished yurts and cabins. There is even a genuine *hale nui,* a grass shack on the beach. The Laie side is a public beach park with a pretty, tree-fringed beach curving toward Kalanai Point. Restrooms, showers, and picnic facilities are located on both sides of the park.

Malaekahana is popular with local fishermen. There are two flat reefs along the shoreline that attract fish. Older Hawaiians say the *anae holo* (a salt water mullet found in Pearl Harbor) used to make an annual migration around the Windward Shore, stop at Makahoa Point, reverse direction, and return to Pearl Harbor by the same route. Local shorecasters still favor Makahoa Point.

Island Sanctuaries

Offshore from Malaekahana there are two uninhabited islands dedicated as seabird sanctuaries: the **Kihewamokui Island Seabird Sanctuary** and the **Makuauia Seabird Sanctuary (Goat Island).** The smaller island, **Kihewamokui,** lies northeast of Malaekahana. The larger island, **Mokuauia,** is only about one-eighth of a mile from the beach near Kalanai Point. It is known locally as **Goat Island** because Mormon settlers from Laie once kept goats there.

Mokuauia is the top of a large stranded coral reef. Unlike islands formed by volcanoes, it is a low, flat surface inside the main coral reef. The 13-acre coral shelf is a sanctuary for ten species of seabirds, including burrowing shearwaters. It is open to the public during daylight hours. You can walk around the perimeter of the island and see the burrowing birds with eggs resting in their nests. Remember Rule No. 9—stay on the trail and do not disturb the nesting sites.

From the beach near Kalanai Point, you can wade at low tide or swim at high tide to Mokuauia. Be sure to wear water shoes and check the tide table and water conditions before you go. For greater comfort, make the passage on a bodyboard, surfboard or kayak.

Mokuaula Beach

There are three picturesque beaches on Mokuauia. The two beaches on the windward side are exposed to the open ocean, where the water is usually rough. There is a **left break** there that is frequented by surfers and sailboarders, but it is not suitable for swimming.

On the protected, leeward side of the island, to the left of the welcome sign as you come ashore, **Mokuaula Beach** is an ideal place for a relaxing swim. A long barrier point protects it from the ocean waves, the bottom is sandy, and the slope is gradual. Relax on the sandy white beach and enjoy the view of Malaekahana before wading or swimming back the way you came. After all, how often will you find yourself on an uninhabited island in the Pacific?

A Perfect Day on the Northeast Shore

Take an early morning walk along the deserted shoreline from Turtle Bay to Malaekahana Bay. Catch The Bus back to your car. Relax over lunch at the Turtle Bay Resort or at Romy's or Giovanni's shrimp truck in Kahuku. Then return to Malaekahana, swim or paddle over to Mokuauia, walk around the perimeter of the island seabird sanctuary, and enjoy a swim at Mokuaula Beach. Finish the day with a round of golf at the Kahuku Golf Course and "talk story" with the locals.

LAIE

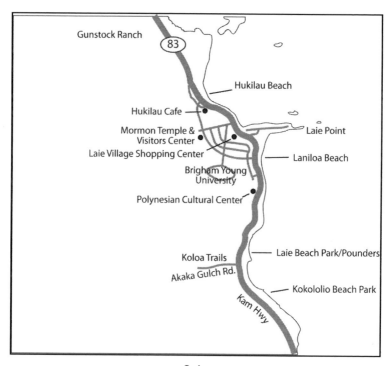

Laie

Laie's Story

The *ahupuaa* of Laiewai ("leaf of the ieie vine") was named for a legendary Hawaiian princess, Laieikawai, who was said to be so beautiful that she was hidden away in the secret chamber of a fresh-water pool to protect her from mortal men. Laiewai was heavily ter-raced and cultivated by the early Hawaiians. At least two *heiau* were located there, but they were lost through years of sugar cane plant-ing. In addition to farming, the Hawaiian population used net fish-ing to harvest abundant seafood.

The entire community participated in the *hukilau* and shared the harvest. *Huki* means hook; *lau* means fish with a net. Some members of the group waded into the water with a long weighted net and stretched it across the bay. The net was lined with *ti* leaves to scare the fish toward the center. Other members of the group went ahead to splash the water and drive the fish into the center of the net. A third group on the beach pulled the ends of the net into shore, landing the catch.

Today, Laie is a Mormon community. The LDS Church started sending missionaries to Hawaii in 1850. Despite considerable opposition from the Protestant power structure, they converted many Hawaiians and organized a "City of Joseph" on the island of Lanai. In 1861, a controversial character named Walter Murray Gibson arrived in Lanai. Gibson represented to the native converts that he was the Church's "Chief President of the Islands of the Sea and of the Hawaiian Islands" and had been sent to revive the settlement. He asked the Hawaiian Mormons to work and contribute to buy the valley of Palawai as the permanent home of the LDS Church in Hawaii. After contributing generously for several years, the Hawaiians discovered that Gibson had registered the land in his own name. In 1864, a committee from Utah arrived to investigate the matter. Gibson was excommunicated from the LDS Church but refused to give up Palawai. Turning his ambition toward the Hawaiian royalty, the artful Gibson eventually became an influential minister of King Kalakaua. After holding every ministerial post in the kingdom, he was named Premier of Hawaii.

In the meantime, Brigham Young sent Francis Hammond and George Nebeker to Hawaii to find another site for a Mormon colony. Former U.S. Consul Thomas Dougherty owned the entire *ahupuaa* of Laiewai and agreed to sell it to them. In 1865, the Church purchased 6,000 acres in Laie, and most of the Hawaiian Mormons left Lanai for the new settlement. Nebeker served as president of the Laie Mission from 1865 to 1873.

The LDS Church started the Laie Sugar Plantation in 1872 with 200 acres of cane fields and a primitive mill. The refined sugar was shipped to Honolulu by schooner from a pier at Pounders Beach. In 1896, the Kahuku plantation extended its railroad to Laie, the Laie mill was abandoned, and the Laie-grown cane was hauled to the Kahuku mill for processing. In 1931, the Laie Plantation's cane fields were leased to the Kahuku Plantation Company, which continued cultivating them until the Kahuku mill closed in 1971.

The LDS Church flourished in Laie. By 1880, one in ten Hawaiians was a Mormon. In 1919, a striking white temple built of local coral and lava rock was dedicated after years of construction. The Church College of Hawaii, now known as Brigham Young University-Hawaii (BYUH), was founded in 1955. Mormon missionaries built the 42-acre Polynesian Cultural Center in 1963. The Church's commercial arm, Hawaii Reserves, Inc., manages its land in the Laie area.

Gunstock Ranch

As you leave Malaekahana, turn left (south) on the Kam Highway and watch *mauka* for the **Gunstock Ranch**. The pretty, 400-acre ranch in the shadow of the Koolau Mountains was founded by Dr. Max Smith, DVM, an Arizona rancher who moved to the islands in 1965 and became the state meat inspector. Dr. Smith served as state veterinarian from 1975 until 1994, and was inducted into the Paniolo Hall of Fame. Still owned and operated by the Smith family, Gunstock Ranch hosts many high school rodeos, the Paniola O Koolauloa 4-H Club, American Barrel Race Association events, and roping and sorting events.

Gunstock Ranch Trails offers horseback riding for all ages and skill levels, including *keiki* pony rides for young children and guided trail rides through spectacular scenery. Guided moonlight rides are offered each full moon. **Gunstock Aquatics** conducts swimming programs for all ages in a solar heated pool.

Continuing south on the Kam Highway, TT's Surf Shop is now the **Hukilau Surf Shop**. TT sold the business and went surfing at the age of 74. Next door, **Cackle Fresh Eggs** sells eggs to passersby, as well as supplying many local stores and restaurants. Watch *makai* for the colorful sign marking Hukilau Beach, and pull into the parking lot.

Hukilau Beach

Hukilau Beach, from Kalanai Point

Hukilau Beach is a very pretty strand curving about 1.5 miles from Kalanai Point to Laniloa Point. The sand is deep and extremely fine, and the bottom as flat as a floor. A small reef lies off the northern portion of the beach, *makai* of a shady campground. The center portion, *makai* of the parking lot, is unprotected by a fringing reef. The resulting shorebreak is popular for bodyboarding and bodysurfing. About 50 yards south of the parking lot, where homes line the shore, a wide, shallow reef creates a calmer entry for small children. This area is sometimes referred to as **Laie Beach,** which was once the name for the entire shoreline.

Where the homes along the shore stand now, there were sand dunes known as *Puuahi,* which means "hill of fire." The name referred to cooking fires where local fishermen and their families would cook their "catch of the day." The sand dunes were leveled for home sites, but the name was retained in Puuahi Street, which runs inland from the "hill of fire."

From 1947 until 1972, a traditional Hawaiian *hukilau* was held at Hukilau Beach every month. A wooden monument *makai* of the parking lot tells the story. A local resident, Viola Kehau Kawahigashi, started the monthly *hukilau* to raise funds to restore an LDS chapel that had been destroyed by fire. A local fisherman named Hamana Kalili supplied the nets for fishing, and the congregation contributed food, talent and time. Everyone who attended the *hukilau* participated in pulling the fish-filled nets to shore, and enjoyed a traditional *luau* and hula dancing afterward. When songwriter Jack Owens attended the *hukilau* in 1948, it inspired him to write the famous *"Hukilau"* song. Unfortunately, this lovely tradition ended when taxes were imposed and the event could not sustain the expense. Nonetheless, the chapel funded by the *hukilau* still stands in Laie, the *"Hukilau"* song is still sung at *luaus* everywhere, and Hukilau Beach still retains its captivating beauty. My husband and all of his brothers can still do the *"Hukilau* hula dance" in unison, having learned it as children at Hukilau Beach.

Laie Town

The Hukilau Cafe

If you are hungry as you approach Laie Town, look *mauka* for the large sign welcoming you to Laie. Turn *mauka* at the sign, proceed to the traffic circle, go around the circle looking to your right, and you will see the **Hukilau Café** at the corner of Loala and Wahinepee Streets. This cute little cafe is a gathering place for locals, and a great spot for breakfast or lunch on weekdays and breakfast on Saturday. Notice the photos of Hamana Kalili and other local heroes along the walls.

The Mormon Temple and Visitors Center

Continuing south on Kam Highway, look *mauka* for a sign to the **Mormon Temple and Visitors Center**. Hale Laa Boulevard leads straight up the hill, affording a clear view of the temple from the highway. Access to the interior of the LDS temple is restricted to church members, but non-members can tour the Visitors Center. The gardens are accented with fountains, waterfalls, a reflecting pool, exotic flowers, and stately palm trees. Admission is free and tours are available.

In front of the temple, Hale Laa Boulevard intersects with Naniloa Loop. Turn right on Naniloa and proceed to the traffic circle. On the other side of the traffic circle, turn left on Poohaili Street. The Laie Cemetery is off to the right. Veer left at the intersection. Here the road narrows as it passes aquaculture ponds, horse pastures, and views into the valley.

Laie Village Shopping Center

Returning to the Kam Highway, look *mauka* for the **Laie Village Shopping Center** at 55-510 Kam Highway. The **Laie Theater** is the only movie house on the North Shore except for the IMAX cinema at the Polynesian Cultural Center. It shows first run films in two theaters. A well-stocked **Foodland Grocery Store, Ace Hardware Store, Napa Auto Parts store, and Laie Post Office** are also located in the Laie Village Shopping Center. Services include a well-managed **Launderette** that offers large coin-operated washers and dryers and off-premise dry cleaning, a **Haircut Store, nail salon, flower and balloon shop,** and **Ohana Video.** Eateries include a **Subway Sandwich and Salad Shop, Laie Chop Suey, Pizza Hut, Taco Bell,** and **Angel's Ice Cream,** which sells shave ice and smoothies. Next to the Kam Highway, there is an **auto repair shop** and **L & L Drive In Chopstick Express,** a local chain that offers plate lunches and sandwiches. The shopping area is closed on Sundays and does not sell alcoholic beverages. In fact, it is virtually impossible to purchase alcoholic beverages anywhere in Mormon Laie.

Dr. Marc Schlacter, M.D., "the Country Doctor," has his office in the shopping center. It contains a wonderful photo gallery of his patients and their families that is a veritable museum of Laie's history.

Laie Family Dental Center, optometrist Dr. Kevin Baize, O.D., and D. A. Pharmacy are also located in the Laie shopping center.

Spectacular Hiking Trails

There are some spectacular hiking trails in the mountains above Laie. The 12-mile **Laie Trail** leads to a lovely swimming pond with waterfalls above and below it and breathtaking views of both sides of the island. The **Koolau Summit Trail** extends for 18.5 miles along the top of the Koolau Mountain Range. These trails are difficult, and permission must be obtained from Hawaiian Reserves, Inc.

Laie Point

Laie Point is a popular photo spot. The Point affords sweeping views of the Koolau Mountains descending seaward along the Windward Shore. Waves crash against the rocky point and islets offshore, including **Kukuihoolua Island** with its picturesque arch. In contrast to arches in the Southwest that take many years to form, this arch was formed in a single day by the tsunami of 1946.

Kukuihoolua Island from Laie Point

To reach Laie Point, take the Kam Highway to the traffic light at the Laie Village Shopping Center and turn *makai* on Anemoku Street to the **Laniloa Peninsula**. Follow Anemoku Street uphill to the stop sign and turn right again on Naupaka Street. Park at the end of the road.

This is a windy spot and the water can be wild. During the winter or stormy weather, huge waves crash against the rocks, throwing spray skyward. The spray against the arched rock and the lovely views of the Windward Shore to the south are enough to excite any photographer, but please do not go out on the rocks to take your pictures. Local fishermen cast their lines from the rocks, but walking on them can be very dangerous. Remember Rule Number 5!

Laniloa Beach

Backtrack from Laie Point to the Kam Highway and turn left (south). On the *makai* side of Kam Highway, large homes obstruct the view of **Laniloa Beach**, which extends from Laie Point to Kehukuuna Point. There is a public right of way at 55-470 Kam Highway. Except for two sandy pockets, the entire shoreline is covered with coral. The bottom is rocky, but the water is protected by the outer reef and safe for swimming once you manage to get in.

BYU Hawaii

Back on Kam Highway, watch *mauka* for the turnoff to BYU Hawaii (BYUH). The LDS Church opened the school as "Church College of Hawaii" in 1955. Today, the four-year college is operated as a branch of Brigham Young University in Provo, Utah. The student body includes about 2,200 undergraduates, mostly from Asia and the Pacific. BYUH offers liberal arts degrees and professional programs in business and education. Campus walking tours are available weekdays except holidays from 9 a.m. to 4 p.m., and take about an hour. Weekday visits to the **Museum of Natural History on the BYUH campus** can also be arranged by calling 293-3816.

Returning to the Kam Highway from BYUH, you will pass the **Laie Inn, a Chevron station,** and **McDonald's.** Immediately ahead is the huge parking lot of the Polynesian Cultural Center. *Makai* of the Polynesian Cultural Center, there is a **little surf break** that is surfable for short boards and body boards most of the winter.

The Polynesian Cultural Center

The Polynesian Cultural Center is a 42-acre park dedicated to the cultures of Hawaii, Easter Island, the Marquesas, Samoa, Tonga, Tahiti, and New Zealand. Each culture is presented in its own village, built with authentic native structures. Polynesian students from BYUH finance their education by working at PCC. Presentations include native games, traditional music and dances, arts and crafts, and a colorful canoe pageant. A canoe tour provides a cooling respite. The IMAX movie theater shows spectacular films. The day ends with a boat ride to the dining areas, where a variety of dinner options, including the delightful Alii Luau with Hawaiian food and entertainment, are provided.

The evening show, "Horizons, Where The Sea Meets The Sky," is spectacular. What sets it apart from the Polynesian shows found in Waikiki and other tourist areas is the authenticity of the costumes and dances, charm of the singers and dancers, and deep respect for the cultures presented. My favorite number is not the sensational finale performed by firewalkers and fire knife champions, but the tender moment in the Hawaiian show when the dear old Hawaiian "aunties" dance a lovely hula in their traditional *muumuus* and are escorted back to their chairs by their young escorts, a moment of sweet *aloha*.

A day at PCC is certainly entertaining, but this is not just a tourist attraction or amusement park. It is an excellent presentation of fascinating cultures. Some packages allow you to return for a second visit without additional charge (subject to certain restrictions)—a good deal if you are staying on the North Shore.

Laie Beach Park Or Pounders Beach

South of Laie on the Kam Highway, **Laie Beach Park,** known locally as **Pounders Beach,** stretches from **Kehukuuna Point** on the north to **Pali Kilo Ia Point** on the south. Originally, this beach was known as **Pahumoa** in honor of a highly regarded fisherman who lived near **Koloa Stream,** which flows into the sea near Kehukuuna Point. Pahumoa arranged many *hukilaus* and gave fish to everyone who helped him draw in the nets as well as neighbors in need. Spotters stood on the ridges on each end of the beach and directed the fishermen with nets offshore as they surrounded a school of fish. In fact, the traditional name of the limestone ridge on the south end of the beach, Pali Kilo Ia, means "fish watcher's cliff." Fishermen still frequent this shoreline to fish for *moi* and other good eating fish.

A shallow sandbar on the southern end of the bay near the limestone cliff produces a rough shorebreak. White waves crash on a dark ledge with the pine forested Koolau Mountains rising vertically above it. When Church College opened in 1955, the students soon discovered that this was a stellar place for bodysurfing. They named it **Pounders** for the pounding shorebreak caused by the shallow sandbar.

On the north end of the beach, you can see the remnants of the pier where interisland steamers and schooners stopped to deliver passengers and supplies and pick up sugar and other local crops. This part of the bay is usually calmer and safer for swimming than the southern section. The beach park has parking, picnic tables and showers, but no restrooms.

The Koloa Trails

Across the road from the house at 55-147 Kam Highway, Akaka Gulch Road leads *mauka* into the Koolaus. **Akaka Gulch** lies to the south and **Koloa Gulch** lies to the north of the ridgeline. There are several challenging hiking trails in this area.

The **Koloa Ridge Trail** leads along the ridge and then ascends uphill toward the crest of the Koolaus. The **Koloa Gulch Trail** is a difficult, seven-mile round trip that begins on the ridge and descends into the gulch, crossing the Koloa Stream several dozen times before it ends at the **Koloa Double Waterfall**. A fork off the main trail leads to another pool and waterfall. The rock hopping is hard on the ankles, the rocks are slippery, and there is a significant danger of flash floods and rock falls. As a somber reminder of this danger, the trailhead is marked by a memorial in honor of Jonathan Taylor, a Boy Scout who was killed in Koloa Gulch when the stream flash flooded in 1994. A permit from Hawaii Reserves, Inc. is required for access to the trails.

Kokololio Beach Park

Continue south on Kam Highway .3 miles past Akaka Gulch Road to Kokololio Beach Park, at 55-017 Kam Highway. The beach park lies at the foot of a valley and stream named Kokololio, meaning "gusty." The tree-fringed beach curves from Pali Kilo Ia Point on the south end of Pounders to Kaipapau Point, with lovely views of the Windward Shore.

This shorefront was owned privately for generations. The southern end was part of an estate owned by the family of James Castle; for that reason it was called Kakela ("castle"). The luxurious home was surrounded by extensive gardens and statuary. The Hawaiian Electric Company purchased the northern end in 1952 for the use of company executives. The City and County of Honolulu acquired both properties and created the beach park in 1991.

The Kakela end of the beach has a protective reef, making it suitable for recreational swimming close to shore. The beach park has restrooms, showers, a nice lawn, and picnic facilities. Camping at five beachfront campsites is allowed by county permit.

A Perfect Day in Laie

Spend the morning at Hukilau Beach, or if you have teenagers take them bodyboarding at Pounders. Drive up to Laie Point, then have a plate lunch at the Hukilau Café. Spend a fascinating afternoon at the Polynesian Cultural Center and stay for the Alii Luau and Polynesian review.

Alternative: Hike the Laie Trail or take the luncheon trail ride at Gunstock Ranch. Go swimming at Kokololio Beach Park or use your return pass for another afternoon at the Polynesian Cultural Center. Stop at Laie Chop Suey for takeout and enjoy a picnic supper at a beach park.

HAUULA TO PUNALUU

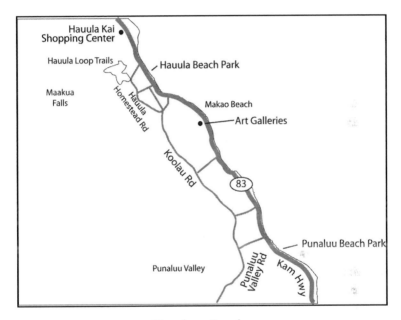

Hauula to Punaluu

Hauula Town

The name Hauula means "red *hau*," referring to the *hau* trees that blossomed profusely in this area during the summer months before the land was cleared for agriculture. Like hibiscus, *hau* blossoms bloom only for a day. They are yellow in the morning and turn to a brilliant red by evening.

The Hauula Kai Shopping Center at 54-316 Kam Highway is the site of **Tamura's Market,** which has a popular *poke* and sushi counter. **Papa Ole's Kitchen, Domino's Pizza, a post office, and**

gas station are also located in this shopping center. The **Hawaiian Seafood Grill & Bar** specializes in fish and chips and shrimp dishes. It is breezy and clean, with excellent service. Non-Mormons who feel a little parched after a day in Laie may enjoy the bar, which stocks a good selection of beer, wine, and other alcoholic beverages. The old Hauula BBQ is across the highway at 54-295 Kam Highway.

The shoreline across from the shopping center, **Kaipapau Beach,** is frequented mainly by fishermen. With little sand and a shallow, rocky bottom, it is not a good place to swim.

Hauula Beach Park

About ¼ mile south of the Hauula Kai Shopping Center, a white concrete wall marks Hauula Beach Park at 54-135 Kam Highway. The beach is long and sandy and protected by a long reef, but the bottom is rocky. At high tide, local kids enjoy the **Kilia surf break**. On the south end of the beach, Maakua Stream runs down toward the sea. A barrier sand bar blocks the stream from the ocean and creates a *muliwai*, a pond of standing, brackish water. The nine-acre beach park contains restrooms, showers, picnic tables, and a wide lawn. Camping is allowed by county permit at 15 beachside campsites. There is a playground across the street at Hauula Community Park, 54-050 Kam Highway.

The Hauula Loop Trails

Several excellent hiking trails lead through the pine-covered mountains above Hauula. Watch for the green "Hauula" community sign across Kam Highway from the north end of Hauula Beach Park. Turn *mauka* at the sign onto Hauula Homestead Road. As the name suggests, Hauula Homestead Road runs through Hawaiian-homestead land reserved for the Hawaiian people. Please respect the residents' privacy and remember Rule No. 9. The road is a loop that runs back into the Kam Highway at the southern end of Hauula. Where the paved road turns left (south), continue *mauka* (straight ahead) on the dirt road named Maakua Road, park at the gate, and walk through the Hawaiian-homestead property to the trailhead at the end of Maakua Road.

The **Hauula Loop Trail** is one of the most popular and beautiful hikes on Oahu, providing breathtaking views of the Windward Shore. The **Papali Loop Trail** does not provide such sweeping views, but it takes you through native vegetation and a stand of *kukui* trees.. The two loop trails are each about 2.5 miles long, with only a 600-foot gain in elevation. The six-mile **Maakua Gulch Trail** is a much more difficult hike, with a 900-foot gain in elevation. It follows the streambed to a waterfall, with numerous stream crossings and rock hopping from boulder to boulder. In essence, the trail *is* the streambed for most of the way. The valley narrows so dramatically that you can reach out and touch the sides. The reward is a lovely waterfall that drops into a pool about four feet deep. Do not attempt these hikes alone or if it is raining or rain is predicted.

The Shoreline From Hauula To Punaluu

Retrace your route and turn south (right) on Kam Highway to continue your tour. Remember that Hauula Homestead Road is a loop and stay on the north (left) side to rejoin Kam Highway at the same place.

Across Kam Highway from Hauula Beach Park, look *mauka* for the **Hauula Congregational Church** on Lanakila Hill, at 54-311 Hauula Homestead Road. The stone **ruins of King Lanakila Church,** built in 1853, lie next to the new church. King Lanakila Church was constructed with stones from the reef along the beach park. Lime made from nearby coral was mixed with sand for the mortar. As the population shifted southward in the late 19th century, wood removed from King Lanakila Church was used to build a smaller church in Kaluanui and the old church was left in ruins.

As the road curves eastward, look *makai* for tiny **Aukai Beach Park** at 54-071 Kam Highway. The raised coral reef along the shoreline makes swimming impossible, but a small bay with a sandy beach and bottom is accessible from the park. When the ocean is calm, it is safe to swim in the bay. When the ocean is rough, strong rip currents can form along the shore.

Continuing south, look *mauka* for **Wu's Sundries,** 54-060 Kam Highway, and the "**Ching Store**" (now **Hauula Gift Shop and Art Gallery**), 54-042 Kam Highway, remnants of the days when Chinese plantation workers relied on mom and pop "Ching stores" for supplies.

South of Kalaipaloa Point, Makao Road intersects the highway. The records of missionary Levi Chamberlain record that the natives called this location Makao because trading ships from the Portuguese-owned island of Macao near Hong Kong used it to load provisions and cargo. An offshore reef protects **Makao Beach**, but the bottom is shallow and rocky and the beach is practically covered at high tide. Notice the little fishing shrines that local fishermen have placed on the rocks along the shoreline facing Makao Road.

Two pleasant art galleries are located in the Makao area. The **Kim Taylor Reese Gallery** displays the portraits of Hawaiian *wahine* (women) for which this artist is famous. The **Lance Fairly Gallery** represents a number of local artists. Turn *mauka* on Hulahula Place for parking next to the Kim Taylor Reese Gallery. From there you can walk across the Kam Highway to visit the Lance Fairly Gallery.

Continuing south on Kam Highway, look *mauka* for the Kamamalama O Keao Church. As you cross the bridge over Kaliuwaa Stream, notice the old sign to **Sacred Falls State Park**. This was the site of a popular hiking trail that followed the Kaluanui Stream as it rushed down the mountainside. The hike ended at a refreshing swimming pond under an 87-foot waterfall. The Sacred Falls park and trail were closed permanently after a fatal rockfall in 1999.

The *ahupuaa* of Kaluanui extends from Kaliuwaa Stream to Waiono Stream. The Kaluanui shoreline is sandy, shallow, and safe for swimming and snorkeling near the shore when the streams are not running. The most popular section for swimming and fishing is in the middle, where a channel cuts through the reef into a large, sandy bay. However, this is not much of a beach. Where the Kam Highway opens on the shoreline, there is a breakwall with steps leading down to the shallow water. The only other improvement is a water fountain.

Punaluu

The fertile *ahupuaa* of Punaluu lies between the Waiono and Punaluu Streams, which descend precipitously from the towering Koolau Mountains to the ocean. The average rainfall in the forests of Punaluu is over 250 inches a year.

The early Hawaiians enjoyed a comfortable lifestyle here. Fishing was plentiful. Bananas and breadfruit grew in the upper valley and taro filled the terraces below. There were at least five *heiau* in the highlands, with the famous Kaumakaulaula *heiau* located near the present beach park.

Punaluu means "to dive for coral," a reference to the practice of Hawaiian women who dove for coral to prepare a lime-based bleach for their hair. To produce the lime, they burned pieces of coral in an *umu* (kiln). Later, the same process was used to obtain lime for construction mortar.

Tragically, the Hawaiian population of Punaluu was decimated by disease after the arrival of Westerners. By the beginning of the 20th century, Chinese farmers settled in Punaluu and planted rice where the taro ponds had been. Eventually, James Castle's Koolau Agricultural Company planted sugar cane in the coastal plains all the way to Kahana Bay, and Punaluu became a plantation community. The Koolau rail line stopped in Punaluu and hauled the cane to the Kahuku mill.

Today, Punaluu is a sleepy town with deep Hawaiian roots. Members of the Kawananakoa family, descendants of Hawaiian royalty, own several homes along the shoreline. The Hanohano family built the Hanohano Hale high-rise condominium at 53-549 Kam Highway. Queen Liliuokalani's Children's Center, on the hill *mauka* at 53-516 Kam Highway, is operated by the Trust established by Hawaii's last monarch.

Across the highway from pretty St. Joaquin's Church is **Kaya's General Store**, 53-534 Kam Highway. William Kaya, a plantation worker's son who served in World War II with the legendary 100th Infantry Battalion, started the business in 1946 when he returned from the War. If you're hungry or thirsty, you can pick up some shrimp scampi, a cold drink, and other refreshments at Kaya's.

To get a feel for this quiet part of Oahu, take a pleasant detour into the scenic **Punaluu Valley**. Just turn *mauka* off the Kam Highway at Green Valley Road or Punaluu Valley Road and enjoy the pastoral views of ranch buildings, horses, flocks of egrets, and cultivated banana plots.

Punaluu Beach Park

Punaluu Beach Park is a narrow, three-acre enclave at 53-309 Kam Highway. Waiono Stream (sometimes called Punaluu Stream) flows into the ocean at the north end of the beach. Before the waters of Waiono Stream were diverted to the upland valley for agriculture, it was a deep, swift river. Local children used the bridge across it as a diving platform. Where the fresh water and salt water met, the brackish mix teemed with fish. The deep channel that the swift-moving stream cut in the sea floor was used as a stopping place where coastal steamers delivered supplies and picked up rice and other local crops. Today, Waiono is just a small muddy stream and the pier where the steamers once landed is gone.

Punaluu Beach is narrow, straight, and safe for swimming and snorkeling when the stream is not running. Inshore, the water is shallow and protected by a reef where locals like to fish for octopus. Offshore, there are currents where a channel crosses the reef *makai* of Waiono Stream. The beach park provides restrooms, showers, and a shaded picnic area beneath pretty coconut palms.

Before Western contact, the Kaumakaulaula *heiau* was located near the area the beach park occupies today. The name Kaumakaulaula comes from a Hawaiian legend that the eyes of all the pigs near the *heiau* turned red on certain sacred nights.

Mauka of the beach park, **Tropicaina Bar & Grill** offers local fare and smoothies. The name is a misnomer, as alcoholic beverages are not available. In the rear of the building, a pretty patio fronting a horse pasture affords an impressive view of the Koolau Mountains towering above it.

A Perfect Day in Hauula and Punaluu

Go hiking or mountain biking on the Hauula Loop Trail. Have lunch at the Hawaiian Seafood Grill & Bar or Papa Ole's, or pick up some poke at Tamara's and have a picnic. Visit the art galleries and the ruins of Lanikila Church, then relax, swim and snorkel at Punaluu Beach Park.

KAHANA TO KAAAWA

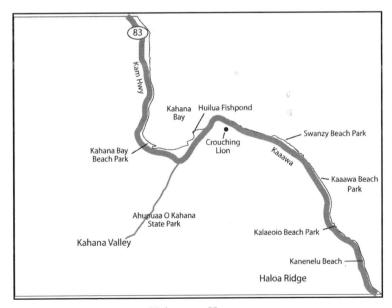

Kahana to Kaaawa

South of Punaluu, the Kam Highway travels along **Mamalu Bay** and around **Makalii Point** to the beautiful vista of **Kahana Bay**. Pull over to the side of the road to absorb the views in all directions. Above the highway, the Koolau Mountains slope steeply, sending the clear waters of Kahana Stream tumbling toward the sea.

Kahana Bay Beach Park

The eight-acre state beach park at 52-222 Kam Highway is one of the safest beaches on Oahu. A sandy beach extends the entire length of the bay from Makalii Point to Mahie Point. The bottom is sandy with a gentle slope. A small shorebreak sometimes provides ideal conditions for young or novice bodysurfers. When a swell runs across the offshore reefs at the mouth of the bay, waves suitable for beginning board surfers can form outside the shorebreak. The wide, sand-bottom channel that runs out to the middle of the bay provides good entry and exit for the Kapaeleele Boat Ramp. The bay is broad and calm, though the water is sometimes cloudy near the mouth of the Kahana Stream. The estuary where the stream flows into the bay is still popular with locals for fishing, squidding, and crabbing. There are restrooms, showers, ten campsites, and a lovely picnic area in a shady coconut grove.

On the north end of the bay, there is a fishing shrine where early Hawaiians performed ceremonies and made offerings to ensure bountiful catches, and a *kilo* built for *kilo ia* who scanned the sea to locate schools of food fish and signal their location to fishermen. At low tide, you can see the Huilua Fishpond on the south end of the bay.

Huilua Fishpond

At one time there were three fishponds along the lower reaches of Kahana Stream: two *puone* (inland ponds) and Huilua Fishpond, which is the only surviving *kuapa* (open-sea pond enclosed by a rock wall) in northern Oahu.

Huilua Fishpond is a National Historic Landmark. Historians believe it was built between 1400 and 1600 A.D. It probably started forming when crosscurrents between the ocean and the mouth of the stream formed a sandbar. The early Hawaiians fortified the exterior wall of the sandbar with rocks from the streambeds and valley slopes. They didn't use any mortar, but they knew how to lock the rocks together so the wall could withstand the daily wave action. The loose cobble and sand fill allowed water to move through the wall. Standing three to four feet wide and about four feet above the high tide, the 500-foot wall enclosed seven acres of ocean water adjacent to the estuary. The early Hawaiians used the fishpond to cultivate fish as well as to hold catches. Two sluice gates made of lashed poles allowed water to circulate. The spaces between the poles were wide enough to let small fish swim into the pond, where they grew too big and fat to swim out. Fingerlings were raised in a separate pond and then released into the larger pond. When water flowed seaward with the tides, the fish collected at the sluice gates, where they were easily netted.

The pondkeeper lived next to the pond. From 1924 until 1948, Sam Pua Haaheo was the pondkeeper, the *kilo* who watched for fish in the bay, and the fishing *konohiki* who organized the *hukilau*. The pond's location in the bay protected it, but flooding and tsunamis caused major damage in the 20th century. Since the tsunami of 1960, Huilua Pond has not been used and has filled with sand and vegetation. It is only visible from the shore at low tide. You can visit the Huilua Fishpond from the east side of the bay, but please do not walk on it. If you would like to learn more about Hawaiian fish ponds, continue south on the Kam Highway to Kualoa Ranch, where the Molii Fishpond is still in operation, and to Heeia State Park, where you can get a good view of the 88-acre Heeia Fishpond, a brackish pond that was used as late as the 1950s.

Ahupuaa O Kahana State Park

Kahana Stream flows the length of the *ahupuaa* of Kahana, from the crest of the Koolaus down to Kahana Bay. The valley is one of the wettest spots on Oahu. With up to 300 inches of rain a year, the upper slopes are often shrouded in mist.

In ancestral days, extensive agriculture, fishing, and aquaculture supported a large native community in this valley. Kahana Stream provided a steady source of water for upland taro patches. Fishing with surround nets was relatively easy. The water was much calmer than at Laie and Hauula, where strong currents made maneuvering more difficult. From *kilo* on the ridges above the bay, *kilo ia* looked for sun reflecting off the fish like a mirror and signaled with a white flag when a school entered the bay. As the fishermen waiting on the beach paddled into the bay in canoes laden with nets, the *kilo ia* directed their movements from the lookout with arm signals or flags. Following their signals, the fishermen encircled the school with nets and pulled the catch to shore. Fishponds were used not only to hold the abundant harvests, but also to cultivate food fish. Sometimes the catches were so large that corrals were made of nets to hold them. The fishermen of Kahana also used hook and line with fishhooks made of bone and pearl shell. Fish could even be caught from the shore with scoop nets and dip nets.

Unfortunately, the Kahana Valley was decimated by the spread of foreign diseases. By 1850, the Hawaiian population had declined so much that the taro patches and fishponds fell into disuse. With the native population gone, the *Mahele* of 1848–1850 resulted in the transfer of large parts of the Kahana Valley to *haole* entrepreneurs. James Castle extended his Koolau Railroad to Kahana, planted his Kahana land in sugar cane, and hauled the harvested cane to the Kahuku mill. Soon the entire coastline from Kahana to Kahuku was planted in sugar cane, and imported plantation workers constituted the majority of the population. When the Koolau Agricultural Company and Koolau Railroad closed down in the 20th century, Kahana became a backwater.

During World War II, the United States Army leased the Kahana Valley to train American soldiers for jungle warfare. It built a road into the interior of the valley, installed concrete bunkers, and erected guns and searchlights at the entrance to the bay. When the war ended, the valley was returned to the property owners and the *ahupuaa* of Kahana reverted to a ghostly vestige of Hawaiian life.

Today, the entire *ahupuaa* of Kahana is owned by the State of Hawaii. The 5,300-acre Ahupuaa O Kahana State Park was created to revive and restore the traditional Hawaiian way of life. The park surrounds a small area of Hawaiian homestead land.

Ahupuaa O Kahana State Park is a 'living park" intended to foster native Hawaiian traditions and the culture of rural windward Oahu. Thirty Hawaiian families live in the valley. There are no regularly scheduled programs or activities for tourists. The restrooms near the parking area are open, but the Visitors Center is closed. If you are interested in a cultural program at the park, call 237-7767.

Koa and Kilo Loop Trail

An easy 1.2-mile loop trail leads along the western side of the valley floor to the Kapaeleele Koa fishing shrine and Keaniani Kilo lookout over Kahana Bay. The Koa and Kilo Loop Trail affords terrific views of the bay. Just park in the designated parking area and follow the signs.

The Kahana Valley Trails

Trails leading into the valley require greater effort and preparation. This is the wettest valley on Oahu, so the ground can be muddy, the rocks slippery, the streams dangerous, and rain and mosquitoes a trial. There are many archaeological sites, including a *heiau*, fishing shrines, house sites, irrigation channels, and agricultural terraces, but most of them are not easily accessible. If you plan to explore the backcountry trails, obtain trail maps before you go or take a group hike with a knowledgeable guide. Let others know the route you intend to take, and do not hike alone. Be sure to wear shoes with a good tread and bring mosquito repellent and a rain parka. Be aware that there is a significant population of feral pigs in the valley and take precautions during hunting season. The gate from the parking area to the trailhead is open from 7:00 a.m. until 6:45 p.m. Remember that the hiking distances for the valley trails are extended by the .6-mile walk from the designated parking area to the trailhead. Also remember Rule No. 2.

The **Nakoa Trail** is a fairly easy hike with a wonderful reward. The route is a 3.5-mile loop that leads across Kahana Stream and a number of sidestreams to an inviting swimming hole. The **Puu Piei Trail** is a rugged climb up a peak overlooking Kahana Bay. It is only a three-mile round trip, but it has an elevation gain of 1,700 feet. The reward is a spectacular view of the bay from a *kilo* used by Hawaiian fish spotters. Another ancestral fishing shrine is a short detour from the Puu Piei trail. The **Puu Manamana Trail** is an extremely challenging four-mile loop along the steep ridges surrounding the valley, with an elevation gain of 2,100 feet.

The Crouching Lion

Continuing around Kahana Bay, the Kam Highway turns east toward Mahie Point. The *ahupuaa* of Makaua lies between Mahie Point and Kaaawa Point. Makaua means "eye of the rain," a very appropriate name for the wettest part of the island. The picturesque rock formation on the ridge above Mahie Point is called the **Crouching Lion** because it resembles a lion at rest. The early Hawaiians called this soaring rock formation *Kauhiimaka o kalani,* which means "the observant cover of the heavens."

Look *mauka* for the **Crouching Lion Inn** at 51-666 Kam Highway. Built in the 1920s, this handsome building passed through a number of owners until it became a restaurant in 1951. A generation ago, people drove here from all over the island for elegant dining. The building could use an update, but the food and service are still passable and there is a great view of the water from the British pub and outdoor patio.

Tiny **Makaua Beach Park** is a small, undeveloped strip of land between the Kam Highway and the ocean near Kaaawa Point. Fishing shrines placed by local fishermen stand on the rocks along the shore. The "beach" is so narrow it disappears completely during high tide. The bottom is a shallow reef with a sand bottom channel cutting through it. The channel provides a good fishing ground for divers and pole fishermen and an anchorage for small boats. Surfers and bodyboarders sometimes paddle out to surf the tubes that form on the outer reef, which is also called Crouching Lion.

Swanzy Beach Park

Swanzy Beach Park is marked by a masonry seawall fronted by a rocky shoreline at 51-392 Kam Highway. There is not much of a beach. Most of the sand was washed away before the seawall was built, and it is usually under water at high tide. The shoreline and sea bottom are rocky. The park is more popular with locals hunting for octopus and squid in the shallows than with tourists. The five-acre park contains restrooms, showers, a playground, picnic pavilion, basketball court, and nine campsites for weekend use by county permit.

Swanzy Beach Park was named for Julie Judd Swanzy, who had the good fortune to inherit all of Kualoa and Kaaawa from her father, missionary doctor Gerrit P. Judd. For $1.00, Mrs. Swanzy gave the county this five-acre parcel and a narrow, two-acre strip of land a mile down the beach, plus one acre inland for a school. In consideration for the gift, the county abandoned plans to develop a public park near her home in Kualoa.

During World War II, Swanzy Park was used for the headquarters of the U.S. Army's jungle warfare training program in the Kahana Valley. *Mauka* of the beach park, **Uncle Bobo's Smoked BBQ** is located at 51-480 Kam Highway (next to the post office).

Kaaawa

Continue past Swanzy Beach Park and Kaaawa Point to the little town of Kaaawa. The name is taken from *aawa,* the Hawaiian name for the yellow wrasse that was abundant in earlier times and is still fairly common here. As you drive south along the water's edge, you will see large boulders placed to protect the highway from erosion. Notice the difference from the North Shore, where the big surf would tower over such minor impediments.

Kaaawa Beach Park

Kaaawa Beach Park, at 51-237 Kam Highway, is the narrow two-acre strip of shoreline that Julie Judd Swanzy donated to the county in her deal to avoid having a public park near her home in Kualoa. Although the beach has been eroded, it is still a pleasant and safe place to swim and snorkel near the shore. Locals fish for octopus on the shallow reef offshore. The park contains restrooms, showers, and picnic facilities. Look *mauka* for Kaaawa Elementary School on the one-acre parcel donated by Mrs. Swanzy.

Kalaeoio

As you continue south on the Kam Highway, the dramatic mountain ridge separating Kaaawa from Kualoa towers over Kaiaka Bay. According to Hawaiian legend, the most famous burial cave in Oahu extended from these cliffs all the way through the Koolau Mountains to Kahuku. One of the entrances was supposed to be on the cliff above Kalaeoio, but none of the entrances has been located in modern times.

Kalaeoio Beach Park takes its name from **Kalaeoio Point**, which separates Kaaawa from Kualoa. Kalaeoio means "the point of the bonefish." The point is still popular with shorecasters fishing for *moi, oio,* and *papio,* as well as surfers enjoying the small waves off the point. The beach park is a one-acre strip with a narrow sand beach. The bay is shallow, sandy, and safe for swimming when the ocean is calm and the stream is not running. Where Kaaawa Stream runs into the bay, it has cut a wide channel through the reef.

The park ends at **Makahonu Point**, which is marked by a small grove of ironwood trees. The name Makahonu means "eye of the turtle," referring to times when this was a feeding and nesting ground for sea turtles. This small beach park has shaded picnic tables, but no restrooms or bathhouse. It is easily accessible from Kam Highway, with roadside parking. Beyond Makahonu Point, there are wonderful views of Kaneohe Point and Rabbit Island.

Kanenelu

Kanenelu, meaning "the marsh," is a former wetland on the *mauka* side of Kam Highway from Kalaeoio Beach Park. The beachfront at the boundary between Kaaawa and Kualoa is known as **Kanenelu Beach**. The narrow beach is sandy but the sea bottom is rocky in spots. The water is safe for swimming and the small offshore waves are good for young or novice surfers. Be sure to stop and catch the view up the Windward Shore, with the dramatic ridges of the Koolau Mountains descending to white beaches as far as the eye can see.

South of Kanenelu Beach, the Haloa Ridge descends all the way down to the highway. As you round the ridge, look *mauka* for the ruins of an old sugar mill. This was the first sugar mill erected on the island, in about 1864.

To the south, Kualoa Regional Park, the Mokolii Fishpond, and Chinaman's Hat mark the northern end of Kaneohe Bay. The Kam Highway continues south along the shore; the Kahekili Highway (Route 83) cuts *mauka* along the dramatic *pali*, where waterfalls tumble toward temple gardens when it rains. Both roads will take you to the H-3 Freeway. To complete the "Circle Tour," you can return to Honolulu on H-3. To return to the North Shore, you can either retrace your route up the Kam Highway or take H-3 west to H-1, H-1 west to H-2, and H-2 back to northern Oahu.

A Perfect Day in Kahana and Kaaawa

Enjoy a guided hike or bike ride in the beautiful Kahana Valley, followed by a picnic lunch in the pretty coconut grove. Then spend the afternoon walking, swimming, kayaking, and exploring the Huilua Fishpond and Kahana Bay. Drive to the Haloa Ridge and enjoy the wonderful views of the Windward Shore as you complete your circle tour of northern Oahu.

III. MAJOR TOURIST ATTRACTIONS

DOLE PINEAPPLE PLANTATION

Although the days of pineapple growing on Oahu are coming to an end, the Dole Pineapple Plantation, 64-1550 Kam Highway, (808) 621-8408, www.dole-plantation.com, is still an attractive stop. It offers three interesting entertainments. The red and yellow **"Pineapple Express" train** departs every half hour for a two-mile, narrated trip through the pineapple fields. Passengers hear the history of pineapple and the story of James Dole, who pioneered the pineapple industry in Hawaii. The **Pineapple Garden Maze**, recognized by the Guinness Book of World Records as the "world's largest maze," contains nearly two miles of paths lined by more than 11,000 colorful Hawaiian plants. Prizes are awarded to those who find the six "secret stations" in the maze in the fastest time. The **Plantation Garden Tour** is a walking tour that affords a close-up look at a variety of crops, such as bananas, coffee, mango, papaya, and hibiscus, as well as handicrafts and cultural activities. The attractive gift shop contains an incredible variety of pineapple products, souvenirs, and treats. Try the chocolate-covered pineapple. Ship some of the delicious fruit to family, friends, or yourself. Outdoor kiosks offer additional local products, such as the kukui nut body oils that are made in Waialua. The Dole Pineapple Plantation is open daily from 9:00 a.m. until 5:30 p.m.

WAIMEA VALLEY HISTORICAL NATURE PARK

Waimea Valley Historical Nature Park, 59-864 Kam Highway, provides a delightful introduction to the natural beauty and history ui Πawaii. Take a leisurely walk along lovely Kamananui Stream. The ¾-mile self-guided trail passes a lily pond, native and tropical gardens, a fishing shrine, an ancient Hawaiian living site, agricultural terraces, a Hawaiian games site, and several sacred areas. At the top of the valley, **Waimea Falls** (also known as Waihee Falls) cascades over a cliff into a fresh water pond. Wear your bathing suit and enjoy a refreshing swim. There are changing rooms and lifeguards at the pond.

Waimea Valley is one of the richest repositories of pre-contact Hawaiian artifacts on Oahu. Guided tours of Hawaiian living and games sites help visitors understand how the early Hawaiians lived in this sacred valley.

This is also one of the best places on the island to observe native flora and fauna. With a range of habitats stretching from the dry, salty seashore to the cool, misty uplands, Waimea Valley is the home of a vast array of ferns, flowering plants, invertebrates, birds, stream life, and Oahu's only native land mammal, the hoary bat.

The plant collections focus on native Hawaiian plants and Polynesian introductions. The Waimea Arboretum collects and grows rare specimens of Hawaii's endangered plants, which can be enjoyed from the paths winding along Waimea Stream. Stroll through the Hawaiian collection, just beyond the Visitors Center, and enjoy an assortment of plants found only in Hawaii. Many of them are very rare; every plant with a red label is an endangered species. You can see what ancient Hawaiian lowland vegetation might have looked like in the Ogasawara collection, which features close relatives of now-extinct Hawaiian flora. Meander through the Hawaiian ethnobotanical garden, which features one of the best collections of Polynesian plants found anywhere. The gardens contain over 35 distinct collections with 5,000 taxa of tropical plants, all carefully documented and labeled. A **guided moonlight walk** provides a unique opportunity to see mysterious night-blooming tropical flowers come to life before your eyes. Come early and bring flashlights and bug spray.

Visitors can also observe the Hawaiian animals that make their home in the valley. Four of the five species of *oopu* (Hawaiian goby), Hawaii's only freshwater fish, thrive here. Native birds include the *aukuu* (black-crowned night heron) and the endangered *alae ula* (Hawaiian moorhen), a black water bird with a red faceplate. Native damselflies, dragonflies, fruit flies, and other invertebrates also abound. Various species of migratory birds, including plovers and turnstones, winter here. Many introduced species also inhabit the valley, including peacocks and the ubiquitous Indian mongoose.

The park is open daily from 9:30 a.m. to 5:00 p.m. Wheelchair access is provided. An attractive grill serves sandwiches, salads, plate lunches, and drinks on a pleasant deck near the entrance and gift shop. Another snack bar near the waterfall offers snacks and drinks. Check the bulletin board outside the gift shop or call 638-7766 in advance for the schedule of guided tours and other events.

POLYNESIAN CULTURAL CENTER

The 42-acre Polynesian Cultural Center in Laie, 293-3333 or 1-800-367-7060, www.Polynesia.com, is Oahu's most popular tourist attraction. It contains seven authentic native villages that bring to life the cultures of Polynesia's seven island nations: Hawaii, Fiji, New Zealand, Samoa, Easter Island, Tonga, Tahiti, and the Marquesas. "Go Native" activities allow visitors to learn to climb a coconut tree, make fire from sticks and coconut husks, throw spears, and practice the warrior training exercises of Aotearoa (New Zealand). Kid-friendly activities, such as Hawaiian hula lessons, Samoan fire making, Tongan drumming, Tahitian fishing, and wash-offable Marquesas cultural tattoos, are scheduled in each village throughout the day. A canoe pageant along the lagoon adds to the entertainment. Thrilling IMAX films are shown in the IMAX movie theater. A canoe ride offers a cooling rest. The day ends with a boat ride to the dining areas, where a variety of dinner options, including a delightful Alii Luau with Hawaiian food and entertainment, are offered. The Polynesian review, "Horizons, Where The Sea Meets The Sky," is fabulous. With more than 100 performers in native attire, it is highlighted by the performances of firewalkers and fire knife champions.

The shops are open from 11:00 a.m. until 9:00 p.m. The villages are open from 12:00 noon until 6:00 p.m. Dinner is served from 5:00 until 7:00 p.m. The evening show begins at 7:30 p.m. Gift shops offer a wide variety of merchandise and recordings of the performances. Transportation is available by minibus or motorcoach for an additional fee. The Center is closed on Sundays. Wheelchairs and strollers are available for rent.

The LDS Church operates the Polynesian Cultural Center. Eighty per cent of the entertainers and workers are Polynesian students attending the church-owned Brigham Young University-Hawaii in Laie. Profits are used to fund student scholarships. Alcoholic beverages are neither available nor permitted in the park.

Packages

The Center offers a variety of packages, from the all-inclusive Ambassador Package to simple admission. Check with the Center on current packages and pricing. The longstanding offerings are:

The Ambassador: VIP Tour of Park, Dinner or Luau, and Show

The **Ambassador Package** is the most expensive and all-inclusive. It is best for those who want to see and learn as much as possible regardless of cost. This premium package includes a kukui nut *lei* greeting, a small group guided tour of the seven villages, the canoe pageant, canoe rides, IMAX movie, a choice of the Ambassador dinner (see the Dining Options below) or the Alii Luau dinner and show with a fresh flower *lei*, and premium seating at the Horizons Night Show with a pineapple dessert at intermission and souvenir video and program. This can be upgraded further to the "Super Ambassador" or "Romance Package." The **Twilight Ambassador Package** includes village access from 4:00 p.m. to 6:30 p.m., canoe rides, an IMAX film presentation, a choice of the Ambassador dinner or the Alii Luau dinner and show with a fresh flower *lei*, and premium seating at the Horizons Night Show with a pineapple dessert at intermission and souvenir video and program.

The Alii: Park, Luau, and Show

The **Alii Luau Package** provides full-day access to the villages in walkabout style, at your own pace without a guide. It also includes the canoe pageant, canoe rides, IMAX movie, Alii Luau dinner and show with a fresh flower *lei*, and preferred seating at the Horizons Night Show. If you want to see the villages at your own pace and attend the *luau*, this is the best package. The **Twilight Alii Luau Package** includes access to the villages from 4:00 p.m. to 5:15 p.m., canoe rides, the IMAX movie, the Alii Luau dinner and show with a fresh flower *lei,* and preferred seating at the Horizons Night Show.

Admission/Show: Park and Show, with Dinner On Your Own

The **Admission/Show Package** includes full-day access to the villages, the canoe pageant, canoe rides, IMAX movie, and reserved seating at the Horizons Night Show. With this package, you can purchase dinner separately at any of the on-premise restaurants or snack bars. The **Twilight Admission/Show Package** includes access to the villages from 4:00 p.m. to 6:30 p.m., canoe rides, the IMAX movie, and reserved seating at the Horizons Night Show.

Ohana Adventure: Park and Lunchtime Luau

The **Ohana Adventure Package** is specially tailored for families with children who want to limit their visit to daytime hours. It begins with a lunchtime *Keiki Kaukau* (children's feast), and includes full-day access to the villages with kid-focused presentations, special children's activities, the canoe pageant, canoe rides, and IMAX movie. If you want to combine the children's activities with the Alii Luau and Horizons Night Show, the Ohana package can be upgraded.

Admission only

Admission only tickets can also be purchased.

Free Return Visit And Tram Tour

The full-day packages (the Ambassador, Alii Luau, Admission/ Show, and Ohana packages) allow you to return within a specified time to enjoy the villages, family activities and games, and IMAX movie. Transportation, meals, and the night show are not included in the extra day. The full-day packages also include free tram tours of Laie focusing on the Visitors Center of the LDS Church.

If you want to get a feel for the place before buying a package, walk through the entrance area. Without paying an admission fee, you can stroll through the shops, watch local artisans create handmade crafts, and have lunch at the Island BBQ or lunch buffet.

Dining Options

Dinner

The Ambassador Restaurant

The most expensive option, the Ambassador Restaurant serves first-class American fare from 5:00 to 7:00 p.m. The menu includes shrimp cocktail, prime rib, crab legs, scallops, fresh fruits and vegetables, and desserts, but no entertainment.

The Alii Luau

Only available with the Ambassador and Alii Luau packages, the *luau* features traditional Hawaiian food, including fire-pit roasted kalua pig, chicken long rice, fresh fish, native fruits and vegetables, and traditional Hawaiian desserts. There is also a nice salad bar. The *luau* begins at 5:15 p.m. with Hawaiian entertainment and dancing.

The Gateway Restaurant

If you do not want heavy food or Hawaiian entertainment, the Gateway Restaurant's buffet dinner offers a variety of entrees, vegetables, a fresh salad bar, fruits, and desserts from 5:00 to 7:00 p.m.

The Banyan Tree Snack Bar

Open for lunch and dinner from 11:00 a.m. until 7:00 p.m., the Banyan Tree Snack Bar features fast food, island style, including burgers, fish, chicken, pizza, salads, and desserts.

Lunch

Suggestion: To maximize your expensive day at the PCC, arrive early, buy your tickets before lines form, and tour the villages that interest you most as soon as they open. The crowds grow as the afternoon passes. When you get hungry, have lunch and a nice rest at one of these delightful eateries. The canoe ride and IMAX theater are also pleasant ways to get off your feet and cool off.

The Keiki Kaukau (children's feast)

This family-friendly Hawaiian-style buffet is designed to provide a *luau* experience for families with children who need to be home by evening.

Island BBQ

For a quick, healthy lunch, the Island BBQ serves island-style barbecued chicken and shrimp and fresh fruits from 11:00 a.m. to 1:30 p.m.

Soup, Salad and Sandwich Buffet

This lunchtime buffet offers soups, salads, a sandwich bar, and desserts from 11:30 a.m. to 1:30 p.m.

The Banyan Tree Snack Bar

Open from 11:00 a.m. until 7:00 p.m., the Banyan Tree features fast food, island style, including burgers, fish, chicken, pizza, salads, and desserts.

IV. BEACHES

*All of Hawaii's beaches, up to the highest high-water
mark, are public property. Where the shoreline has been developed,
access is provided by public rights of way. All terrain wheelchairs
are available for persons with disabilities; call the City and County
of Honolulu Department of Parks and Recreation, telephone
768-3027. Remember that you are responsible for your own
safety when you enter the water. Follow the "Ten Commandments"
in Chapter I. Make sure the water conditions are appropriate
for your ability.*

SHORT LIST OF GREAT SWIMMING BEACHES

*Subject to changing conditions, these are the most popular
swimming beaches.*

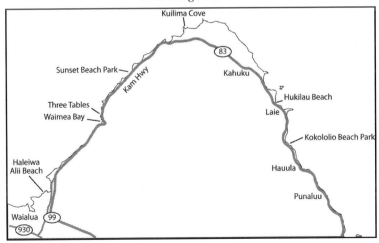

Best Beaches for Recreational Swimming

For Recreational Swimming:

Haleiwa Alii Beach Park (inshore of the surf break)

Waimea Bay Beach Park

Three Tables Beach

Sunset Beach Park

Hukilau Beach

Kokololio Beach Park (the Kakela (southern) side)

For Families With Young Children:

Waimea Bay Beach Park

Three Tables Beach

Kuilima Cove

Hukilau Beach (the southern end where the houses are)

For Older Kids And Teenagers:

Jumping off the rock at Waimea Bay Beach Park

Bodyboarding in the shorebreak at Waimea, Sunset, and Hukilau Beaches

Bodysurfing and bodyboarding at Pounders, Ke Waena, and Ehukai Beaches

Snorkeling and scuba diving at Three Tables and Shark's Cove

Reef-protected Kuilima Cove is safe for swimming year-round.

Lifeguarded Beaches:

Alii Beach Park

Haleiwa Beach Park

Laniakea Beach Support Park

Chun's Reef Support Park

Waimea Bay Beach Park

Ke Waena Beach Park

Ehukai Beach Park

Sunset Beach Park

In addition to these lifeguard stations, the Sunset Fire Station at Pupukea Beach Park responds to emergencies including shore rescues.

For current information on lifeguarded beaches, check oceansafety-soest.hawaii.edu.

THE NORTHWEST SHORE

Get lost on this secluded six-mile coastline where the television show "Lost" was filmed. Explore deserted beaches and sand dunes where turquoise water tops purple reefs.

YMCA Camp Harold Erdman Beach
69-385 Farrington Highway, Kaena
Swimming, diving and snorkeling when calm; fishing on west end of beach; YMCA conference center and summer camp

The YMCA owns the shoreline along the western end of the Farrington Highway. The Y's Camp Harold Erdman is a year-round conference center and summer camp for children. Access to the facilities is restricted to authorized users. The YMCA provides lifeguard service, but only for those in its charge. The beach is sandy, but the offshore reef is broken. Strong currents and turbulent water make it unsuitable for swimming during the winter or stormy weather. The area west of the camp is a popular fishing spot. Roadside parking on Farrington Highway.

Mokuleia Army Beach
Farrington Highway, Kaena
Swimming and diving when calm, fishing, surfing

The shoreline along the Farrington Highway across from Dillingham Airfield was developed as a recreation area for military personnel. The State of Hawaii has taken over the property with plans to restore it. The beach is wide and sandy, but breaks in the offshore reef make it dangerous for swimming during the winter or stormy weather. A surf spot offshore is known for quick left tubes in northwest swells. Roadside parking on Farrington Highway. No improvements or lifeguards.

Kealia Beach

Farrington Highway, Kealia
Swimming and diving when calm, fishing

The wide sandy beach between the Army Beach and Mokuleia Beach Park is popular for fishing. The offshore reef provides enough protection for swimming and diving on calm days, but there are strong currents and it is too rough for recreational swimming during winter surf or stormy conditions. The beach is accessible from the highway via well-worn paths through the brush. There are no improvements or lifeguards. Roadside parking on Farrington Highway.

Mokuleia Beach Park

68-919 Farrington Highway (also called Kaena Point Road), Mokuleia.
Swimming, snorkeling and diving when calm; fishing; kitesurfing; windsurfing; picnicking. Camping has been suspended until further notice.

An offshore reef protects this 38-acre beach park. Purplish reefs and shallow aquamarine water color the picturesque shoreline. Sea turtles feed on the *limu* that grows on the rocks. The beach is sandy. The section of beach directly in front of the parking lot lies on the leeward side of a sandy point, affording some protection from the wind. The sea bottom is rocky with a few sand pockets. The shallow reef near the shore is suitable for snorkeling when the water is calm. Winter waves and currents can be treacherous. Children must be closely supervised, as the shoreline is easily accessible from the picnic and parking areas but hidden from view by sand dunes. Mokuleia is great for windsurfing and kitesurfing. It is also popular with short boarders. Several surf spots are accessible from this park, including Park Rights directly offshore and Day Star (also known as The Boat) on the reef about 200 yards to the west. Mokuleia is frequented by local shorecasters. The park contains restrooms, showers, a playground, lawn, and picnic facilities, but no lifeguards. Camping has been suspended until further notice.

Mokuleia Polo Field Beach
68-411 Farrington Highway, Mokuleia
Swimming and diving when calm, fishing, horseback riding, polo lessons, polo matches

The Hawaii Polo Club owns the shoreline along its 100-acre ranch in Mokuleia. The beach is sandy and safe for swimming when the ocean is calm. There are strong currents during the winter months, especially when the big surf is running. Restrooms and refreshments are available during polo matches. There are no lifeguards. Polo lessons and horseback riding on beachfront trails can be arranged by reservation. Devil's Rock, the only rock island on the Mokuleia shoreline, lies offshore.

Makaleha Beach Park
68-539 Farrington Highway, Mokuleia
Swimming and diving when calm, surfing, fishing

This is a 28-acre pasture with no improvements bordering Makaleha Stream where it runs into the ocean. The public right of way from the Farrington Highway leads to a long, sandy beach used mainly by local fishermen. The Sylva Channel surf break lies offshore. There are no improvements or lifeguards.

Crozier Drive Beach
Crozier Drive, Waialua
Swimming, snorkeling, diving, fishing

The shoreline in front of the quaint Crozier Drive beach colony is a wonderful long, sandy beach. The entire area is protected by the offshore reef and safe for swimming. The reef comes all the way up to the shore, but there are several sandy pockets where you can get into the water. There are no improvements, lifeguards, or crowds. There is a public right of way on Crozier Drive .2 miles west of Olohilo Street, but parking is difficult.

Aweoweo Beach Park
68-197 Au Street, Waialua
Swimming and diving when calm

Aweoweo Beach Park has a steep, sandy beach with small waves near the shore east of the Crozier Drive residential community. There are wonderful views of the shoreline curving toward Haleiwa on one side and Kaena Point on the other. Watch out for rocks and triangular tank traps along the base of the beach. The offshore reef, beachrock, and seawall can be sharp and slippery. The park has restrooms and showers but no lifeguards. To reach Aweoweo Beach Park, take Waialua Beach Road to Apuhihi Street. Turn *makai* on Apuhihi and drive to the T intersection. Turn left on Au Street and continue west to the beach park. Parking is limited.

HALEIWA

Well-maintained beach parks offer year-round swimming, surfing, fishing, canoeing, kayaking, and numerous other recreational facilities.
Locals enjoy fishing, crabbing, and camping on Kaiaka Bay.

Kaiaka Bay Beach Park
66-449 Haleiwa Road, Haleiwa
Fishing, crabbing, camping

This 53-acre park lies on the northeast side of Kaiaka Bay. The baysidse beach is used mainly by local fishermen and neighborhood children. Two large streams empty into the bay. The wave action is gentle, allowing silt carried by the streams to accumulate near the shoreline. The beach is narrow and the sand is often brown from the flow of silt. When heavy rains fall, the entire bay becomes muddy. Most swimmers prefer the wide sand beach fronting the ocean on the north side of the park. The Hammerheads surf break lies offshore. The park contains restrooms, showers, picnic facilities, seven campsites, and parking. There are no lifeguards.

Waialua Beach
Haleiwa Road, Haleiwa
Swimming, surfing

The shoreline between Kaiaka Bay Beach Park and Kupaoa Point is known as Waialua Beach. West of Alii Beach Park, the beach is sandy, with fringing trees, a gently sloping bottom, and a great view of the shoreline. The Walls surf break lies offshore from the Haleiwa Surf Condos at 66303 Haleiwa Road. For access, take Haleiwa Road to Walikanahele Road and turn *makai* on Walikanahele into a parking lot with restrooms. Alternatively, you can park at Alii Beach Park or along Haleiwa Road and walk along the shore. There are no lifeguards.

Alii Beach Park
66-167 Haleiwa Road, Haleiwa, telephone 637-5051
Swimming, longboarding, short boarding, bodysurfing, bodyboarding, first leg of the Triple Crown of Surfing, fishing, picnicking, boat launch

This 20-acre beach park occupies the northeastern end of Waialua Beach. With its deep sand and excellent facilities, it lives up to its name, "Royal Beach Park." The Haleiwa surf break off Kupaoa Point is one of the North Shore's most popular surf spots. The Reef Hawaiian Pro, first leg of the Triple Crown of Surfing, is held there every November. South of the Haleiwa break is Avalanche, where huge sets sometimes occur during the winter. When Avalanche breaks big, it is the scene of tow-in surfing. The best place for swimming is inshore of the surf breaks: either the Kaena end of the beach, where an offshore reef protects the water, or the small, area tucked on the east side of the breakwater. The deeper areas near the breakwater have fringing reef and rocks, along with strong rip currents running seaward when the waves are surfable. The beach park has restrooms, showers, shaded picnic areas, a small boat launch, and lifeguard service. Community meetings and programs are held on the first floor of the John Kahili Surf Center, which was used as a set for *Baywatch*

Hawaii. The parking lot is accessible from Haleiwa Road west of the Haleiwa Boat Harbor.

Haleiwa Beach Park
62-449 Kam Highway, Haleiwa
Swimming, canoeing, kayaking, jet skiing, fishing, picnicking, baseball, softball, lighted basketball and volleyball courts

This 13-acre park on the northern end of Waialua Bay gets plenty of use by locals. The narrow sand beach cannot compete with the lovely deep sand of Alii and Waimea, but it is ideal for launching canoes and kayaks. Shorecasters fish and kids jump off the breakwater. The picnic facilities, lawn, playground, lighted basketball and volleyball courts, and baseball and softball fields in the north end of the park are heavily used. Swimming is safe year-round and lifeguard service is provided. The park is also a great place to enjoy the sunset. Public restrooms and showers are located near the playground and basketball court. Paved parking is accessible from the Kam Highway on both sides of the park.

KAWAILOA

The shoreline of Kawailoa extends from Puaena Point on the northern tip of Waialua Bay to the tiny Wananapaoa Islands at the entrance to Waimea Bay. This lovely coast is graced with famous surf breaks and picturesque beaches, many unseen from the road.

Papailoa Beach
61-785 Papailoa Road, Kawailoa
Swimming in sand pockets when calm, diving, surfing, turtle watching, fishing

Papailoa Beach lies in front of the pretty residential neighborhood of Papailoa Road. It cannot be seen from the Kam Highway. On the southern end of the beach, the shoreline is too rocky for recreational swimming. The reef is broken and low, and currents can be

strong close to shore. When the surf is high, the currents are powerful. The shore drops off steeply, creating backwashes and rip currents in big surf or storm conditions. The northern end of Papailoa
Beach is a lovely strand for walking or wading. Huge *honu* sometimes
come out of the water to bask in the sun. There are several good sand
pockets between the reefs where it is safe to swim when the water is
calm. A spit of land that collects sand in the summer creates a surf
spot called the Point, where there are little left breaks in the winter.
Papailoa Beach is accessible through a public right of way at 61-785
Papailoa Road, a loop off the Kam Highway. There is limited parking on Papailoa Road. There are no improvements or lifeguards.

Laniakea Beach

Kam Highway between Papailoa Road and Pohaku Loa Way,
Kawailoa

*Swimming and snorkeling when calm, diving, surfing, turtle
watching, fishing*

Across the Kam Highway from the Kawailoa Ranch, the road
opens to a picturesque cove fronted by a low reef. This scenic shoreline attracted mostly surfers and artists until an influx of sea turtles made it a top tourist destination. The rocky shore is covered
with *limu* that sea turtles love. Giant *honu* congregate in the cove
and sometimes crawl up on the beach to bask in the sun. A small
freshwater spring that gave the area its name is located among the
rocks on the south end of Laniakea. On the north end, a sandy area
affords access to the water. The reef makes swimming difficult, and
turbulence and currents can be dangerous in winter and stormy conditions. When northwest swells arrive, surfers crowd the Himilayas
and Laniakea surf breaks offshore from the Kawailoa Ranch. When
the surf is up, there is a rip current through the channel on the west
side of Laniakea. The **Laniakea Beach Support Park** consists of
three acres of undeveloped land on the *mauka* side of Kam Highway.
Park there and be very careful crossing to the *maikai* side. A lifeguard
station has been installed, but there are no other improvements.

Laniakea Beach

Chun's Reef Beach

Kam Highway north of Pohaku Loa Way, Kawailoa
Swimming and snorkeling when calm, diving, surfing

Chun's Reef is one of the most popular surfing locations on the North Shore, attracting longboarders, short boarders, and body-boarders. Until recent years, this shoreline was regarded strictly as a surf spot. The shallow reef comes all the way up to the beach, with just a few sandy spaces suitable for wading or a quick dip. Nevertheless, Chun's Reef has become popular for swimming, snorkeling, and picnicking. There is limited roadside parking on the *mauka* side of the Kam Highway. If you park there, be very careful crossing to the *makai* side. The City and County of Honolulu has acquired a small piece of land on the *mauka* side designated as **Chun's Reef Support Park**, and several beachfront lots designated as **Kawailoa Beach Park**, but they are still undeveloped. There is a lifeguard station on the north side of the beach, but no other improvements.

Kapaeloa Beach

Kam Highway between Chun's Reef and Waimea Bay,
Kawailoa

Diving, surfing, fishing

Hidden from the highway, this last section of Kawailoa Beach stretches in front of the private homes between Chun's Reef and the Wananapaoa Islands at the entrance to Waimea Bay. The entire shoreline is rocky, with Alligator Rock forming a landmark in the middle. Although there are some sand pockets, Kapaeloa is generally unsuitable for recreational swimming. When the surf is up, there are powerful rip currents. Surfers flock to half a dozen surf breaks and shorecasters fish along the rocky shore. Access is through **Leftovers Beach Access Park**, east of the Pidley's surf break. There are no improvements or lifeguards. Roadside parking along the Kam Highway.

WAIMEA BAY BEACH PARK

61-031 Kam Highway, Waimea

The Crown Jewel of North Shore Beaches

Swimming and snorkeling when calm; bodyboarding and bodysurfing in the shorebreak; expert longboarding and short boarding; surf contests; hook and line fishing from the shore; turtle, spinner dolphin, and whale watching; picnicking; beach volleyball

Horseshoe-shaped Waimea Bay Beach Park is one of Hawaii's most beautiful beaches. It features incredibly deep white sand and a sandy sea floor with a gradual descent. During the summer the water is calm, clear and luminescent, except when the Waimea Stream breaks through the barrier reef and muddies the shoreline on the north end of the beach. Despite a sign prohibiting it, youngsters continually climb up the back of Jumping Rock and leap into the water below. Turtles and spinner dolphins frequent the bay year round. Humpback whales are sometimes seen offshore during the winter. The shorebreak is popular for bodyboarding and bodysurfing, but can be dangerous during winter swells. Waimea is famous for big winter surf. On the northeastern end of the bay, the inside break named Pinballs is surfable in small swells. In large swells, the outside break called Waimea Bay produces giant, bowl-shaped waves that sometimes close out the entire width of the bay. During the winter, a strong rip current runs seaward straight out through the middle of the bay. Waimea Bay is part of the Pupukea Marine Life Conservation District (MLCD). Fishing is restricted to hook and line from the shore. The beach park has restrooms, showers, picnic facilities, beach volleyball, and lifeguard service. A memorial to local hero Eddie Aikau, who was one of the first lifeguards at Waimea, is located at the beach end of the parking lot. An invitation-only surf contest is held in his honor when the waves are over 20 feet high. The paved parking lot is *makai* of the Kam Highway north of Waimea Stream and the entrance to the Waimea Valley. It fills up early. Additional parking can be found at Sts. Peter and Paul Mission Church to the north and along the Kam Highway on the bluff to the south. Observe the signs; fines are imposed for violations.

PUPUKEA BEACH PARK

59-727 Kam Highway, Pupukea, telephone 638-7213
Pupukea Beach Park contains over 80 acres of spectacular shoreline teeming with sea life, including Three Tables Beach, a shallow tide pool, and Shark's Cove. The park lies within the Pupukea Marine Life Conservation District; no fishing is allowed.

Three Tables Beach
South end of Pupukea Beach Park
Swimming, snorkeling, diving, exploring tidal pools, bodyboarding, picnicking, lighted basketball and volleyball courts, bicycling

Three Tables Beach

This small sandy beach is named for three table-shaped sections of reef visible at low tide. The pretty cove is bordered by a rock outcropping on one side and shallow tidal pools on the other. Fringing trees shade part of the beach. Swimming conditions are good from April through October. The sea floor is sandy and the reef protects the cove from the open water. Little tots can play in the sand and frolic in the shallow water. Older kids can snorkel and bodyboard. It is easy to keep an eye on them within the circumference defined by the rocks, tidal pool, and reef. Snorkeling is excellent around the tables, where the water is about 15 feet deep. The area outside the tables is ideal for scuba diving, with lava tubes and arches. Many visitors like to wade in the shallow lagoon on the north side of Three Tables. If you do so, be sure to wear water shoes and avoid stepping on the delicate coral. During winter swells, large waves wash over the tables and sometimes flood the walls of the lagoon. As the water level rises, a current drains into Shark's Cove. It is best to stay out of the water when waves are washing over the outer wall, as the current can sweep you off your feet and drag you across the coral. The park has restrooms, showers, volleyball and basketball courts, and picnic facilities. The Ke Ala Pupukea bicycle path begins at Pupukea and runs all the way to Velzyland. The parking lot is accessible from the Kam Highway south of the Sunset Fire Station. Additional parking can be found along the access road between Three Tables and Shark's Cove and at Sts. Peter and Paul Mission Church.

Shark's Cove
North end of Pupukea Beach Park
Swimming, snorkeling, diving, exploring tidal pools, picnicking, lighted basketball and volleyball courts, bicycling

This is the premier snorkeling and diving spot in northern Oahu. A short downhill hike is required to reach the rocky outcroppings surrounding the cove. The entry can be a little difficult at low tide. Wear your sandals or water shoes and find a sandy area to enter the water. Once you are in, the magic begins. Coral and sea life are abundant. Schools of colorful tropical fish drift by you. *Honu* swim along the rocks nibbling on *limu.* The water is approximately 20 feet deep inside the cove and 45 feet deep outside. Sea caves are located outside the northeastern corner. The shallow tide pool immediately south of the cove provides additional opportunities to observe sea life. To avoid the tourists and dive tours that come up from Honolulu, it is best to visit Shark's Cove early in the morning or late in the afternoon. There is nothing more beautiful than snorkeling in the quiet coves of Pupukea on a clear, sunny morning. But if you find yourself there at a crowded time, don't be intimidated. Once you are in the water, most of the crowds you see will be schools of fish. During the winter months, turbulence and currents often make the cove and tide pool unsafe. The park has restrooms, showers, lighted basketball and volleyball courts, and picnic facilities. There are no lifeguards, but the Sunset Fire Station responds to emergencies including water rescues. The parking lot is accessible from the Kam Highway north of the Fire Station. Additional parking can be found along the access road between Shark's Cove and Three Tables Beach and at Sts. Peter and Paul Mission Church. Snorkel gear can be rented at Planet Surf or Shark's Cove Surf Shop on the *mauka* side of the Kam Highway.

SUNSET

The shoreline from Pupukea to Sunset Beach is the longest stretch of wide beach on Oahu. A number of legendary surf spots occupy this spectacular strand.

Ke Iki Beach
Shoreline fronting Ke Iki Road, Sunset
Fishing
On the other side of Kulalua Point from Shark's Cove, a rough shorebreak and huge winter surf piles lovely soft sand on Ke Iki Beach. Even in the summer months, the steep dropoff, sharp rocks, and strong rip currents make swimming hazardous. The beach lies off Ke Iki Road. **Kahawai Beach Support Park** is on the *mauka* side of the Kam Highway.

Ke Waena Beach
Shoreline fronting Ke Waena Road, Sunset
Swimming when calm; surfing, bodyboarding, and bodysurfing
This surfing mecca is best left to expert board surfers and body-surfers. Turbulence and strong currents make it unsuitable for recreational swimming. Even in the summer, this is not a good beach for children or inexperienced swimmers. The winter surf carves steep drop-offs in the beach and ocean bottom, and the strong currents and rough water are dangerous. Still, it's a beautiful place to walk and watch the surfing. It got the name Kodak Beach because of all the film wrappers left there. The Outer Log Cabins surf break is on the deepwater reef off the south end of the beach. The Log Cabins break is closer to shore. The large lava rocks on the south end of the beach are called Rock Pile or Banzai Rocks. The shoreline north of those rocks is sometimes called Banzai Beach. The Rock Pile surf break lies

about 250 yards offshore from Banzai Rocks. Off the Wall or Kodak Reef is directly in front of the Ke Waena lifeguard tower. Access is through a public right of way near the Ke Waena lifeguard tower at 59-475 Ke Waena Road (a loop that runs along the beach parallel to Kam Highway); **Banzai Rock Support Park**, an undeveloped 2.3-acre parcel between Ke Waena Road and Ke Nui Road: or along the shore from Ehukai Beach Park. There is a lifeguard station but no other improvements. Restrooms, showers, and picnic tables can be found at nearby Ehukai Beach Park.

Banzai Beach
Shoreline between Ke Waena and Ke Nui Roads, Sunset
Surfing and bodysurfing

The shoreline between Ke Waena Road and Ke Nui Road, on the north side of Banzai Rocks, has become known as Banzai Beach. It is popular with long boarders, short boarders, and bodysurfers. During the winter, the surf and currents can be extremely dangerous. Even in the summer, the water is turbulent and there are sometimes strong currents. The Backdoor surf break is a right break from the Banzai Pipeline. Access is through **Banzai Rock Support Park**, an undeveloped 2.3-acre parcel between Ke Waena Road and Ke Nui Road, or along the shore from Ehukai Beach Park. There are no improvements, but lifeguard towers at Ke Waena Beach on the south and Ehukai Beach Park on the north straddle the beach. There are restrooms, showers, and picnic tables at Ehukai Beach Park.

The Banzai Pipeline
Shoreline fronting Ke Nui Road south of
Ehukai Beach Park, Sunset
*Surfing and bodysurfing, third leg of the Triple Crown
of Surfing and other surf contests*

The Banzai Pipeline lies between Banzai Rocks and Ehukai Beach Park, in front of Ke Nui Road. It cannot be seen from the Kam Highway. A shallow coral shelf that extends about 50 yards into the ocean produces the iconic curl of the wave. During winter swells, the waves rolling through the deep water offshore jump to tremendous heights when they hit this coral shelf. The incoming surf is so strong that the crest of each wave is thrown forward as it breaks, forming a tube. Pipeline is the site of the Billabong Pipeline, third leg of the Triple Crown of Surfing, the Pipeline Masters, and the Monster Energy Pipeline Pro. Due to the sharp coral, rough water, and strong currents, there have been many injuries and even a few fatalities. Pipeline is unsafe for swimming and novice surfers. There are no improvements, but lifeguard towers at Ke Waena Beach on the south and Ehukai Beach Park on the north straddle the Pipeline. Restrooms, showers, and picnic tables are located at Ehukai. Access is through **Banzai Rock Support Park**, an undeveloped 2.3-acre parcel between Ke Waena Road and Ke Nui Road, or along the shore from Ehukai Beach Park. Additional parking can be found at Sunset Beach Neighborhood Park and Elementary School on the *mauka* side of the Kam Highway. Watch for children and observe signs.

Ehukai Beach Park
59-337 Ke Nui Road, Sunset, *maikai* of Sunset Beach
Neighborhood Park
and Elementary School
Swimming when calm, surfing, bodyboarding and bodysurfing
Ehukai is a one-acre beach park adjacent to the Banzai Pipeline. Near the lifeguard tower, the beach and sea floor are sandy. However, the winter surf often causes severe erosion, leaving steep dropoffs and exposing large boulders. The dropoffs and turbulence make the water unsuitable for children and casual bathers, even in the summer. Conditions are hazardous during the fall and winter months, with strong rip currents and backwash. On the north end of the beach, rocks and coral on the shore and bottom can be slippery. The park has restrooms, showers, picnic tables, a lawn, and lifeguard service. The

lifeguard tower is visible from the Kam Highway. There is a small parking area at 59-337 Ke Nui Road, *makai* of the Kam Highway. Additional parking can be found at Sunset Beach Neighborhood Park and Elementary School on the *mauka* side of Kam Highway. Watch for children and observe signs.

Kammieland
Shoreline south of Sunset Beach Park
Surfing

This popular surf spot can be seen from the south end of Sunset Beach Park. It is accessible through a right of way *makai* of the Kam Highway at the site of the old Kammie's Market or along the shore from Sunset Beach Park. There are no improvements. Park roadside on the Kam Highway, at Sunset Beach Park, or at Sunset Beach Support Park.

Sunset Beach Park
59-100 Kam Highway, Paumalu
Swimming and snorkeling when calm; surfing, bodyboarding and bodysurfing; second leg of the Triple Crown of Surfing and other surf contests; bicycling

Sunset Beach is a beautiful, crescent-shaped beach with fine, deep sand. During the summer, it is a great place for swimming, snorkeling, bodyboarding, and bodysurfing close to shore. Be aware that the bottom drops off quickly and there is a strong current toward Waimea and out to sea. Keep your eye on children, pets, plastic floats, and other items that might sail away to Kauai. The best spot for bodyboarding and bodysurfing is at Val's Reef on the north end of the beach. The lineup is *makai* of the curved coconut tree and the telephone pole on the other side of Kam Highway. Further out the coral reef makes the surf unsuitable for amateurs. During the winter, Sunset Beach has some of the longest and heaviest waves in the world. It is the site of the Roxy Pro Sunset, second leg of the

Triple Crown of Surfing, the O'Neill World Cup, and other major surf competitions. When the big surf is running, Sunset Beach can be extremely treacherous for swimmers and amateur surfers. On the Waimea side of the surf break, a channel runs out to sea where the Paumalu Stream once flowed into the Pacific. The shorebreak and rip currents in this channel are extremely powerful in a big swell. The "Sunset rip" has necessitated many rescues and caused some fatalities. The 18-acre beach park has parking and lifeguard service. Additional parking, restrooms, and showers are located in **Sunset Beach Support Park** on the *mauka* side of the Kam Highway.

Sunset Point Beach Park
Shoreline north of Sunset Beach Park
Swimming when calm, watching surfing action at Sunset,
surfing, windsurfing

Sunset Beach ends at a wide sandy point that is partially protected by a wide fringing reef. The Point is suitable for recreational swimming from April through October, but there are strong currents during the winter. The Backyards surf break on the north side of the Point is popular with surfers and sailboarders. The Point is a great place to watch the surfing action and contests at Sunset, but access is difficult because the entire shoreline is developed and parking is very restricted. There are rights of way among the private homes on Kahauola Street and Makanale Street, where the unimproved, one-acre Sunset Point Beach Park is located. Take the Kam Highway and (1) turn *makai* on Kahauola Street, or (2) turn *makai* on Oopuola Street, turn right on Makanale Street, and continue to the beach park on Makanale Street. Observe the parking restriction signs. If you can't find a parking space near a right of way, you can park in the Sunset Beach Support Park lot and walk along the beach to the Point. No improvements or lifeguards.

SUNSET POINT TO TURTLE BAY

As the shoreline heads north toward Kahuku, sandy coves and secluded beaches alternate with rocky outcroppings and popular surf spots.

Kaunala Beach or Velzyland
Shoreline fronting Sunset Bay Colony in 58-100 area of Kam Highway
Swimming when calm, diving, surfing, fishing

Kaunala Beach lies in front of the Sunset Bay Colony development of luxury homes at approximately 58-100 Kam Highway. The beach is long, curving and sandy, but is lined with sections of coral reef and rocks. There is a small pocket at the mouth of Kaunala Stream where it is feasible to swim in the summer. The rest of the bottom is too rocky. The currents are strong when the surf is big. There are three popular surf breaks here: Freddyland, Velzyland, and Phantoms. Velzyland is the main attraction, and nowadays most locals use that name rather than the historic place name for this beach. Access from Kam Highway is through a public right of way to the right of the car gate into the Sunset Bay Colony. There is limited roadside parking along the Kam Highway. No improvements or lifeguards.

Waialee Beach Park
Shoreline along Kam Highway north of University of Hawaii Livestock Research Farm
Surfing, fishing

North of the University of Hawaii's Livestock Research Farm, the Kam Highway opens to rocky Waialee Beach with little Kukaimanini Islet lying offshore. Coral reef and rocks extend along the entire shoreline and ocean bottom, with only a few sand pockets where swimming is feasible. Currents can be strong when the winter surf comes in. Kukaimanini Islet is completely rocky and covered with sparse vegetation and a few small trees. Locals sometimes wade out to fish there. Bong's surf break is on the offshore reef. There are no improvements or lifeguards.

Pahipahialua Beach
Shoreline between Waialee and Kawela Bay
Fishing

The rocky shoreline between Waialee Beach Park and the western point of Kawela Bay is called Pahipahialua. Locals sometimes call it West Kawela. The shoreline is dotted with private homes and there is no convenient public access. The shoreline and ocean floor are as rocky as Waialee, making it unsuitable for swimming. There are no improvements or lifeguards. Access is along the shore from Waialee Beach Park.

Kawela Bay Beach Park
Shoreline between Waialee and Turtle Bay
Swimming, snorkeling, kayaking, fishing, horseback riding from Turtle Bay Resort

Kawela Bay is an idyllic, horseshoe-shaped bay protected by an outer reef. This lovely lagoon is rarely visited by tourists. A gated residential development borders the west side of the bay. The homes that once lined the east side were removed to make way for a hotel that was never built. A sandy beach lined with graceful coconut palms and ironwood trees runs almost the entire length of the shoreline. The water is tranquil. The bottom is sandy with coral heads and mud sediment in some spots. The best place for swimming and snorkeling is the middle and west side, where there are fewer coral heads. Occasionally, strong trade winds or heavy surf beyond the reef create an inshore current, but it is not dangerous. In *kona* winds and a west swell, rights and lefts break on the point off Kawela Bay. When the big surf hits the reef, it produces small waves inshore. The only problems are that the water is fairly shallow and the stream flowing into the bay sometimes muddies the water. To reach Kawela Bay, follow the trail from the Turtle Bay Resort along Turtle Bay and around the point to Kawela. The 25-minute walk is well worth the effort. A charming alternative is to kayak to Kawela from the Resort or Waialee. There are no improvements or lifeguards.

Turtle Bay
Shoreline between Kawela Bay and Kuilima Point, on the south side of the Turtle Bay Resort hotel
Fishing, surfing, surf contests, horseback riding

Turtle Bay is a crescent-shaped bay with a rocky shoreline between the northern point of Kawela Bay and the Turtle Bay hotel on Kuilima Point. This is not a swimming beach—the shoreline is full of aa (lava rock), the sea bottom is covered with rocks and raised coral reef, and there are dangerous currents. During the winter months, large waves cross the bay in irregular patterns. In recent years, Turtle Bay has become somewhat popular for surfing, with the Resort sponsoring several championships. The Resort's pretty cabanas line the shore. The Hang Ten Surf Bar provides a very civilized place to watch the surfing and sunset at day's end. There are no lifeguards.

Kuilima Cove
Shoreline between Kuilima Point and Kalaeokamanu Point, on the north side of the Turtle Bay Resort hotel
Swimming, snorkeling, kayaking, beach volleyball

On the Kahuku side of the Turtle Bay hotel, Kuilima Cove offers safe swimming and good snorkeling year-round. Protected by a reef, this tranquil bay is ideal for small children. It was a favorite swimming place of the old Hawaiian community in Kahuku, who called it Kalokoiki ("the little pool"). The bottom is a bit rocky close to the shore, but sandy at the water's edge. Swimmers have to avoid coral outcroppings, but it is possible to find an unobstructed route to the reef and back on the breakwater side of the cove. The best snorkeling is also on the breakwater side. There is a current running out to sea along the rocky point. Food and beverages are available at Ola's beachfront restaurant, and the Resort rents beach chairs, kayaks, paddle boats, and other beach equipment. There are restrooms and showers, but no lifeguards. Park in the beach access section of the Resort's parking lot.

TURTLE BAY TO MALAEKAHANA

*Unseen from the highway, this pristine coastline
harbors ancient fishing grounds,
bird refuges, uninhabited islands, and a tree-fringed beach park.*

Kaihalulu Beach
Shoreline between Kalaeokamanu Point and Kahuku Point
Swimming in one protected cove, wading, fishing

Kaihalulu is a curving, mile-long beach between Kuilima Cove and Kahuku Point, the northernmost point on Oahu. The beach is sandy, but the entire shoreline is lined with coral reefs and rocks. The sea bottom is rocky and the offshore reef is broken, affording little protection from the strong currents. A small, protected cove in the middle of the beach known as Keiki Cove is the only safe place to swim. During the summer of 2006, a mother monk seal used this protected cove as a nursery for her newborn pup. Accessible only on foot from the Turtle Bay Resort, Kaihalulu is frequented mainly by beachcombers and fishermen. There are no improvements or lifeguards.

Hanakailio Beach
Shoreline between Kahuku Point and Kalaeuila Point
Diving, fishing

A long stretch of isolated beach extends from Kahuku Point to Kalaeuila Point. On the eastern side of Kahuku Point, there is a small cove similar to Kuilima Cove, but not as protected. The reef is broken and irregular, allowing currents and turbulence. East of the cove, adjacent to the ruins of the Kahuku Airstrip from World War II, a sandy beach with a few outcroppings of rock and coral extends for about half a mile. Here the deep sand will give your legs a good workout, but the rocky bottom and strong currents make it unsafe to swim. At the Laie end of the beach, there is an old drainage pipe at the water's edge that was installed by the American Marconi Company. On the other side of the pipe, the shoreline is completely rocky. Just inside Kalaeuila Point, there is a small cove that is protected enough to let divers enter the water. Hanakailio is accessible on foot from the Turtle Bay Resort or Kahuku Golf Course. You can drive up Kahuku Airport Road *makai* of the Kam Highway and walk to the beach from the old airfield, but it is an isolated area with no maintained path. There are no improvements or lifeguards.

Keawaawaloa
Shoreline between Kalaeuila Point and Kahuku Golf Course Beach
Fishing

Between Kalaeuila Point and the Kahuku Golf Course Beach, the shoreline becomes straighter, with reaches of sand interrupted by coral and rock outcroppings. The offshore reef is broken and irregular, but swimming is feasible at a few carefully chosen spots on calm days. This section of the shore contains the traditional fishing grounds of Puanui, Keawaawaloa, Kii, and Kaluahole, which are still frequented by local fishermen. For many years it was the site of a nudist colony. The shoreline is accessible on foot from the Turtle Bay Resort or Kahuku Golf Course. There are no improvements or lifeguards.

Kahuku Golf Course Beach
Shoreline between the Japanese graveyard and Makahoa Point, Kahuku

Diving, surfing, fishing

The Kahuku Golf Course Beach begins *makai* of the Japanese cemetery and runs east to Makahoa Point. The shoreline of sand and bedrock is bordered by picturesque sand dunes. The Seventh Hole surf break lies directly offshore from the seventh hole of the golf course. In the middle of the beach, a large channel cuts through the offshore reef and comes all the way into the shore. The backwash often creates a strong rip current out to sea, making it unsafe for swimming. The shoreline is accessible on foot from the Turtle Bay Resort, Kahuku Golf Course, or Malaekahana State Recreation Area. There are no improvements or lifeguards.

Malaekahana State Recreation Area
Shoreline between Makahoa Point and Kalanai or Cooke's Point
Swimming, bodyboarding, kayaking, fishing, picnicking,
wading and swimming to Goat Island, camping

Malaekahana State Recreation Area extends along a beautiful bay between Makahoa Point and Kalanai Point. The sandy beach is over a mile long and shaded by trees. There are two flat reefs along the shoreline. The bottom is sandy, with a gradual descent, and safe for swimming near the shore. The park is divided into two sections. The Kahuku side is a gated, 37-acre campground operated by a community-based, non-profit organization called Friends of Malaekahana. The camping facilities range from bare tentsites to furnished yurts and beach houses and even a little grass shack. The Kalanai Point side is a public beach park. Two picturesque islands lie offshore: Kihewamoku is off the western portion of the beach. The larger Mokuauia, or Goat Island, is closer to shore off the eastern end of the beach. Both islands are bird sanctuaries. From the east end of the beach near Kalanai Point, you can wade or swim to Goat Island. Shorecasters fish from Makahoa Point and Kalanai Point. Restrooms, showers and picnic facilities are located on both sides of the park. There are no lifeguards. Malaekahana State Recreation Area is well marked and easily accessible from the Kam Highway. The Kahuku side is 1.3 miles north of Laie Town. The Kalanai Point side is .6 miles north of Laie Town.

Mokuaula Beach
North shore of Mokuauia Island (Goat Island), Laie Bay, Laie
Swimming, snorkeling, diving, bird watching, fishing

The sandy bay on the leeward side of Mokuauia has a wide, curving beach protected by a reef. The bottom is sandy and slopes gently toward the north. The beach is accessible by wading at low tide or swimming or paddling a board from the Kalanai Point side of Malaekahana State Recreation Area. Wear water shoes to protect your feet from coral and rocks and explore the island comfortably. A trail winds around the shoreline, providing intimate views of the nesting birds. The beach is only accessible from the water, with no improvements or lifeguards. Overnight camping is prohibited.

THE WINDWARD SHORE

This scenic coastline is marked by the dramatic Koolau Mountains, where sparkling streams and waterfalls descend through verdant hillsides to the sea. Due to onshore winds, swimmers should be on the lookout for jellyfish and Portuguese man of war.

Hukilau Beach

Kam Highway between Kalanai Point and Laniloa Point, Laie
Swimming, bodyboarding, bodysurfing, fishing, picnicking, camping

Hukilau Beach

Curving about 1.5 miles from Kalanai Point to Laniloa Point, Hukilau Beach has fine sand and a bottom as flat as a floor. A small reef lies off the northern portion of the beach, *makai* of a shady campground. The center portion, *makai* of the *hukilau* monument, is unprotected by a fringing reef. The resulting shorebreak is popular for bodyboarding and bodysurfing. A channel comes into the shoreline and sometimes creates strong currents along the shore in this section. The southern portion of the beach, where homes line the shore, is great for families with young children. A wide, shallow reef along this section keeps the water calm and safe for swimming. This part of the beach is sometimes referred to as Laie Beach, which once was the name for the entire shoreline. Hukilau Beach is well marked and the parking lot is accessible from the Kam Highway. Restrooms are open to the public. Camping is allowed with a permit from Hawaii Reserves, Inc. There are no lifeguards.

Laniloa Beach

Shoreline between Laniloa Point and Kehukuuna Point, Laie
Swimming in sandy pockets, snorkeling, diving, fishing

Laniloa Beach is a long, sandy beach in front of the homes between Laie Point and Kehukuuna Point. On the Laie Point side. a channel runs through an inshore reef, making two sandy pockets where its tributaries hit the shore. Except for the two pockets, the entire shoreline is covered with coral. The bottom is rocky, but an outer reef makes the water suitable for swimming if you manage to get in. The beach cannot be seen from the road, but there is a public right of access at 55-470 Kam Highway. There are no improvements or lifeguards.

Laie Beach Park, aka Pounders Beach

Kam Highway between Kehukuuna Point and Pali Kilo Ia
Point, Laie
Swimming, bodyboarding, bodysurfing, fishing

Laie Beach, better known as Pounders, is a long, wide beach stretching from Kehukuuna Point to Pali Kilo Ia Point. The Kehukuuna (north) end of the beach is usually calm and safe for swimming. The remains of the pier where coastal steamers once stopped can be seen there. Fishermen frequent this part of the shoreline to fish for *moi* and other good eating fish. At the south end of the beach, near the limestone cliff, a shallow sandbar creates a bruising shorebreak that is popular for bodyboarding and bodysurfing. When BYUH was founded in 1955, the students soon discovered this spot and gave it the name "Pounders" for the rough waves and strong rip currents created by the sandbar. The bottom is sandy, but shallow. The beach park has parking, picnic tables and showers, but no lifeguards, restrooms, or other improvements.

Kokololio Beach Park
55-017 Kam Highway, Laie
Swimming and snorkeling when calm, fishing, camping

Kokololio Beach Park lies on the opposite side of the limestone cliff from Pounders. This 15.5-acre park is a lovely place to spend a lazy afternoon or weekend. Fringing trees shade the sandy beach. The sea floor is sandy. There are lovely views of the Windward Shore. The north end of the beach is exposed to the open sea and the bottom drops off sharply. When the ocean is rough, there can be dangerous currents there. The south end is protected by a reef, and good for swimming in the shallow water *makai* of the sand dunes. The beach park has parking, restrooms, showers, a large lawn, and picnic facilities, but no lifeguards. Camping is permitted by county permit.

Kaipapau Beach
Kam Highway across from Hauula Kai Shopping Center
Snorkeling, diving, fishing

The shoreline along the Kam Highway across from the Hauula Kai Shopping Center has very little sand and a shallow, rocky bottom.

This section of shoreline is used mostly by local fishermen. There are no improvements, lifeguards, or convenient public access.

Hauula Beach Park
54-135 Kam Highway, Hauula
Swimming, snorkeling, diving, surfing, fishing, picnicking, volleyball, camping

Hauula Beach Park has a long, narrow beach inside a shallow reef that is a popular fishing site. The bottom is shallow and rocky. On the north end of the beach, a channel crosses the reef and comes into shore. At high tide, local kids enjoy the Kilia surf break. On the south end of the beach, Maakua Stream runs down toward the ocean. A barrier sand bar blocks the stream from the sea and forms a *muliwai*. The nine-acre beach park contains restrooms, showers, a wide lawn, beach pavilion, picnic facilities, and a volleyball court, but no lifeguards. Camping is allowed by county permit. The parking area is accessible from the Kam Highway. There is a playground across the Kam Highway in Hauula Community Park, 54-050 Kam Highway.

Aukai Beach Park
54-071 Kam Highway, Hauula
Swimming and wading when calm

The raised coral reef along the shoreline of this tiny park (.2 acres) makes swimming impossible. However, a small bay with a sandy beach and bottom is accessible from the park. When the ocean is calm, it is safe to swim in the bay. When the ocean is rough, strong currents along the shore can form fast rip currents. Aukai Beach Park is accessible from the road at 54-071 Kam Highway. There are no improvements or lifeguards.

Makao Beach
Kam Highway across from Makao Road, Hauula
Diving, fishing

Across from Makao Road, the Kam Highway runs along a narrow sand beach protected by an offshore reef. The bottom is shallow and rocky, and the beach is practically covered at high tide. The shoreline is accessible from Kam Highway, with roadside parking. There are no improvements or lifeguards.

Kaluanui Beach
53-500 Kam Highway, Kaluanui
(between Hauula and Punaluu)
Swimming, snorkeling, diving, fishing

Kaluanui Beach extends from Kaliuwaa Stream to Waiono Stream. It is sandy, shallow, and safe for swimming and snorkeling near the shore when the streams are not running. The most popular section for snorkeling and fishing is the middle, where a channel cuts through the reef into a large sandy bay. Further out, there are sometimes strong rip currents in the channels through the offshore reefs, especially in winter surf or stormy conditions. There is not much of a beach, especially at high tide. Where the Kam Highway opens up on the shoreline there is a breakwall with steps leading down to the shallow water. The only other improvement is a water fountain. There are no lifeguards. Kaluanui Beach is accessible from the Kam Highway, with roadside parking. There is also a public right of way along Kaliuwaa Stream.

Punaluu Beach Park
53-309 Kam Highway, Punaluu
Swimming, snorkeling, fishing, picnicking

Punaluu Beach Park is a narrow three-acre park. Waiono Stream (also called Punaluu Stream) flows into the ocean at the western end of the park. The beach is narrow, straight, and safe for swimming and snorkeling when the stream is not running. The water inshore is shallow and protected by a reef. Offshore, there are some dangerous currents where a channel crosses the reef *makai* of Waiono Stream. The beach park has restrooms, showers, and a pleasant picnic area beneath pretty coconut palms, but no lifeguards. The parking lot is accessible from the Kam Highway.

Kahana Bay Beach Park
52-222 Kam Highway, Kahana
Swimming, snorkeling, bodyboarding, bodysurfing, surfing, fishing, kayaking, boat ramp, picnicking, camping

Kahana Bay is one of the safest and most popular beaches on Oahu. The bay is broad and calm. The shoreline is a long barrier beach. The bottom is sandy with a very gentle slope. When a swell is running across the offshore reefs at the mouth of the bay, waves suitable for beginning board surfers sometimes form outside the shorebreak. The small shorebreak can provide ideal conditions for young or novice bodysurfers. The wide, sand-bottom channel that runs out to the middle of the bay provides good entry and exit for the Kapaeleele Boat Ramp. The water is sometimes cloudy where Kahana Stream enters the bay. This eight-acre state park is popular for swimming, snorkeling, bodyboarding, bodysurfing, fishing, kayaking, and camping. There are restrooms, showers, a lovely picnic area in a shady coconut grove, and a boat launch, but no lifeguards. The parking lot is easily accessible at about 52-222 Kam Highway.

Makaua Beach Park
51-541 Kam Highway, Makaua (between Kahana and Kaaawa)
Diving, bodyboarding, surfing, fishing, boating

Makaua Beach Park occupies the shoreline between Kahana Bay and Kaaawa, across the Kam Highway from the Crouching Lion Inn. The park is small and undeveloped. The beach is narrow and sometimes disappears completely when the tide comes in. The ocean bottom is shallow and lined with coral, and there are strong rip currents offshore. A large sand-bottom channel cuts through the reef, providing a good fishing ground for divers and pole fishermen. Surfers and bodyboarders sometimes paddle out to the tubes on the outer reef at Crouching Lion on the north and Razor Reef on the south. This channel also accommodates small fishing boats that anchor off the point. The tiny .14-acre beach park does not have any improvements or lifeguards. It is accessible from the road at 51-541 Kam Highway, with roadside parking.

Swanzy Beach Park
51-392 Kam Highway, Kaaawa
Swimming, snorkeling, fishing for octopus and squid, picnicking, basketball, weekend camping

A masonry seawall with a shorefront full of rocks and small boulders marks this little park. There is not much of a beach. Most of the sand was washed away before the seawall was built, and it is usually under water at high tide. The water is safe for swimming and snorkeling, but not very appealing since both the beach and sea floor are rocky. Swanzy is more popular with locals hunting octopus and squid on the offshore reef than it is with swimmers. If you decide to swim or snorkel at Swanzy, stay inside the reef on the northern end of the beach park. Offshore in the fringing reef, beyond the houses on the south end of the beach, there is a break in the reef where a channel creates a dangerous rip current running out to sea. The five-acre park has restrooms, showers, a playground, picnic pavilion, basketball court, and nine campsites for weekend use by county permit. There are no lifeguards. The parking lot is accessible from the Kam Highway.

Kaaawa Beach Park
51-369 Kam Highway, Kaaawa
Swimming, snorkeling, diving, picnicking

Kaaawa Beach Park is a two-acre strip of shoreline at 51-369 Kam Highway. Although the beach has been eroded, it is still a pleasant and safe place to swim and snorkel. The water inshore is shallow and protected by a reef. On the edge of the reef , there is a strong rip current in the channel. The park has restrooms, showers, and picnic facilities, but no lifeguards. The parking lot is accessible from the Kam Highway.

Kalaeoio Beach Park

51-237 Kam Highway, Kaaawa

*Swimming when calm and the stream is not running, surfing,
fishing, picnicking*

Kalaeoio Beach Park is a one-acre strip of shoreline beneath the
soaring Haloa mountain ridge. The inshore waters are shallow, sandy,
and safe for swimming when the ocean is calm and the stream is
not running. When the ocean is rough or the tides are changing, a
strong rip current runs out through the channel. The beach park was
named for Kalaeoio Point, which separates Kaaawa from Kualoa on
its southern end. The point is a popular with shorecasters fishing for
moi, oio, and *papio,* and surfers who enjoy the small waves there. This
tiny, one-acre beach park has shaded picnic tables, but no lifeguards
or other improvements. It is accessible from the Kam Highway, with
roadside parking.

Kanenelu Beach

50-000 area of Kam Highway, at the southern boundary
of Kaaawa

Swimming, diving, surfing, fishing

Kanenelu Beach lies *makai* of the Kam Highway at the boundary between Kaaawa and Kualoa. It is a narrow, sandy beach with a
shallow bottom that is rocky in some spots and sandy in others. The
water inshore is safe for recreational swimming. Occasionally there
are strong currents offshore. Kanenulu's small offshore waves are popular with young and novice surfers. Kanenelu is also popular with
shorecasters fishing for *moi, oio,* and *papio.* There is a great view of the
Windward Shore, but no improvements or lifeguards. The beach is
accessible from the Kam Highway.

V. ACTIVITIES ON THE WATER

BOATING

Boat charters are available at Haleiwa Boat Harbor. **North Shore Catamaran Charters** offers whale watching, sunset, snorkeling, picnic, and charter cruises along the North Shore on a large catamaran, the Hoo Nanea. Contact North Shore Catamaran Charters, LLC, PO Box 400, Haleiwa, HI 96712, telephone 351-9371, fax 637-9757, E-mail: info@sailingcat.com, www.sailingcat.com. **Chupu Charters,** Haleiwa Boat Harbor, slip 312, Haleiwa, telephone 637-3474, www.chupu.com, and **Kuuloa Kai Sport Fishing,** telephone 637-5783, are primarily fishing charters, but also offer whale watching, sunset cruises, and custom trips. **North Shore Diving and Deep Ecology,** 66-460 Kam Highway (in the same building as Café Haleiwa), telephone 73-SCUBA, offers whale watching and eco-tours. Haleiwa Harbor is the only harbor in northern Oahu. There are boat launching ramps at Alli Beach Park in Haleiwa and Kahana Bay Beach Park and a small boat anchorage off Makaua Beach Park. The boat ramp at **Wahiawa Freshwater State Recreation Area,** 380 Walker Avenue, Wahiawa, is limited to fishing.

BODYBOARDING AND BODYSURFING

A bodyboard is a small rectangular piece of foam with an aerodynamic shape. It is usually ridden lying down, but it can also be ridden standing up or with one knee touching the board. Most bodyboarders wear swim fins to control their speed and trajectory and help them paddle out and catch the wave. **Surf 'n' Sea,** 62-595 Kam Highway, Haleiwa, HI 96712, telephone 637-SURF (7873), www.surfnsea.com, offers body boarding lessons and rentals. Bodysurfing is the art of riding the waves without a board, using the shape of the body to control speed and trajectory. Popular spots for bodyboarding and bodysurfing include Alii Beach Park, the Waimea Shorebreak, Three Tables, Ke Waena, Ehukai, Val's Reef at Sunset Beach Park, Pounders Beach, and Kahana Bay Beach Park.

CANOEING

The traditional Hawaiian canoe has an outrigger on one side and a number of paddlers who stroke in unison under the direction of a leader in the bow. Many canoe clubs participate in regattas and races in canoes with and without sails. The Manu O Ke Kai Canoe Club of Haleiwa practices on the beach behind Surf 'n' Sea, usually on Saturday mornings and late afternoons. Members range in age from 10 to 70.

FISHING

Shorecasting is available all along the northern Oahu coastline except the Pupukea Marine Life Conservation District (MLCD). MLCD rules prohibit any fishing whatsoever in the waters off Pupukea and anything except hook and line fishing from the shore at Waimea. Fishing for octopus and squid is best on the Windward Shore, especially at Punaluu, Kahana Bay, Swanzy, and Kaaawa Beach Parks. Bass fishing from shore or boat is available at **Wahiawa Freshwater State Recreation Area**, 380 Walker Avenue, Wahiawa. Deep-water fishing charters out of the Haleiwa Boat Harbor are offered by at least three outfitters: Captain Jesse Lovett and Sara Voll Lovett, **Chupu Charters**, Slip 220, Haleiwa Boat Harbor, Haleiwa 96712, telephone 637-3474, fax 636-2405, E-mail chupu@ hawaii.rr.com, www.chupu.com; **Kuuloa Kai Big Game Sport Fishing Charters**, 66-195 Kaamooloa Road, Waialua 96791, telephone 637-5783, E-mail fishing@kuuloakai.com; and **Go Fishing Hawaii**, P.O. Box 1176, Haleiwa 96712, telephone 637-9737,

E-mail gofishinghawaii@mail.com. Offshore fishing from Haleiwa is ideal because the waters are not crowded with boats. Opportunities include trolling for big gamefish, jigging for tuna, and bottom fishing for reef dwellers. Full and half-day charters and custom trips are available.

JET SKIING

Jet skis can be rented from **Surf 'n' Sea,** 62-595 Kam Highway, Haleiwa, HI 96712, telephone 637-SURF (7873), www.surfnsea. com, and **The Watercraft Connection,** Haleiwa Boat Harbor, Haleiwa, telephone 637-8006, www.jetskihawaii.net. Haleiwa Beach Park is a popular launch site.

KAYAKING

Sea kayaks can be rented from **Surf 'n' Sea,** 62-595 Kam Highway, Haleiwa, HI 96712, telephone 637-SURF (7873), www. surfnsea.com, and the **Turtle Bay Resort,** 57-091 Kam Highway, Kahuku, telephone 293-8811, www.turtlebayresort.com.

KITESURFING

Kite High, North Shore Marketplace, Haleiwa, telephone 637-0025, specializes in kite surfing and offers kite surfing lessons. Mokuleia Beach Park is the best location in northern Oahu for this exciting sport.

SAILING

Sailing excursions on a large catamaran are offered by **North Shore Catamaran Charters,** Haleiwa Boat Harbor, Haleiwa, HI, telephone 638-8279, 351-9371, www.sailingcat.com.

SCUBA DIVING

Surf 'n' Sea, 62-595 Kam Highway, Haleiwa 96712, telephone 637-SURF (7873), www.surfnsea.com, offers introductory dives for those with no experience and three-day PADI certifications from open water to dive master. Boat, shore, night, and advanced dive tours are available. Surf 'n' Sea carries a full line of diving accessories and air fills. **North Shore Diving Headquarters,** 66-456 Kam Highway, Haleiwa, telephone 637-7946, offers similar packages. **North Shore Diving and Deep Ecology,** 66-460 Kam Highway, telephone 73-SCUBA, offers six-passenger boat dives, shore dives, night dives, introductory dives, and PADI three-day certifications. The **Turtle Bay Resort** offers introductory diving lessons in its pool and ocean dives for hotel guests. The best spots for diving from shore are Shark's Cove and Three Tables outside the reef.

SNORKELING

Snorkelers employ a diving mask, snorkel tube, and usually swimfins to observe underwater plants and sea life while swimming on the surface. **Surf 'n' Sea,** 62-595 Kam Highway, Haleiwa 96712, telephone 637-SURF (7873), www.surfnsea.com, offers snorkeling lessons, tours, equipment and rentals. **North Shore Catamaran Charters** in Haleiwa Boat Harbor, telephone 638-8279, offers snorkel and picnic cruises along the North Shore on a large catamaran. **North Shore Diving and Deep Ecology,** 66-460 Kam Highway, telephone 73-SCUBA, also offers snorkeling tours. Two shops near Shark's Cove rent snorkel equipment: **Planet Surf,** on the corner of Kam Highway and Pupukea Road, telephone 638-5060, and **Shark's Cove Surf Shop,** 59-672 Kam Highway (across the street from Shark's Cove), telephone 638-7980. The **Turtle Bay Resort** also rents snorkel equipment. The best places for snorkeling from shore are Shark's Cove, Three Tables around the tables, and Kuilima Cove along the breakwater, but you can enjoy snorkeling just about anyplace you enter the water.

SURFING

Surfing at Waimea Bay

Surfing is a water sport in which the surfer catches a breaking wave and rides it on a surfboard. The early Hawaiians invented surfing and rode the waves of northern Oahu on wooden longboards of 12 feet or more. Most modern surfers use short boards, which let them ride a greater variety of waves and do tricks. Today's surfboards are made of hard foam, polyester resin, and fiberglass. Fins help surfers control the direction of their boards. Leashes help them recover their boards after a wipeout. Wax makes the boards easier to grip. These developments have greatly increased the size and type of waves that can be surfed. Tow-in surfing uses mechanized watercraft to tow surfers onto extremely large waves. Kitesurfers and windsurfers add the element of wind to the sport.

If you are on the North Shore during a major surf contest, don't miss it. Big time surfing is big entertainment, with major corporate sponsors, rock music, bikini contests, and other attractions. Competitors are judged by the size of the waves they catch, the length of the ride, and the difficulty of the maneuvers they complete. The Triple Crown of Surfing is held on the North Shore each year in November and December, with the first leg at Alii Beach, the second leg at Sunset Beach, and the third leg at the Banzai Pipeline. The Quicksilver In Memory Of Eddie Aikau International is held at Waimea in honor of Eddie Aikau when the waves are higher than 20 feet. Other world-class surfing competitions on the North Shore include the Pipeline Masters, Turtle Bay Resort Pro, and Monster Energy Pipeline Pro. The exact dates depend on the surfing conditions.

Tropical Rush maintains a surf report line giving current information for all of Oahu. The telephone number is 638-7874. Surf reports are also available on the internet.

Surf Equipment And Lessons

Surf 'n' Sea, 62-595 Kam Highway, Haleiwa 96712, telephone 637-SURF (7873), www.surfnsea.com, rents a wide variety of surfboards; sells new, used and custom boards; and provides 24-hour ding repair. It offers surfing lessons, surf tours, and surf safaris. It also provides lessons and rentals in body boarding and packs boards for shipping. **Surf Hawaii Surf School**, North Shore Marketplace, 66-250 Kam Highway, Suite D204, Haleiwa 96712, telephone 295-1241, www.surfhawaii4u.com, offers three-hour surf lessons by certified lifeguards. **Planet Surf**, on the corner of Kam Highway and Pupukea Road, Pupukea, telephone 638-5060, offers surf lessons and surfboard rentals. **Shark's Cove Surf Shop**, 59-672 Kam Highway, Pupukea (across the street from Shark's Cove), telephone 638-7980, offers surf lessons, surfboard rentals, and ding repair. **Sunset Suzy**, telephone 781-2692, www.sunsetsuzy.com, a female lifeguard, specializes in surf lessons for beginners and children. **Turtle Bay Resort** arranges surf lessons and rentals for hotel guests. Call the concierge at 293, 8811. **North Shore Eco-Surf Tours**, P.O. Box 1174, Haleiwa 96712, telephone 638-9503, www.ecosurf-hawaii.com, offers surfing and windsurfing lessons. For more information, call Stan Van Voorhis at 638-9503 or E-mail stanvanvoorhis@yahoo.com.

Surf Breaks

The most popular North Shore surf spots are well known: Haleiwa, Laniakea, Chun's Reef, Waimea Bay, Banzai Pipeline, Sunset Beach, Velzyland. With surfers from around the world crowding those spots, many other breaks are now being surfed. The following list includes most of the breaks now being surfed on northern Oahu. They are listed in clockwise order from northwest to southeast. Before going out, be sure your abilities match the break and the conditions that day. For current conditions, call the Surf Hotline at 638-7874 or check online.

Kaena Point

Arguably the world's largest and most dangerous waves occur off Kaena Point in winter swells. The waves sometimes reach 50 feet (15 meters) and the fast-moving current is extremely dangerous. No one has ever ridden the monster waves off Kaena Point successfully. Do not even think about descending to the shore, much less surfing there.

Mokuleia Army Beach

The break offshore from the Army Beach is known for quick left tubes in northwest swells. Park roadside on Farrington Highway.

Day Star (The Boat)

The shallow reef about 200 yards west of Mokuleia Beach Park produces short left shoulders and long right walls. The surfing is best when the waves are four to twelve feet. Access is from Mokuleia Beach Park, 68-919 Farrington Highway.

Park Rights (Mokuleia)

Directly offshore from Mokuleia Beach Park, there are fast, hollow rights in northern swells. The surfing is best when the waves are three to eight feet. Access is from Mokuleia Beach Park, 68-919 Farrington Highway.

Sylva Channel

Sylva Channel is a wrapping left reef *makai* of Makaleha Beach Park in Mokuleia. Access is through Makaleha Beach Park or the public right of access on Crozier Drive about .2 miles west of Olohilo Street.

Hammerheads

The Hammerheads break off Kaiaka Bay Beach Park often has challenging left tubes in the winter. However, most surfers go elsewhere because, as the name implies, it is a breeding area for hammerhead sharks. Access is from Kaiaka Bay Beach Park, 66-449 Haleiwa Road, Haleiwa.

Walls

A north swell produces a right wall straight out from the Haleiwa surf condos at 66303 Haleiwa Road. The surf is best up to seven or eight feet. If you can't find a parking space there, take Haleiwa Road to Walikanahele Road and turn *maikai* to the parking lot at the end of Walikanahele Road.

Avalanche

On the outside reef at Alii Beach Park, south of the Haleiwa break, Avalanche sometimes has huge waves in the winter. When Avalanche breaks big, it is suitable for tow-in surfing. Strong currents can be dangerous. Access is from Alii Beach Park, 66-167 Haleiwa Road, Haleiwa.

Haleiwa

The Haleiwa break off Kualoa Point (to the left of the breakwater) in Alii Beach Park provides fast hollow rights into the "Toilet Bowl" and some lefts for beginners. Surfing conditions are best in west and northwest swells. The inside lineup breaks on a shallow reef shelf that can be hazardous at low tide. Haleiwa is only suitable for beginners when the surf is small; in bigger waves there is a heavy current. Popular with longboarders, short boarders, and bodysurfers, Haleiwa is the site of the **Reef Hawaiian Pro, first leg of the Triple Crown of Surfing,** every November. Access is from Alii Beach Park, 66-167 Haleiwa Road, Haleiwa.

Puaena/Puaena Point

The break off the northeastern tip of Waialua Bay has fast hollow rights with some lefts for beginners. The surf is best at three to ten feet. The outside right break called Puaena Point is for experts only. It can carry a board all the way into Puaena, but only if you manage to clear the dangerous rocks in the way. For access, drive to the north end of Haleiwa Beach Park, turn left, follow the street until it dead ends near the water, park, and follow the dirt path to the point.

The Point

On the northern end of Papailoa Beach a spit of land that collects sand in the summer creates a surf spot called the Point, where there are little left breaks in the winter. For access, take Kam Highway to Papailoa Road, park roadside, and use the public right of way at 61-785 Papailoa Road.

Himalayas

Off the southwest end of Laniakea, Himalayas produces long lefts on the outside. It is dangerous when the surf is big. Access is from Laniakea Beach Support Park or roadside parking on Kam Highway.

Laniakea

In northwest swells, there are fast rights and lefts offshore from the Kawailoa Ranch. The fun ride attracts a big crowd of longboarders, short boarders, and body boarders. The outside break known as Laniakea can provide a long ride that connects to an inside right tube, but beware of bruising closeouts. During big winter swells, the wide channel on the Haleiwa side of the break develops a powerful rip current running straight out to sea. Access is from Laniakea Beach Support Park or roadside parking on Kam Highway.

Hulton's (also known as Off the Rocks)

In northwest swells, there are nice rights and lefts at Hulton's or Off the Rocks. The break lies offshore from Pohaku Loa Way, northeast of Laniakea. Access is from Pohaku Loa Way, Laniakea Beach Support Park, or roadside parking on Kam Highway.

Jocko's

In northwest swells Jocko's offers fast, steep lefts off the end of the reef for short boards, but there are dangerous rip currents and a long paddle. The break lies northeast of Hulton's, across the channel from Chun's Reef where the beachfront parking opens up again. Access is from Chun's Reef Support Park or roadside parking on Kam Highway.

Chun's Reef

With consistent surf that is suitable for longboards, short boards, and bodyboards, Chun's Reef is one of the most popular surf spots on the North Shore. Four different breaks produce right tubes and short lefts all winter. Access is from Chun's Reef Support Park, Kawailoa Beach Park, or roadside parking on Kam Highway.

Pidley's

A west swell produces nice little lefts over a lava and sand bottom northeast of Chun's Reef. Access is from Chun's Reef Support Park or Kawailoa Beach Park on the southwest, Leftovers Beach Access Park on the northeast, or roadside parking on Kam Highway.

Left Overs/Right Overs

Located in front of the beachfront homes north of Chun's Reef, Left Overs produces a fast left in north, northwest and west winter swells. Right Overs is just south of Left Overs. Access is through Leftovers Beach Access Park or roadside parking on Kam Highway.

Alligator Rock/Baby Sunset

There are nice rights near the landmark rock formation in front of the private homes. On the outside, the big right break called Baby Sunset has a right takeoff followed by a long wall. Access is through Leftovers Beach Access Park or the public right of way at the third break in the beachfront homes along Kam Highway north of Chun's Reef.

Marijuana's

Marijuana's has shallow right tubes off large rock outcroppings *makai* of the beachfront homes about 1.3 miles up the shore from Left Overs. Access is through the public right of way between the beachfront homes.

Uppers (Elephants)

A north swell produces a right wall, with some lefts. Access is through the public right of way between the beachfront homes.

Waimea Shorebreak

Waimea's famous shorebreak is popular for bodyboarding and bodysurfing, but its steep drop and huge power can be dangerous in winter conditions despite the sandy bottom. For a spot in the parking lot, you must arrive early or wait for someone to leave. There is some additional parking on the Kam Highway along the bluff to the south and at Sts. Peter and Paul Mission Church to the north.

Pinballs

On the northeastern side of Waimea Bay near the cliffs, the inside break named Pinballs is surfable in smaller swells. Park in the Waimea Bay Beach Park lot, on Kam Highway along the bluff to the south, or at Sts. Peter and Paul Mission Church to the north.

Waimea Bay

The huge right off the outside break known as Waimea Bay is one of the world's most famous big-wave surf spots. In a northwest swell, giant, bowl-shaped waves form on the offshore reef and rocks along the cliff. Sometimes these huge waves close out the entire width of the bay, trapping surfers inside. Only experts should attempt Waimea when the big surf is running. A dangerous rip current lurks near the shore and runs seaward through the middle of the bay, making it unsafe for amateurs to go near the water then. The Quicksilver in Memory of Eddie Aikau International surf contest is held at Waimea when the waves are consistently over 20 feet. Park in the Waimea Bay Beach Park lot, on Kam Highway along the bluff to the south, or at Sts. Peter and Paul Mission Church to the north.

Pele's Followers

Nice rights can be found on the south side of Kulaloa Point, at the northeastern tip of Shark's Cove. Access is through Shark's Cove.

Outer Log Cabins

On the far left of Ke Waena Beach, a massive long right break sometimes occurs on the outside deepwater reef in northern swells. The reef pushes western swells toward Pipeline, but northern swells into a huge right break. Outer Log Cabins is famous for tow-in surfing. Some of the largest waves in history were ridden there in January of 1998. Access is through a public right of way near the Ke Waena lifeguard tower at 59-475 Ke Waena Road (a loop that runs along the beach parallel to Kam Highway); Banzai Rock Support Park, an undeveloped 2.3-acre parcel between Ke Waena Road and Ke Nui Road; or along the shore from Ehukai Beach Park, 59-337 Ke Nui Road.

Log Cabins

Inshore from Outer Log Cabins, there are big rights and lefts in north, northwest, or west swells. The bottom is extremely uneven. Flat lava tables alternate with sand and dangerous rock spikes, making the wave action challenging and wipeouts treacherous. For access, see the directions for Outer Log Cabins.

Rock Pile

About 250 yards offshore from Banzai Rocks, the Rock Pile reef sometimes produces challenging waves in a northern swell. For access, see the directions for Outer Log Cabins.

Off the Wall (Kodak Reef)

Directly in front of the Ke Waena lifeguard tower, Off The Wall (formerly known as Kodak Reef) offers fast action with shallow rights and occasional lefts over a bottom of lava and sand. The lineup is off the stone wall of a beachfront home. For access, see the directions for Outer Log Cabins.

Backdoor

The right break from the Pipeline is called Backdoor. In a northwest swell, Backdoor can sometimes produce a deep right barrel that is longer and faster than the Pipeline itself, but it does not have a channel back out like the Pipeline has. The break is between Ke Waena and Ehukai, about 50 yards west of Pipeline. Park at Banzai Rock Support Park, an undeveloped 2.3-acre parcel between Ke Waena Road and Ke Nui Road; at Ehukai Beach Park, 59-337 Ke Nui Road; Sunset Beach Neighborhood Park on the *mauka* side of Kam Highway, or roadside on Kam Highway.

Banzai Pipeline

Winter swells over a shallow coral shelf produce the famous left tube known as the Banzai Pipeline. This world-class left break challenges expert board surfers. Pipeline is for experts only. The sharp, shallow coral bottom, powerful waves, and strong currents have caused many injuries and even a few fatalities. Pipeline is the Site of the **Billabong Pipeline, third leg of the Triple Crown of Surfing, the Pipeline Masters, and the Monster Energy Pipeline Pro,** which is held on the four best wave days in late January and early February. Park at Banzai Rock Support Park between Ke Waena Road and Ke Nui Road; at Ehukai Beach Park, 59-337 Ke Nui Road; at Sunset

Beach Neighborhood Park and Elementary School on the *mauka* side of Kam Highway, or roadside on Kam Highway.

Ehukai

In front of the Ehukai lifeguard tower, the surf breaks left and right over a sandy bottom. This area is popular with bodysurfers as well as board surfers. Access from Ehukai Beach Park, 59-337 Ke Nui Road.

Pupukea

Immediately north of Ehukai Beach Park, Pupukea provides solid rights and smaller lefts over a sandy bottom during north swells. This is a good spot for bodysurfing, with a shallow inside section and a sandy beach. Access is from Ehukai Beach Park, 59-337 Ke Nui Road.

Gas Chambers/Turkey Bay

Gas Chambers is one of the first breaks on the North Shore to be surfed consistently. There is a nice left on a west swell. When conditions are right, Gas Chambers breaks into Rocky Point. There is also a right break off Gas Chambers known as Turkey Bay. The bottom is coral. Park roadside on Ke Nui Road or Kam Highway and use the public right of way on Ke Nui Road, or park at Ehukai Beach Park, 59-337 Ke Nui Road, and walk north along the beach.

Rocky Point/Arma Hut

Rocky Point is a shallow, sharp reef offshore from the Haleiwa side of the Chevron station between Ehukai Beach Park and Sunset Beach Park. In northerly swells, the fast right wall and left close to shore are popular with short boarders and bodyboarders. A similar reef section east of Rocky Point is known as Arma Hut. Park roadside on Kam Highway and watch out for the sharp bottom.

Kammieland

This popular surf spot off the south end of Sunset Beach has left and right breaks, depending on conditions. Park roadside on Kam

Highway near the wall marking the site of the old Kammie's Market and use the public right of way, or park at Sunset Beach Park and walk south along the beach to Kammieland.

Val's Reef

Inside the coral shelf on the northeast side of Sunset Beach, where the water is relatively shallow, there are sharp rights and lefts over Val's Reef. This is a good spot for bodyboarding and bodysurfing when the waves are three to six feet. The lineup is in a direct line with the curved coconut palm before the first house and the telephone pole on the *mauka* side of the Kam Highway. There are parking lots on both sides of Kam Highway at Sunset Beach Park and Sunset Beach Support Park.

Sunset Beach/Sunset Point

Sunset has some of the heaviest and longest waves in the world. During winter swells, Sunset Beach produces a world-class right, with steep peaks reaching 15 to 20 feet. Huge right breaks form further out at **Sunset Point**. Sunset can be treacherous: huge waves can appear suddenly and throw surfers into the jagged coral reef and underwater caves. On the Waimea side of the break, a channel runs out to sea where the Paumalu Stream once flowed into the Pacific. The rip currents in the channel are extremely powerful when a big swell is running. The "Sunset rip" has necessitated many rescues and caused some fatalities. At times Sunset Point closes out and surfers have to battle their way into shore or let the current take them out and hope for a helicopter rescue. The **Roxy Pro Sunset, second leg of the Triple Crown of Surfing, O'Neill World Cup,** and other professional surf contests are held here every winter. There are parking lots on both sides of Kam Highway at Sunset Beach Park and Sunset Beach Support Park.

Backyards

Backyards has fast rights and difficult lefts for expert short boarders. It is very popular for sailboarding and windsurfing. Backyards is northeast of Sunset Beach, off the intersection of the Kam Highway and Comsat Road. To reach it, walk along the shore north from Sunset Point or south from Velzyland.

Freddyland

On the south side of the channel off Kaunala Beach, in front of the Sunset Bay Colony housing development, Freddyland has short rights and long lefts in a north swell. Park roadside on Kam Highway and use the public right of way to the right of the car gate into the Sunset Bay Colony.

Velzyland

Velzyland was named for Dale Velzy, one of the first commercial manufacturers of surfboards. Located on the north side of the channel off Kaunala Beach, it breaks on a shallow reef shelf that has cracked many boards and bruised many surfers. With long lefts and hollow rights in winter swells, Velzyland is popular for short boarding and bodyboarding with windsurfing on the outside. Park roadside on Kam Highway and use the public right of way to the right of the car gate into the Sunset Bay Colony.

Phantoms

On the outer reefs beyond Velzyland, there is a big winter break the locals call Phantoms. Park roadside on Kam Highway and use the public right of way to the right of the car gate into Sunset Bay Colony.

Bong's

The shallow reef offshore from Waialee Beach Park and Kukaimanini Islet creates the little break called Bong's. Access is from Waialee Beach Park.

Kawela Bay

In *kona* winds and a west swell, rights and lefts break on the point off Kawela Bay. Access is through the Turtle Bay Resort; park in the "beach access" section of the Resort's parking lot and follow the trail to Kawela Bay, or paddle around from Turtle Bay.

Turtle Bay

Small rights and lefts inshore are suitable for beginners who are not daunted by the lava rock entry and coral and rock bottom. Access is through the Turtle Bay Resort; park in the "beach access" section of the Resort's parking lot and follow the paved trail past the cabanas.

Kuilima

Waves rolling past Kuilima Point cross the raised coral reef in irregular patterns, producing short rights next to the Turtle Bay Resort's swimming pool. An audience gathers at the poolside Hang Ten Surf Bar every evening to watch the surfers and sunset. This spot has become more popular in recent years, with the resort sponsoring several championships. Access is through the Turtle Bay Resort; park in the "beach access" section of the Resort's parking lot.

Seventh Hole

Directly offshore from the seventh hole of the Kahuku Golf Course, the Seventh Hole surf break produces big lefts and short rights in north and east swells. Turn *maikai* off Kam Highway at Kahuku High School, park at the Kahuku Golf Course, and paddle out from the 7th hole.

Mokuauia (Goat Island)

Surfers and windsurfers escape the crowds on the windward side of Mokuauia (Goat Island). Long lefts can be found here all year, but conditions are best in the winter, especially in north, east, and large northwest swells. Park in the Kalanai Point section parking lot in Malaekahana State Recreation Area, about .6 miles north of Laie Town, and paddle across to the windward side of the island.

Laniloa

Makai of the Polynesian Cultural Center in Laie, short boarders and bodyboarders can enjoy long fast lefts and short rights all year. Conditions are best in the winter, especially in north, east, and large northwest swells. Park roadside on Kam Highway. There is a public right of access at 55-470 Kam Highway.

Pounders

The shorebreak on the southern end of Laie Beach Park provides short rights and lefts for bodyboarders and bodysurfers who do not mind getting roughed up. Park at Laie Beach Park.

Kilia (Hauula Beach Park)

At high tide, local kids enjoy the Kilia surf break on the offshore reef. Park at Hauula Beach Park.

Secrets (Kahana Bay)

Swells along the offshore reefs at the mouth of Kahana Bay sometimes produce ideal waves for beginning board surfers. The shorebreak is often good for novice bodysurfers. Park at Kahana Bay Beach Park.

Crouching Lion

The outer reef *makai* of the Crouching Lion rock formation offers nice tubes suitable for short boarders and bodyboarders willing to paddle that far. Conditions are best in *kona* winds and east, northeast, and north swells. Park roadside near the Crouching Lion Inn, 51-666 Kam Highway.

Razor Blades

South of the Crouching Lion, a wide sandy channel in Razor Reef off Makaua Beach produces tubes suitable for surfing and bodyboarding. Park roadside on Kam Highway.

Kaaawa

The point separating Kaaawa from Kualoa south of Kalaeoio Beach Park often produces small waves that are surfable with short boards and bodyboards. Park at Kalaeoio Beach Park or roadside on Kam Highway.

Kanenelu

The small offshore waves off Kanenelu Beach provide nice right walls suitable for longboards, short boards, and bodyboards. Conditions are best in north, northeast, and east swells during the winter. Park roadside on the Kam Highway south of Kaaawa Elementary School.

SWIMMING

For recreational swimming in the ocean, see Chapter IV. Serious swimmers swim laps across Waimea Bay and Sunset Bay in the summer and along the breakwater at Kuilima Cove in the winter. For competitive swimming, contact the North Shore Swim Series, telephone 372-8885. A public swimming pool and children's pool are located at **Waialua District Park**, 67-180 Goodale Avenue, Waialua 96791, telephone 637-6061.

Swimming lessons in a solar heated pool are available at **Gunstock Aquatics**, 56-250 Kam Highway, Laie, telephone 341-0788, www.gunstockaquatics.com. Classes include Baby N Me Swimming, Preschool Swimming, Youth Swimming, Teen Swimming, Adult Swimming, Competitive Stroke Workshops, American Red Cross Lifeguard Certification, CPR Certification, First Aid Certification, American Red Cross Lifeguard Instructor Certification, and American Red Cross Water Safety Instructor Certification.

WHALE WATCHING

Whale watching cruises are offered in the winter by **Chupu Charters,** Haleiwa Boat Harbor, Haleiwa 96712, www.chupu.com, telephone 637-3474; **North ShoreCatamaran Charters,** Haleiwa Boat Harbor, Haleiwa, telephone 351-9371, www.sailingcat.com; and **North Shore Diving & Deep Ecology,** 66-460 Kam Highway, telephone 73-SCUBA.

WINDSURFING

Surf 'n' Sea, 62-595 Kam Highway, Haleiwa 96712, telephone 637-SURF (7873), www.surfnsea.com, offers windsurfing lessons, equipment sales and rentals, and repairs. **North Shore Eco-Surf Tours,** P.O. Box 1174, Haleiwa 96712, telephone 638-9503, www.ecosurf-hawaii.com, also offers windsurfing lessons. For more information, call Stan Van Voorhis at 638-9503 or E-mail stanvanvoorhis@yahoo.com. Popular windsurfing locations include Mokuleia, Sunset Point, Backyards, Velzyland, Malaekahana, and Mokuauia (Goat Island).

VI. ACTIVITIES ON LAND

BASEBALL

Baseball fields are located at **Waialua District Park**, 67-180 Goodale Avenue, Waialua, telephone 637-9721; **Haleiwa Beach Park**, 62-449 Kam Highway, Haleiwa; and **Kahuku District Park**, 56-170 Pualalea Street, Kahuku, telephone 293-5116.

BASKETBALL

Outdoor basketball courts are located at **Haleiwa Beach Park**, 62-449 Kam Highway, Haleiwa; **Pupukea Beach Park**, 59-727 Kam Highway, Pupukea, telephone 638-7213; **Sunset Beach Neighborhood Park**, 59-360 Kam Highway, Sunset, telephone 638-7051; **Kahuku District Park**, 56-170 Pualalea Street, Kahuku, telephone 293-5116; and **Swanzy Beach Park**, 51-369 Kam Highway, Kaaawa, telephone 638-7051. **Waialua District Park**, 67-180 Goodale Road, Waialua, telephone 637-9721, has both indoor and outdoor basketball courts.

BIKING

Biking opportunities on the North Shore range from the paved Ke Ala Pupukea Bicycle Path to scenic mountain trails, dirt cane roads, and even a motocross track. Group rides and commercial tours are available. If you plan to go mountain biking on your own, obtain trail maps and information on current conditions in advance. Be aware of hazardous conditions that may occur on mountain trails, including landslides, flash floods, trail surface instability, and hunting and military operations in some areas. Be sure to bring water, a hat, sunscreen, mosquito repellent, and bike lock. In the

Koolaus, rain gear may also come in handy. Do not attempt to ford streams if the water is more than knee-high and do not bike in the Koolaus if it is raining or rain is predicted. Note that cell phones often do not work on mountain trails.

Information and Permits

For backcountry trails:

Hawaii Division of Forestry and Wildlife

151 Punchbowl Street, Honolulu 96813, telephone 587-0166, fax 587-0160, or

2135 Makiki Heights Road, Honolulu, HI 96822, telephone 973-9778, fax 973-9781.

For state parks:

Hawaii Division of State Parks

1151 Punchbowl Street, Room 131, P.O. Box 621, Honolulu 96809, telephone 587-0300.

Bicycle Rentals

Bikes can be rented from **Barnfield's Raging Isle Surf & Cycle**, 66-250 Kam Highway, Building B, Haleiwa, HI 96712, telephone 637-7707, ragingislebikes@hawaii.rr.com; **Country Cycles** on Pupukea Road, telephone 638-7400; and **Planet Surf**, corner of Pupukea Road and the Kam Highway, Pupukea, telephone 638-5060.

Group Rides

The non-profit **Hawaii Bicycling League** hosts group rides and other biking events. For information, contact the Hawaii Bicycling League, 3442 Waialae Avenue, Suite 1, Honolulu, HI 96816, telephone 735-5756, www.hbl.org. **Bike Hawaii**, a division of Ohana Adventure Tours, offers guided mountain bike tours on private land in the Kaaawa Valley. One package lets riders coast five miles downhill through a rain forest; another combines biking with kayaking and snorkeling; a third option includes a short, guided hike to a 200-foot waterfall. Bicycle rentals and helmets are included in the package. Contact Bike Hawaii, P.O. Box 240170, Honolulu 96824, telephone 734-4214, E-mail: tours@bikehawaii.com, www.bikehawaii.com.

Bike Paths

The paved **Ke Ala Pupukea Bicycle Path** extends along the North Shore from Pupukea Beach Park to Velzyland. So far, the Ke Ala path is the only portion of the North Shore bikeway system that has been completed. The master plan calls for a coastline route stretching from the Leeward Shore around Kaena Point and all the way up the North Shore and down the Windward Shore, a route through Haleiwa Town, and routes along the Haleiwa Bypass and Haleiwa and Waialua Roads. Potential additional bikeways include Paalaa Road in Haleiwa and Puuiki Street, Cane Haul Road, and Kealohanui Street in Waialua.

Mountain Bike Trails

The following brief descriptions are intended to give you a feel for the most popular mountain biking trails in northern Oahu. The trails are listed in clockwise order from northwest to southeast. Please remember that the information provided here is incomplete. You are responsible for informing yourself about current conditions and taking appropriate precautions before heading into the backcountry. Detailed trail maps, proper equipment, and good judgment are essential for the safe enjoyment of these trails.

The Kaena Point Trail

This rutted jeep trail follows the old roadbed of the OR&L Railway around the northwestern corner of Oahu. From the Kaena parking area, it is 2.5 miles to Kaena Point and five miles to Yokohama Beach on the Leeward Shore. The views of the Pacific are magnificent. The ride is fairly flat and suitable for beginning to advanced riders. There is no shade, so start in the morning and bring water, sunscreen and a hat. Also bring a lunch, bathing suit, and bike lock for stops at the Kaena Point Natural Area Refuge and Yokohama Beach. Remember that it is unsafe to descend toward the sea or any area exposed to the breaking waves. Between the parking area and Kaena Point, the sandy *makai* trail is preferable to the rockier, clay-like *mauka* trail, especially in wet weather. Bikes are only allowed on the main trail, as the coastal lowland dune ecosystem is quite fragile. As you near Kaena Point, look for the **Pohaku o Kauai**, the huge boulder that the god Maui dropped as he tried to unite the islands of Oahu and Kauai. Another highlight of this trip is the Kaena Point Natural Area Refuge. Park your bike at the gated boulder barricade on the *makai* side of the path and walk through the refuge to see the endangered plants and animals that depend on this delicate ecosystem. The trail continues around Kaena Point to Yokohama Beach. If you ride down the Leeward Shore, look for the sea arch and the small blowhole in the rocks. There is one section where you may have to dismount and carry your bike over a washout. Showers and restrooms are available at Yokohama Beach, where you can enjoy a refreshing ocean swim before starting your return trip. Begin at the dirt parking area at the end of the Farrington Highway or leave your car at Dillingham Airfield and set out from there.

The Kealia Trail Down The Bluff Above Dillingham Airfield

The Kealia Trail is a one-way technical descent down the volcanic bluff above Dillingham Airfield. The terrain is too loose and the grade too steep to ride this trail uphill. The downhill is strictly for experts: it drops 1,700 feet in 2.8 miles, with rough 180-degree switchbacks, steep cliffs on both sides, and loose rocks demanding skill and vigilance. There are sweeping views of the North Shore and Mokuleia. As you descend, you may see gliders, aerobatic biplanes, and hang gliders passing before you and kitesurfers and windsurfers in the ocean below. Please dismount before you take your eyes off the winding, precipitous trail! To reach the Kealia Trail from above, take the Mokuleia Access Road to Peacock Flats (see below) or the Kuaokala Forest Reserve Road from the Kaena Point Tracking Station. A permit from the State Division of Forestry and Wildlife is required for access through the Kaena Point Tracking Station. There is no shade on the bluff, so start early and bring water, sunscreen, and a hat. Be aware that hunters frequent the Kuaokala area above the trail. The best time to bike there is between February and April, after pig and bird hunting seasons and before summer.

The Mokuleia Access Road And Kuaokala Access Road Above Mokuleia

The Mokuleia Access road is a paved road up the steep face of the Waianae Range. The first mile is fairly flat and suitable for beginners. After two miles, the grade steepens considerably. There is no shade on the paved road up the bluff, so start in the morning and bring water, sunscreen, and a hat. About 3.8 miles from Farrington Highway, the road reaches the Peacock Flats campground. A four-wheel drive road leads ½ mile from the campground to the boundary of the Pahole Natural Area Reserve. You can leave your bike there and take a short detour on foot to a magnificent overview of the Makua Valley on the Leeward Shore. Do not go into the Makua Valley; it is a military range that is sometimes used for live-fire exercises. From the Peacock Flats campground, the paved road continues approximately .8 miles to the Kuaokala Access Road, which connects to the Kealia Trail and the Kaena Point Satellite Tracking Station. No permit is required for biking on the access road and Kealia Trail, but access through the Kaena Point Satellite Tracking Station requires a permit from the Hawaii Division of Forestry and Wildlife. To reach the Mokuleia Access Road, take Farrington Highway west from Waialua. Continue two miles past Waialua High School and turn *mauka* (left) at the coconut farm. If you come by car, park on the right side as you enter the coconut farm and remember Rule No. 2. If the gates are open, do not drive your car past them as they may be locked when you return. Ride your bike past the three gates. Again, be aware that hunters frequent the Kuaokala area. The best time to bike here is between February and April, after pig and bird hunting seasons and before summer. If you plan to enter or leave through the Kaena Point Satellite Tracking Station, get a permit in advance and also call the Kaena Point Facility at 697-4311 prior to departure to check on access status due to various levels of security.

The Kaunala Trail On The Pupukea Ridge—Weekends and Holidays

The Kaunala Trail is a scenic, six-mile loop through the ridges and gulches of the Pupukea Paumalu Forest Reserve. The elevation gain is only about 500 feet, but sharp drop-offs, protruding roots, stream crossings, and long ascents and descents make this ride unsuitable for young or inexperienced bikers. The rewards are lush tropical vegetation and sweeping views from the clearings. To reach the Kaunala Trail, take the Kam Highway to the traffic light at the Pupukea Foodland and turn *mauka* on Pupukea Road. Continue on Pupukea Road to the end of the pavement and park outside the Camp Pupukea Boy Scout Camp (not in its parking lot). Ride down the dirt road past the Forest Reserve gate to the four-wheel drive road. Continue on the four-wheel drive road to the trailhead on the left. (The trailhead is approximately .7 miles from the end of the paved road.) Stay to the left of the trailhead sign. After a short climb, the trail descends into a copse of paperback trees and winds along ridges covered with thick vegetation. Dismount to observe the native birds and vegetation. Look for the rare sandalwood trees behind the clearing on the last side ridge. The route snakes in and out of lush gulches, which are sometimes muddy. It crosses several streams before rising to join a jeep trail from the Camp Paumalu Girl Scout Camp. Turn right on the jeep trail to return to the starting point near the Boy Scout Camp. Because the trail crosses the Army's Kahuku training area and an active, public hunting area, it is only open on weekends and state and federal holidays. Bring water, hats, sunscreen, and mosquito repellent.

The Kahuku Motocross Track –Weekends and Holidays

The Kahuku Motocross Track is located in Waialee, one mile north of Sunset Beach, on state land leased by the non-profit Hawaii Motorsports Association (HMA). Although it is used mostly for motorcycle racing, the park also contains miles of mountain bike roads and trails through a forest of ironwood trees. It is a great place for daring bikers who enjoy speed and jumps. The routes include steep uphills and fast downhills with plenty of technical riding for trail bikes. The surface is covered with dry twigs. It can be slippery and have cake-like mud in wet conditions. Mountain bikers are required to stay off the racetrack and yield to motorcycles. The helmet requirement is strictly enforced for mountain bikes as well as motorized vehicles. There is a fee of $5 per bike per day to ride. To reach the park, take the Kam Highway one mile north of Sunset Beach. When you see the Sunset Bay Colony residential development *makai* of Kam Highway, look *mauka* for the sign to the Kahuku Motocross Track. Turn *mauka* and follow the dirt road to the entrance. The park is open from 8 a.m. to 6 p.m. on weekends and federal holidays. Portable restrooms are available. Camping is available for HMA members only. For more information, call the Hawaii Motorsports Association Hotline, 668-6276.

The Hauula Loop Trail

This popular 2.5-mile loop trail is suitable for intermediate and advanced bikers. The trail winds up the side of the mountain, crosses the gulch, and rises to the ridge overlooking the beautiful Kaipapau Valley. The elevation gain is about 600 feet. The path climbs through brush and trees, at first open to the sun, then traversing a forest of ironwood that turns to Norfolk pine as you ascend. The flora and fauna are variegated, with wild orchids, native ebony or persimmon, red *hau* trees, and other indigenous vegetation. Clearings afford glimpses of the lovely valley below. As you descend along the top of the ridge, there are breathtaking vistas of Hauula Town and the Windward Shore. The long single track down the ridge provides fantastic views of the verdant Koolaus sweeping down to the sea. After crossing several small streams, the downhill ends at a delightful pond. Stay on the main trail, watch out for drop-offs and roots, and do not ride if it is raining or rain is predicted. To reach the trail, take the Kam Highway to Hauula and turn *mauka* at Hauula Homestead Road. At the fork in the road, turn right and take Maakua Road to the end. Park, follow the dirt road to the left, and the trailhead will be on your right. Follow the right (counterclockwise) fork for the Hauula Loop Trail. The left (clockwise) fork is the Papali Loop Hiking Trail. Bring sunscreen, hats, water, and mosquito repellent. Be aware that this is a very popular hiking trail and watch out for those on foot.

The Maakua Ridge Trail

This 3.3-mile round trip is suitable for intermediate and advanced bikers who are not daunted by a long uphill. Follow the directions for the Hauula Loop Trail. The Maakua Ridge Trail will be on your left after you pass the Hauula Loop Trailhead on your right. You must carry your bike across a streambed to reach the trail. The ride begins with a switchback ascent up the side of Maakua Gulch. Another climb takes you across the Papali Gulch. The rewards are beautiful views of the Windward Shore and Maakua Valley and a single-track downhill return to the starting point. Stay on the main trail, watch out for drop-offs and roots, and do not ride if it is raining or rain is predicted. Bring sunscreen, hats, water, and mosquito repellent. For a full day of biking, tackle the Maakua Ridge Trail while you are fresh, have a picnic lunch and a pleasant rest, then enjoy the Hauula Loop Trail.

BIRD WATCHING

Kaena Point Natural Area Refuge

The Kaena Point Refuge is a coastal lowland dune ecosystem accessible by foot or mountain bike off the north side of the Kaena Point Trail. In November the Laysan Albatross breeds here; the sandy areas in the refuge serve as potential breeding sites. Seabirds, including red-footed and brown boobies, the wedge-tailed shearwater, and the brown noddy, are common. To reach the refuge, park at the end of Farrington Highway and hike or bike to the gated boulder barricade on the *makai* side of the path. See Biking, Mountain Bike Trails, in this Chapter.

Waimea Valley Historical Nature Park

The Waimea Valley Historical Nature Park, 59-864 Kam Highway, telephone 638-7766, is home to several species of native birds, including the black-crowned night heron and the endangered Hawaiian moorhen, a black water bird with a red faceplate that has established populations in two of the park's ponds. Various species of migratory birds, including plovers and turnstones, winter here. Many introduced species also inhabit the park. See Chapter III.

James Campbell National Wildlife Refuge

The James Campbell National Wildlife Refuge lies in the wetlands between the Turtle Bay Resort and Kahuku. The 164-acre refuge is a bird watcher's delight, complete with a visitor kiosk, interpretive signs, and guided and self-interpretive tours. It was established in 1976, when the Kahuku sugar mill closed down and the settling ponds began to dry up, jeopardizing the water bird habitat. Its primary mission is the recovery of Hawaii's four endangered water birds: the Hawaiian stilt, moorhen, coot, and duck. Many wintering migrants are also found here. The refuge is open to the public from the 3rd Saturday in October through the 3rd Saturday in February. Guided public tours are offered on Thursdays from 4:00 to 5:30 p.m., on the first two Saturdays of the month from 9:00 to 10:30 a.m., and on the remaining Saturdays from 3:30 to 5:00 p.m. To reserve a space on the tour, call the Refuge's office in Haleiwa, telephone 637-6330. For more information, contact the Refuge Manager, James Campbell National Wildlife Refuge, 66-590 Kam

Highway, Haleiwa, HI 96712, telephone 637-6330, fax 637-3578. Office hours are 7:30 a.m. to 4:00 p.m. Monday through Friday.

Mokuauia Island (Goat Island)

Mokuauia Island (locally known as Goat Island) is a state bird sanctuary about one-eighth of a mile offshore from Malaekahana State Recreation Area in Laie. The top of a large stranded coral reef, this 13-acre coral shelf is the northernmost offshore Oahu islet with nesting pelagic birds. Ten species of seabirds inhabit Mokuauia. Shearwater burrows fill the interior of the island. A trail winds around the perimeter, providing intimate views of the burrowing birds with eggs resting in their nests. The sanctuary is open to the public during daytime hours. Remember Rule No. 9—stay on the trail and do not disturb the nesting sites. To reach Mokuauia, park on the Kalanai Point (east) side of Malaekahana State Recreation Area. From the beach near Kalanai Point, you can wade at low tide or swim or paddle at high tide to the island. Be sure to wear water shoes and check the tide table and water conditions before you go.

CAMPING

Camping is allowed by permit in a number of state, county, and private campgrounds in northern Oahu. Many locals enjoy camping, so make your reservations and obtain your permits as early as possible.

Beachside Camping

Camp H.R. Erdman

The YMCA of Honolulu operates Camp H.R. Erdman at 69-385 Farrington Highway in Mokuleia. Conferences and camping for groups and families are offered year-round. The YMCA also operates a summer camp for children. Contact Executive Director Josh Heimowitz, telephone 637-4615, fax 637-8874, E-mail: jheimowitz@ymcahonolulu.org, or go to www.ymcahonolulu.org.

Mokuleia Beach Park

This popular beach park at 68-919 Farrington Highway has 15 campsites, but the county has suspended camping there until further notice. For current information about camping at Mokuleia, call the County Parks Permits Section at 523-4525.

Kaiaka Bay Beach Park

Kaiaka Bay Beach Park, 66-449 Haleiwa Road, Haleiwa, has seven campsites. The beach is better for fishing than swimming. Applications for county camping permits must be made in person at the Parks Permits Section on the ground floor of the Frank F. Fasi Municipal Building, 650 South King Street, Honolulu, or at any satellite city hall on the island between 8:00 a.m. and 4:00 p.m. on weekdays. Permits are free. A permit allows a maximum of ten persons, including children, with two family sized tents to occupy a campsite. Camping is allowed five days a week, from 8:00 a.m. on Friday until 8:00 a.m. on Wednesday. There is no camping on Wednesdays and Thursdays, when the campsites are closed for maintenance. It is best to arrive on Friday morning, when maintenance has just been performed. Reservations may be made no earlier than two Fridays prior to the camping period requested. If Friday is a holiday, camping reservations will be accepted on the day before the holiday. Trailers are allowed, but they must be self-contained. There are no electrical or sewer connections. For more information, call the County Parks Permits Section at 523-4525.

Malaekahana State Recreation Area

Malaekahana was once a *puuhonua*, a place of refuge for commoners who broke *kapu*. Today Malaekahana is the most popular campsite in northern Oahu, a place of refuge from the stresses and strains of modern living. The 37-acre camping area occupies a lovely grove of tall trees adjoining a shady white beach on the Kahuku (west) side of Malaekahana State Recreation Area. It is managed by Friends of Malaekahana, a community-based, non-profit organization under the supervision of the Hawaii Department of Land and Natural Resources. There is a gate and 24-hour on-site security. Accommodations include 40 tent sites with picnic tables, firepits, and shared toilets, outdoor hot showers, and kitchen sinks; five furnished yurts with electricity; rustic, furnished beach houses with stoves and refrigerators; eco-cabins; and a genuine *hale nui,* a grass shack with electricity, a private bath, and its own lanai on the beach. No pets or alcohol are allowed. Park on the Kahuku side of Malaekahana State Recreation Area, approximately 1.3 miles north of Laie. Remember Rule No. 2. Contact Friends of Malaekahana, 56-335 Kam Highway, P.O. Box 305, Laie 96762, telephone 293-1736, fax 293-2066, or visit 222. alternativehawaii.com.

Hukilau Campground

A beautiful shady campground overlooks Hukilau Beach in Laie. The LDS Church owns the property. Camping is allowed from Monday to Friday, vacating Saturday. A permit must be obtained from Hawaii Reserves, Inc., 55-510 Kam Highway, Laie (in the Laie Village Shopping Center). There is no fee. For more information, call Serena Johnson-Mailau, telephone 293-6461.

Kokololio Beach Park

Located at 55-017 Kam Highway, Laie, Kokololio has five shady campsites adjacent to a sandy beach. See Kaiaka Bay Beach Park for information on county camping permits.

Hauula Beach Park

Located at 54-135 Kam Highway in Hauula, this beach park has 15 campsites. See Kaiaka Bay Beach Park for information on county camping permits.

Swanzy Beach Park

Located at 51-369 Kam Highway in Kaaawa, Swanzy Beach Park has nine campsites available only on weekends. See Kaiaka Bay Beach Park for information on county camping permits.

Ahupuaa O Kahana State Park

This state park is located at 52-222 Kam Highway on the Windward Shore. There are ten shady campsites near the beach at Kahana Bay. Applications for camping may be made in writing, by telephone, or in person to the Hawaii Division of State Parks, 1151 Punchbowl Street, Room 131, P.O. Box 621, Honolulu 96809, telephone 587-0300. There is a fee of $5 per campsite per night. The maximum stay per permit is five consecutive nights. Applications must be received at least seven days before the camping period, but will not be processed more than 30 days in advance. A 30-day period must elapse before a new permit is issued. Trailers are not allowed.

Mountain Camping

The Hawaii Division of Forestry and Wildlife, operates two campgrounds in the Waianae Mountains. **Kuaokala Campground** is in the Mokuleia Forest Reserve above Dillingham Airfield, near the Kealia and Kuaokala Trails. **Peacock Flats Campground** is located on the bluff above Waialua Intermediate and High School, 2.8 miles up the Mokuleia Access Road from the Farrington Highway. A jeep trail leads ½ mile from the Peacock Flats Campground to the Pahole Natural Area Reserve, where a hiking trail extends to a lookout over the Makua Valley on the Leeward Shore. Locals use this area for pig and bird hunting. The best time to visit is between February and April, after the hunting seasons and before the summer. Applications for camping at Kuaokala and Peacock Flats and for access through the Kaena Point Satellite Tracking Station can be mailed or faxed to the Hawaii Division of Forestry and Wildlife, 151 Punchbowl Street, Room 131, Honolulu 996813, telephone 587-0166, fax 587-0160, or 2135 Makiki Heights Road, Honolulu, HI 96822, telephone 973-9778, fax 973-9781. Campers are advised to call the Kaena Point Facility at 697-4311 prior to departure to check on access status due to various levels of security.

The **Kahuku Motocross Track** in Wailee allows members of the Hawaii Motorsports Association to camp there for a nominal charge. Pick up a permit when you enter the track. See Biking, Mountain Bike Trails, in this Chapter.

FITNESS

Curves

This popular exercise program designed for women has three locations in northern Oahu:

- 935 California Ave. #A-4, Wahiawa, telephone 628-9443.
- Haleiwa Shopping Plaza, 66-165 Kam Highway, Haleiwa, telephone 637-2711.
- 56-565 Kam Highway, Kahuku (in the rear of the Kahuku Sugar Mill Shopping Center), Kahuku, telephone 293-4400.

North Shore Workout

This gym at 66-216 Farrington Highway, Waialua, telephone 637-2005, is open to the public. It offers short-term gym packages, spa and weight loss programs, and surf and strength packages, with personal trainers on staff.

Spa Luana

Located on the ground floor of the Turtle Bay Resort, 57-091 Kam Highway, Kahuku, 293-8811, www.turtlebayresort.com, Spa Luana offers exercise equipment and a variety of fitness classes including yoga, pilates, body sculpting, hula, and water aerobics. Private lessons are also available. Spa Luana also offers a full range of salon services, massages, and other treatments. The Fitness Center is open from 6:00 a.m. to 10:00 p.m. daily. It is accessible to hotel guests with their room keys.

Waialua District Park

This public facility at 67-180 Goodale Avenue, Waialua, 637-9721, has a weight room and free weights.

GOLF

The Links At Turtle Bay Resort

The Turtle Bay Resort, 57-049 Kuilima Drive, Kahuku 96731, telephone 293-8574, fax 293-9094, www.turtlebayresort.com, is the only 36-hole golf resort on Oahu. The hours of operation are 6:30 a.m. to 6:30 p.m. Call 293-8574 for information and tee times. Rental clubs, individual golf lessons, and group clinics are available by appointment. A ten-minute complimentary range lesson is available for hotel guests. Lei Lei's Restaurant serves breakfast, lunch, and dinner adjacent to the golf shop.

The Arnold Palmer Course

Golf Digest consistently rates the 222-acre Palmer course one of Hawaii's top golf courses. The challenging 18-hole layout is a regular stop on the PGA Champions Tour and LPGA Tour. Designed by Arnold Palmer and Ed Seay, the course forms a horseshoe around 100 acres of unspoiled wetlands, passing through a forest of ironwood trees along a magnificent shoreline. There are five sets of tees ranging from 4,851 to 7,218 yards. The front nine has a Scottish Links design, open and exposed to the trade winds. The back nine is tree-lined and more protected from the elements. Six holes border the beautiful Punahoolapa wetland. From the 17th green, there are panoramic views of the coastline.

The tee statistics are:

Championship:	7,218 yards, 72 par, 74.4 rating, and 143 slope
Resort:	6,225 yards, 72 par, 70.0 rating, and 132 slope
Forward:	4,851 yards, 72 par, 64.3 rating, and 121 slope

The Fazio Course

The 167-acre Fazio Course is the only golf course in Hawaii designed by George Fazio. Site of the LPGA Tour's Hawaiian Open and the first Senior Skins Game, the 18-hole resort-style layout features generous fairways, deep bunkers, immaculately sculpted greens, and ocean views. It is challenging, but not as difficult as the Palmer Course.

Tee statistics are:

Championsip:	6,535 yards, 72 par, 71.2 rating, and 131 slope
Resort:	6,083 yards, 72 par, 69.2 rating, and 123 slope
Forward:	5,355 yards, 72 par, 70.2 rating, and 116 slope

Kahuku County Golf Course

The nine-hole, oceanfront Kahuku Golf Course is one of the most unique courses in the world. The Kahuku Sugar Plantation built the course for its workers in 1937. When the county's long-term lease expired, the land was sold to a developer. The county continues to operate the course on a month-to-month basis. If it is still operating when you visit, be sure to give it a try. What this course lacks in landscaping, it makes up for in character. It features the longest hole in Hawaii, a tee on top of an old pillbox from World War II, a green where a miss puts the ball on the beach 60 feet below, and amazing views of a pristine shoreline stretching for miles in each direction. With its flat, sandy terrain and strong ocean winds, it is a true Scottish links course. There are no golf carts, so you must walk the entire 2,699-yard layout. Pull carts and golf clubs are available for rent. If you want to play 18 holes, just go around twice. The fees are unbelievably cheap.

Tee statistics for 18 holes are:

Men:	5,398 yards, 70 par, 65.2 rating, and 111 slope
Women:	5,398 yards, 72 par, 69.0 rating, and 112 slope

The course is open from 7:00 a.m. to 5:00 p.m. daily. Telephone 296-2000 for tee time reservations, 293-5842 for the starter/manager. Soft drink and snack vending machines are available in the clubhouse. Bring your own snacks, lunch, and beverages and dine at the picnic tables with the locals.

Military Golf Courses

There are two 18-hole golf courses attached to Schofield Barracks. **Leilehua Golf Course** is the Army's premiere golf course on the island of Oahu. It sits on a plateau overlooking the Wahiawa Reservoir, surrounded by eucalyptus and palm trees. The Leilehua course is primarily open to authorized military and government personnel and their guests. It is open to Hawaii residents on a limited standby basis. The Leilehua Grill is open from 6:30 a.m. until 9:00 p.m. Monday through Friday and 8:00 p.m. weekends. For more information, contact Manager Rick Ambrose, telephone 655-4653, fax 655-1156, E-mail: lgolfproshop@mwrarmyhawaii.com. The Leilehua course is on Leilehua Road, east of H-2 and the Kam Highway on the south side of Wahiawa. The **Kalakaua Golf Course**, located within the gates of Schofield Barracks, is restricted to military and government personnel and their guests.

Golf Packages

Banzai Golf, telephone 375-2717, will reserve tee times and rent clubs or provide an all-in-one tour package which includes green fees, cart fees, transportation to the golf course, golf clubs and golf balls. **Tee Times Hawaii**, telephone 1-888-675-GOLF, works with numerous courses to arrange tee times and rates.

Golf Lessons

Turtle Bay Golf Academy, Turtle Bay Resort, 57-091 Kam Highway, Kahuku, telephone 293-8574, www.turtlebayresort.com, offers individual lessons and group clinics.

HAWAIIAN HISTORY

Kukaniloko Birthing Stones

The Kukaniloko Birthing Stones

The Kukaniloko Birthing Stones lie among coconut and eucalyptus trees in a field north of Wahiawa. One of the most significant cultural sites on Oahu, Kukaniloko is listed on the National and Hawaii Registers of Historic Places. For centuries, Hawaiian women of royal lineage came here for the birth of their children. Kukaniloko was considered a sacred place imbued with *mana* (spiritual power). A royal child who entered the world in the prescribed manner here was considered *he alii* (a god) with the necessary *mana* to rule. In a feudal society where status depended on the parents' genealogy over many generations, a proper birth at Kukaniloko ensured the child's rank and privileges within the *alii* class as well as his godly status and rights over commoners.

Three dozen chiefs witnessed the royal birth. Two rows of 18 *pohaku* (stones) flanked the birthing stone. One chief stood before each of the 36 *pohaku*. With the help of her attendants, the chiefess leaned against the birthing stone and followed the prescribed regulations for giving birth. An impressive ceremony involving the beating of drums, chants, and the offering of gifts accompanied the royal event. Immediately after the birth, the mother and baby were quickly taken to the adjacent *heiau*, where a larger assemblage of chiefs performed a purification ceremony and cut the umbilical cord. Then the beating of sacred drums informed the common people that a new chief had arrived. After the birth, there were seven days of purification for the royal mother.

The stones were used for centuries. As late as 1797, Kamehameha I made arrangements for the birth of his son and heir, Liholiho (Kamehameha II), to take place at Kukaniloko. Unfortunately, Queen Keopuolani was too ill to make the journey. Many Hawaiians attributed Liholiho's poor health and other problems to his lack of a proper royal birth.

To visit the Kukaniloko Birthing Stones, drive north from the town of Wahiawa on the Kam Highway and stay in the left lane. Where Whitmore Avenue intersects the Kam Highway on the right (east), you will see a red dirt road on the left. Turn left (west) onto this dirt road. In only .2 miles, you will find a convenient parking area directly in front of the sacred stones. Please be aware that this is a sacred site. Remember Rule 9 and do not touch the stones or offerings.

Waimea Valley Historical Nature Park

The Waimea Valley Historical Nature Park, 59-864 Kam Highway, telephone 638-7766, is one of the richest repositories of pre-contact Hawaiian artifacts on Oahu. The ¾ mile self-guided trail includes a fishing shrine, a traditional Hawaiian living site, agricultural terraces, a Hawaiian games site, and several sacred areas. Guided historic tours provide a wonderful opportunity to learn about Hawaiian history and culture and meet people who share that interest. See Chapter III, Waimea Valley Historical Nature Park.

Hale O Lono Heiau

The Hale O Lono Heiau was built in the 15th or 16th century and dedicated to the Hawaiian god Lono. Archaeologists from the Bishop Museum have been restoring the *heiau* since it was discovered in 1974. Visitors can see its original configuration, including the thatched housing for sacred drums, an oracle tower, a storage tower for sacrificial objects, a replica of a typical carved wooden statue, and the refuse pit in which human remains were disposed. The *heiau* is located at the east end of the Waimea Valley parking lot.

Puu O Mahuka Heiau State Monument

This National Historic Landmark occupies 110 acres on the bluff overlooking Waimea Valley. Puu O Mahuka is the largest *heiau* on Oahu. It is part of a complex of temples surrounding the sacred Waimea Valley, which was ruled by the *kahuna nui* of the island. With the help of fierce, tattooed warriors, the *kahuna nui* enforced the law of *kapu* as well as traditional religious beliefs. Historians think that Puu O Mahuka was the site of human sacrifices through the 18th century. It is believed that the unfortunate captain and crewmen who went ashore from the British ship Daedalus met their end here.

The *heiau* consists of three adjoining enclosures. The upper enclosure is a low-walled, court platform-type temple. It held the oracle tower, a tall pole frame covered with *kapa* (tapa cloth) where religious ceremonies were conducted and the gods spoke to the *kahuna* and high *alii*. Offerings to the gods were placed at the *lele* altar near the oracle tower. *Kii* (carved wooden images) stood by the altar and the entrance. There are two adjoining smaller independent structures. The middle enclosure probably held thatched buildings. Outside the buildings, ledges along the walls provided seating for those admitted to the rites. The rocks are unstable, so observe the site from outside the walls and do not enter the *heiau*.

Puu O Mahuka had ties with a *heiau* on the island of Kauai, maintaining regular communications by signal fires. From the west side of Puu O Mahuka, there are magnificent views of Waimea Bay, the North Shore, and the Pacific. As you look out past Kaena Point, imagine the *kahunas* who stood here centuries ago watching for the signal fires from the *heiau* on Kauai, over 50 miles away.

To reach Puu O Mahuka, turn *mauka* (right) from the Kam Highway onto Pupukea Road at the traffic light by Pupukea Foodland. Follow Pupukea Road up the bluff. As you reach the top, Pupukea Road straightens out and a road appears on the right with a sign to the *heiau*. The road winds through heavy brush and may be a bit rough to travel. Keep the faith and you will come to a small parking lot. Remember Rule Number 2!

Ahupuaa 'O Kahana State Park

The *ahupuaa* of Kahana was established as a state park to preserve Hawaiian traditions and foster the culture of rural windward Oahu. It was intended to be a "living park" where 31 families living in Kahana Valley would participate in interpretive programs about Hawaiian culture. There are no regularly scheduled activities or demonstrations. If you have a group interested in a cultural program at the park, call 237-7767.

The rugged Kahana Valley holds many archaeological sites, including a *heiau*, fishing shrines, house sites, irrigation channels, and agricultural terraces. Many of them are inaccessible, but the 1.2-mile **Koa and Kila Loop Trail** leads along the western side of the valley floor to the **Kapaeleele Koa** (fishing shrine) and **Keaniani Kilo** (lookout). The lookout affords terrific views of Kahana Bay. To access the Koa and Kila Loop Trail, drive up Kahana Valley Road, park in the designated location, and follow the signs from the orientation center. For other trails leading to archaelogical sites in the valley, see the Hiking Section of this Chapter.

Huilua Fishpond

This National Historic Landmark is a fascinating structure built between 1400 and 1600 A.D. on the east side of Kahana Bay. The early Hawaiians used the pond to hold catches and cultivate food fish . Huilua is a *kuapa* or open sea pond. It probably started out as a sandbar formed by crosscurrents between the mouth of the Kahana Stream and the ocean. Then the Hawaiians fortified the exterior wall of the sandbar with rocks from the streambeds and valley slopes. They didn't use any mortar; they knew how to lock the rocks together so the wall could withstand the daily wave action. The loose cobble and sand fill allowed water to move through the wall. Standing three to four feet wide and about four feet above the high tide, the 500-foot wall enclosed seven acres of ocean water adjacent to the estuary. Two *makaha* (sluice gates) made of lashed poles allowed water to circulate. The spaces between the poles were wide enough to let small fish swim into the pond, where they grew too big and fat to swim out. Fingerlings were raised in a separate pond and then released into the larger pond. When water flowed seaward with the tides, the fish collected at the sluice gates, where they were easily netted. A pondkeeper lived next to the pond and maintained it. Unfortunately, flooding and tsunamis have caused major damage to the structure. Since the tsunami of 1960, the pond has not been used and has filled with sand and vegetation. It is only visible from the shore at low tide. You can visit the Huilua Fishpond from the east side of the bay, but please do not walk on it.

HIKING

Northern Oahu is a wonderful place for walking, hiking, and jogging. The pristine shoreline is public property, open to everyone. Spectacular mountains and valleys beckon hikers to another world, where trails wind through tropical forests to sparkling waterfalls, inviting swimming ponds, and magnificent vistas.

Hiking Groups

Non-Profit

The following non-profit groups offer group hikes and guided hikes in northern Oahu:

Hawaiian Trail and Mountain Club

P.O. Box 2238, Honolulu 96804, telephone 674-1459 or 377-5442 or 596-4864, htmc.u41.com.

Hawaii Geographic Society

49 S. Hotel St., P.O. Box 1698, Honolulu 96806, telephone 538-3952.

Hawaii Nature Center

2131 Makiki Heights Drive, Honolulu 96822, telephone 955-0100.

The Nature Conservancy

923 Nuuanu Avenue, Honolulu 96817, telephone 537-4508, www.nature.org.

Sierra Club, Hawaii Chapter

P.O. Box 2577, Honolulu 96803, telephone 538-6616, www. hi.sierraclub.org.

Commercial Excursions

North Shore Eco-Surf Tours

P.O. Box 1174, Haleiwa 96712, telephone 638-9503, www.eco-surf-hawaii.com, will take you hiking as well as surfing. For more information, call Stan Van Voorhis at 638-9503 or E-mail stanvan-voorhis@yahoo.com.

Amazing Waterfall Tours

Telephone 375-3137, www.amazingwaterfallbudgettours.com (hikes to waterfalls off the beaten path).

Bike Hawaii

P.O. Box 240170, Honolulu 96824, telephone 734-4214, E-mail: tours@bikehawaii.com, www.bikehawaii.com (a division of 'Ohana Adventure Tours) (excursions on private land in the Kaaawa Valley including hiking, mountain biking, snorkeling and kayaking).

Easy Walks

If you decide to walk, hike or jog along the shore,
beware of sharp coral and lava and crevices that might
contain spiny sea urchins or moray eels. Wear shoes
and remember Rules 3 to 6.

Kaiaka Bay Beach Park

The flat, one-mile loop around this breezy park at 66-449 Haleiwa Road, Waialua, makes a pleasant little walk or jog.

Waimea Valley Self-Guided Trails

There are 3.5 miles of well-maintained trails in the Waimea Valley Historical Nature Park. It is hard to imagine a more beautiful and interesting place to walk or jog. The ¾-mile paved trail through the garden valley is an easy and interesting walk that is suitable for all levels. Guided hikes are available. Check the bulletin board outside the Visitors Center or telephone 638-7766 for the schedule. See Chapter III, Waimea Valley Historical Nature Park.

Ke Ala Pupukea Bicycle Path

The flat, paved Ke Ala Pupukea bike path is also used for walking and jogging. It runs parallel to the Kam Highway from Three Tables Beach in Pupukea Beach Park past Sunset Beach Park to Velzyland. If you get tired, you can take The Bus back.

Turtle Bay Resort Trails

The resort has 12 miles of oceanfront trails. One set heads west along Turtle Bay to lovely Kawela Bay. The other heads east along a secluded shoreline to Kahuku Point, the northernmost tip of the island. These flat, well-maintained trails are suitable for all levels. Trail maps are posted outside the hotel and in the lobby and are available from the concierge.

The Koa and Kilo Loop Trail in Ahupuaa O Kahana State Park

This 1.2-mile loop trail has an elevation gain of less than 100 feet. Ideal for novices, it begins in a grassy area, continues through a dense forest, and ends at a clearing affording a beautiful view of Kahana Bay. The trail is marked with botanical guides and historical sites, including the Kapaeleele Koa (fishing shrine) and Keaniani Kilo (lookout) overlooking the bay. Take Kam Highway to Ahupuaa O Kahana State Park, turn *mauka* on Kahana Valley Road, and park near the Visitors Center. Look for the Koa and Kilo Loop Trail brochure in the weather-resistant box outside the Visitors Center and the metal sign at the small parking lot pointing to the trail.

Backcountry Trails

The following brief descriptions are intended to give you a feel for some of the most popular backcountry trails in northern Oahu. The trails are listed in clockwise order from the northwest to the southeast. The Hawaiian Trail and Mountain Club, Sierra Club, and other groups offer organized hikes. If you prefer to go on your own, please take the necessary precautions. Remember that the information provided here is incomplete. You are responsible for obtaining detailed trail maps and informing yourself about current conditions. If you hike in the mountains, be aware of your own ability and the hazardous conditions that may occur. Volcanic soil and rock can be unstable and crumble under your feet. There may also be a danger of falling rocks and flash floods. Do not attempt to ford streams if the water is more than knee-high, and do not hike in the backcountry when it is raining or rain is predicted. Use appropriate footwear and be sure to bring water, snacks, a hat, sunscreen, and mosquito repellent. Note that cell phones generally do not work on mountain trails.

Kaena Point Trail

See Biking, Mountain Bike Trails. Organized hikes to Kaena Point are conducted by the Hawaiian Trail and Mountain Club and the Sierra Club. This hike has many highlights, including spectacular views, a refreshing swim at Yokohama Beach, and the Kaena Point Natural Area Refuge. The refuge was created in 1983 to preserve the delicate flora and fauna, which had been severely damaged by the railway and all-terrain vehicles. In November the Laysan Albatross breeds here; the sandy areas in the refuge serve as potential breeding sites. Seabirds, including red-footed and brown boobies, the wedge-tailed shearwater, and the brown noddy, are common. The rare Hawaiian monk seal favors the area, along with dolphins and green sea turtles. Humpback whales can be seen breaching offshore during the winter breeding season.

Kealia Trail

This trail is not suitable for young or inexperienced hikers. The seven-mile round trip is a strenuous hike with an elevation gain of 2,000 feet. The first half of the hike is a steep zigzag climb up the volcanic bluff above Dillingham Airfield, with 19 switchbacks and loose rocks demanding caution. There is no shade on the bluff, so begin early and bring plenty of water, hats, and sunscreen. Watch your footing and be sure to stop walking before you enjoy the views of the shoreline and the gliders soaring above the airfield. The ascent ends at a grove of ironwood trees on the ridge. The second half of the route leads through forests to the ridgeline, with an interesting variety of vegetation and birds. Stay on the dirt road that begins on the far side of the ironwood grove until it reaches a T-junction with the Kuaokala Access Road. Turn left (east) on the Kuaokala Access Road and continue on it to a signed four-way junction. At the four-way junction, bear right on the Kuaokala Trail, which takes you along the ridgeline to the summit overlook. The reward is a breathtaking view of the Makua Valley 1,000 feet below, with sheer dark cliffs rising behind it. Further east the ridgeline rises to Mount Kaala, the highest point on the island. Do not walk into the Makua Valley—it is a military range that is sometimes used for live-fire exercises. The Kuaokala Access Road continues eastward to an abandoned Nike missile site and the Makua Rim Trail, and westward to the Kaena Point Satellite Tracking Station, where access is by permit only. Be aware that the Kuaokala area is used for pig and bird hunting. The best time for this hike is between February and April, after the hunting seasons and before the summer heat. To reach the Kealia trailhead, take the Farrington Highway past Dillingham Airfield, turn left at the far west end of the airfield, and drive through the access gate. The gate is open from 7 a.m. to 6 p.m. Drive around to the other side of the runway and park in the paved lot behind the air traffic control building. Walk *mauka* along the wide gravel road, go around a chain across the road, and bear left at the junction, keeping the old concrete aircraft hangar on your right. Continue to the green fence line, where there is a posted trailhead sign.

Kuaokala Trail

The Kuaokala Trail is a six-mile loop along the Waianae ridgeline above Kaena Point. From the Mokuleia side, the hike begins with a zigzag ascent from the coastal plain up the 1,000-foot escarpment above Dillingham Airfield, making the round trip approximately ten miles. This ascent is too difficult for young or novice hikers. At the top, the trail levels out and affords splendid views of both sides of the Waianae Range. The six-mile loop can be taken in either direction. Many native trees and plants, including tapa and yellow hibiscus, decorate the path. The Makua Valley Overlook is spectacular, but remember not to walk into Makua Valley, as it is a military training area that is sometimes used for live fire exercises. The best time to hike this area is between February and April, after pig and bird hunting seasons and before the summer heat. To reach the Kuaokala Trail, follow the directions for the Kealia Trail trailhead. At the beginning of the Kealia Trail, the Kuaokala Trail goes off to the right. Alternatively, you can start at the Kaena Point Satellite Tracking

Station. A permit from the State Division of Forestry and Wildlife is required for this hike. Contact the Hawaii Division of Forestry and Wildlife, 151 Punchbowl Street, Room 131, Honolulu 996813, telephone 587-0166, fax 587-0160, or 2135 Makiki Heights Road, Honolulu, HI 96822, telephone 973-9778, fax 973-9781. It is wise to call the Kaena Point Facility at 697-4311 prior to departure to check on access status due to various levels of security.

Mokuleia Access Road

East of the Dillingham Airfield, the Mokuleia Access Road winds up the volcanic face of the Waianae Range to the Peacock Flats Campground. From the campground, a ½ mile jeep trail takes you to the boundary of the Pahole Natural Area Reserve, where a hiking trail leads to a lookout over the Makua Valley. Again, do not walk into the Makua Valley as it is a military training area that is sometimes used for live-fire exercises. From the Peacock Flats Campground, the paved road continues to the Kuaokala Access Road, which connects to the Kealia Trail and the Kaena Point Satellite Tracking Station. See Biking, Mountain Bike Trails. The climb up the bluff is steep and not suitable for novice hikers. Intrepid hikers can make a challenging day of it by seeding a car at Dillingham Airfield near the Kealia Trail, hiking up the Mokuleia Access Road to the campground, detouring to the lookout over the Makua Valley, continuing along the ridge from the campground to the Kealia Trail, and hiking down the Kealia Trail to the seeded car. Be aware that this area is used for hunting. The best time to hike is between February and April, after pig and bird hunting seasons and before the summer heat.

The Kaunala Trail On The Pupukea Ridge—Weekends and Holidays

The Kaunala Trail is a scenic six-mile loop through lush tropical vegetation on the ridges and gulches of the Pupukea Forest Reserve. The elevation gain is only about 500 feet. See Biking, Mountain Bike Trails.

Laie Trail

Access to the Laie Trail requires a permit from Hawaii Reserves, Inc., 55-510 Kam Highway, Laie 96762 (in the Laie Village Shopping Center), telephone 293-9201, or Serena Johnson-Mailau, 293-6461. This is a 12-mile round trip hike with a 2,200-foot gain in elevation. The trail begins along a red dirt road and climbs to a large hill with a shady grove of Cook pines and a nice view of the shoreline. From there, it contours along the left side of the ridge with strawberry guava trees lining the path. About halfway to the summit, a steep side trail leads to a lovely little swimming hole with waterfalls above and below it. From there, the trail crosses a landslide and passes through a wet native forest to the Koolau summit, where there are breathtaking views of both sides of the island. Below is the junction with the Koolau Summit Trail, an 18.5-mile, poorly maintained expert route along the top of the Koolau Range. If you plan to hike all the way to the summit, bring a lunch and plan to spend the whole day on the trail. To reach the Laie Trail, take the Kam Highway to Laie, turn *mauka* at the Laie community sign onto Naniloa Loop, follow Naniloa Loop to the traffic circle, and exit the circle on Poohaili St. Continue on Poohaili to Laie Field and park by the ballpark. From the ballpark, continue on foot on the paved road, and head right at the fork through the yellow gate to the trailhead at the second gate.

Koloa Gulch Trail

Access to the Koloa Gulch Trail requires a permit from Hawaii Reserves, Inc., 55-510 Kam Highway, Laie 96762 (in the Laie Village Shopping Center), telephone 293-9201, or Serena Johnson-Mailau, 293-6461. This is a seven-mile round-trip hike with a 1,300-foot gain in elevation. After climbing to an open ridge with wonderful views of Oahu's untamed northeastern mountains, the route drops down to Koloa Stream and meanders through a narrow ravine full of native vegetation. The trail crosses Koloa Stream several dozen times. The rocks are slippery, and the trail virtually vanishes as the gulch narrows and steepens and the ridges on each side grow higher. At the fork, keep to the right. About 30 minutes past the fork you will arrive at a deep swimming pool with the Koloa Double Waterfall dropping into it. From the pool, look around the first waterfall to see the second one above it. For a second reward, go back to the spot where the stream splits and take the left fork off the main trail. The left fork leads to another pool and waterfall, but it is a longer hike and not as spectacular as the right fork. This hike is most enjoyable in July and August, when the mountain apples and strawberry guava ripen and the sun is high enough to warm the pools. To reach the trailhead, take the Kam Highway to Aakahii Gulch Road, which runs *mauka* from the highway between Pounders and Kokololio Beach Parks (about .3 miles north of Kokololio Beach Park). Follow Aakahii Gulch Road to the trailhead. A memorial at the trailhead to a Boy Scout who died in a 1994 flash flood is a somber reminder to stay off the trail if there is any danger of flash flooding. Felt-bottomed tabi or good hiking shoes are recommended for traction on slippery rocks.

Koloa Ridge Trail

Access to the Koloa Ridge Trail requires a permit from Hawaii Reserves, Inc., 55-510 Kam Highway, Laie 96762 (in the Laie Village Shopping Center), telephone 293-9201, or Serena Johnson-Mailau, 293-6461. This is a short ridge hike that begins at the same trailhead as the Koloa Gulch Trail. Instead of continuing on the graded trail where it turns right and descends into Koloa Gulch, continue along the ridgeline uphill toward the Koolau crest. The ridge veers to the south and ascends a 680-foot spur to the top of Kaipapau Ridge. This is wild territory, with Koloa Gulch on the north and Aakakii Gulch on the south. To reach the trailhead, follow the directions to the Koloa Gulch Trail.

Hauula Loop Trails

The Hauula Loop Trails are two 2.5-mile loop trails with a 600-foot gain in elevation and good views. They are suitable for novice or intermediate hikers. The route starts at the mouth of Hanaimoa

Gulch and rises gently along its north ridge to the fork where the loops separate. Both loops switchback to the top of the ridge, descend slightly, and cross Waipilopilo Gulch, then climb to the top of the next ridge, which overlooks Kaipapau Gulch.

Hauula Loop

The right (counterclockwise) fork is one of the most popular and beautiful hikes on Oahu. It is also popular with mountain bikers. See Biking, Backcountry Trails.

Papali Loop

The left (clockwise) fork descends into Papali Gulch through native vegetation and a stand of kukui trees. From the loop trail, there is a good view down into Maakua Gulch. Although the Papali Loop is pleasant and easy, many hikers prefer the scenic rewards of the Hauula Loop.

Maakua Gulch Trail

This is a difficult six-mile hike from the same Hauula trailhead, with an elevation gain of 900 feet. It branches off from the Papali Loop and follows the streambed to a lovely little waterfall with a pool about four feet deep surrounded by steep cliffs. The best time to take this hike is July or August, when the mountain apples are in season and the sun is high enough to warm the pool. This trail is very narrow and forces you to crisscross the slippery rocks in the streambed numerous times – in essence, the trail *is* the streambed for most of the way. By the time you reach the waterfall, the gulch is so tight that you can reach out and touch the sides. To get to the pool, you must hike or swim through a short narrows. Before jumping in, look up— you will see a razor-thin slit of sky between the sheer canyon walls. If you do go, take reef-walking shoes and be prepared for numerous stream crossings and rock hopping from boulder to boulder. Do not attempt this hike alone or if it is raining or rain is predicted, as the stream is subject to flash flooding in heavy rains.

The Maakua Ridge Trail

This 3.3 mile trail traverses the Maakua ridgeline. See Biking, Backcountry Trails.

To reach the Hauula trails, take the Kam Highway to Hauula. Watch for the green Hauula community sign across the Kam Highway from the north end of Hauula Beach Park. At the sign, turn *mauka* on Hauula Homestead Road. Where Hauula Homestead Road turns to the left, go straight on Maakua Road, park before the gate where you will not block anyone, and walk through the Hawaiian home-land community to the end of Maakua Road, where a sign marks the trails. Remember Rule No. 2.

Kahana Valley Trails

This is the wettest valley on Oahu, so the ground is often muddy and the rocks slippery. Bring appropriate footwear, mosquito repellent, and raingear. Remember that the dense vegetation makes it easy to get lost. Due to the high ridges on the west, it gets dark early. The valley is home to a large population of feral pigs and a favorite stomping ground for hunters. Note that the hiking distances for the following trails are extended by the .6 mile distance from the parking area to the trailhead.

The Nakoa Trail

This is the most popular trail in Kahana Valley, suitable for nov-ice or intermediate hikers. The 3.5-mile loop leads across Kahana Stream and a number of sidestreams to an inviting swimming hole. The elevation gain is 400 feet. The water tumbling down the moun-tain is clear and cool and the pools are deep and inviting. For a pleas-ant novice hike, walk only the first loop, a round trip of about five miles, and be sure to visit the pool near the bamboo. The second loop can be shortened by turning off the trail toward the deep pool near the mango. Other trails deeper in the valley also pass swim-ming holes and offer good views, but are more difficult. For example, the upper trail leads from the second loop and ends at the intake of the Waiahole Ditch. The Waiahole Ditch Trail continues around the back of the Kahana, Waikane, and Waiahole Valleys.

The Puu Piei Trail

This rugged climb up the peak overlooking Kahana Bay is only a three-mile round trip, but it has an elevation gain of 1,700 feet. The reward is a spectacular view of Kahana Bay from a *kilo* used by Hawaiian fish spotters. A short detour from the Puu Piei trail leads to another ancestral fishing shrine.

Puu Manamana Trail

This extremely challenging four-mile loop traverses the ridges surrounding the valley, with an elevation gain of 2,100 feet. It is steep, dangerous, and strictly for experienced hikers.

To reach the Kahana Valley trailhead, take the Kam Highway down the Windward Shore to Ahupuaa ʻO Kahana State Park. Turn *mauka* into Kahana Valley Road, park at the sign, and walk up the road through the Hawaiian-homeland community to the trailhead. Obtain trail maps and information on current conditions in advance or take a guided hike with an organized group. For more information, call the Honolulu Division of State Parks, 587-0300.

Hikes Requiring A Military Permit

A military permit is required for access to hiking trails on military property. For permission, write to: Commander, U.S. Army Garrison, Hawaii, Schofield Barracks, HI 96857 (attn: APVG-GWY-O).

Wahiawa Trails

In the Wahiawa District, an Army permit is required to access the **three-mile Puu Kaua Trail** in the Honouliuli Preserve above Kunia, the **six-mile Kanehoa-Hapapa Trail** in the Schofield Barracks Forest Reserve and Honouliuli Preserve, the **five-mile Kalena Trail** in the Schofield Barracks Forest Reserve, the **five-mile Wahiawa Hills loop trail** in the ʻEwa 2 Reserve above Wahiawa, the **two-mile Poamoho Ridge Trail** in the Kawailoa and ʻEwa Forest

Reserves above Helemano, and the **seven-mile Schofield-Waikane Trail** connecting Schofield Barracks in Wahiawa and the Waikane Valley on the windward side of the island.

Haleiwa Trails

Kawainui Trail

The Kawainui Trail is an easy six-mile round trip with an 800-foot gain in elevation in the Kawailoa Forest Reserve above Haleiwa. The hike begins on a military road, descends into Kawai Iki Gulch, and crosses Kawai Iki Stream into Kawainui Gulch. Crisscrossing the Kawainui Stream, it passes lovely pools and groves of mountain apple and strawberry guava until it arrives at a swimming pool surrounded by cliffs and *kukui* trees. If you swim across the pool and climb out on the other side, you will find two little waterfalls a short distance upstream. The drive to the trailhead is tougher than the hike. Take the Haleiwa Bypass (Route 83). Turn right on Emerson Road, which is the first right north of the turnoff into Haleiwa Town. Take Emerson Road to the stop sign, turn right, and go through a gate where the pavement ends. Then take a sharp right on a paved road and go through a second gate. The first road on the left after the gate is 'Opae'ula Road. Stop here and reset your tripmeter to 0. Continue 1.5 miles to a fork in the road, take the right fork, continue another mile to the end of the paved road, and go through a third gate. When the road forks again, take the left fork and stay on 'Opaeula Road until it ends at a reservoir 5.2 miles from where you reset your tripmeter. Continue straight on a military road called Paaala Uka Pupukea, which is rutted in spots but passable for two-wheel drive vehicles in dry conditions. Take the military road past Opaeula Lodge on the right. At 6.7 miles, the road turns sharp left and reaches a junction with a side road on the right. Follow the rough side road to the trailheads of the Opaeula and Kawai Iki hikes, continue past Palama Uka Camp on the right at 6.9 miles, and park in the grassy lot on the left at 7.3 miles.

Opaeula Trail

This is another stream hike with the same road access as the Kawainui Trail. An easy, two-mile round trip with only a 200-foot gain in elevation, it passes several appealing swimming holes on the way to another delightful pond. Follow the directions for the Kawainui Trailhead to the Opaeula trailhead. Park on the right side of the main road just past the junction and be sure to leave enough room for military vehicles to pass by. Walk up the rough side road to the Opaeula and Kawai Iki Trailhead.

Kawai Iki Trail

This route is longer than, but similar to, the Opaeula Trail. It begins at the same trailhead, but continues along the ridge past the turnoff for the Opaeula Trail and descends into Kawai Iki Gulch. The irrigation ditch leads to several attractive swimming holes.

HORSEBACK RIDING

Northern Oahu is horse country. Five different equestrian facilities provide a wide range of riding opportunities.

Oceanfront Riding

Hawaii Polo Oceanfront Trail Rides

68-411 Farrington Highway, Waialua, telephone 220-5153, www.hawaiipolo.com.

The Hawaii Polo Club offers oceanfront trail rides and riding and polo lessons on its 100-acre ranch in Mokuleia. All of the mounts are thoroughbred polo horses. The trails wind along the beach with lovely views. Group rides are available on Tuesday, Thursday, and Saturday. Private and full moon rides can be arranged. For reservations, call Jeanna at 220-5153. For polo lessons, call Enrique Diaz at 224-9310.

Turtle Bay Resort

57-091 Kam Highway, Kahuku, telephone 293-8811, www.turtlebayresort.com.

Horseback riding at Turtle Bay begins with a shuttle from the hotel lobby to the charming red stables. The most popular ride is a three-mile venture through an ironwood forest, past a World War II bunker, and along the white sandy beach of Kawela Bay. A 45-minute ride is perfect for young children and dudes. Evening rides, carriage rides, hay wagon rides, and couples-themed rides are also available. Experienced riders can arrange trot and canter rides. All of the mounts are quarterhorses. For reservations, call the concierge at 293-8811.

Mountain Riding

Kawailoa Ranch

61-676 Kam Highway, Haleiwa, telephone 637-4224.

Kawailoa Ranch does not offer trail rides to the public, but has extensive equestrian facilities for boarding, riding, and training horses. The ranch serves as the home of many local equestrian groups and holds numerous riding events and activities, including rodeos and horsemanship and riding clinics. For more information, call Uncle George Ai, the manager, at 637-4224.

Happy Trails Hawaii

59-231 Pupukea Road, Pupukea, telephone 638-7433, E-mail: reservations@HappyTrailsHawaii.com, www.HappyTrailsHawaii.com.

Owner Mark Becker has operated this beautiful horse ranch on the Pupukea Ridge for over a decade. The trail rides navigate tropical forests on the Pupukea and Waimea ridges. Flora and fauna include guava, kukui nut, ironwood, tropical birds, and even wild pigs on occasion. Riders see the gaming stations where Hawaiians use nets to capture female pigs for breeding. The trail guides provide fascinating information about the Hawaiian *alii* who lived in the area. There are spectacular views of the mountains, Waimea Valley, the shoreline, and the huge expanse of ocean below. In the winter, riders on the ridge can sometimes spot the spumes of humpback whales far off in the ocean. Children as young as six can have their own horse. Happy Trails operates Monday through Saturday from 8:00 a.m. to 5:00 p.m. and Sunday from 8:00 a.m. to 3:00 p.m. The maximum weight is 235 pounds. For reservations, call 638-RIDE (7433) or E-mail Reservations@HappyTrailsHawaii.com.

Gunstock Ranch

56-250 Kam Highway, Laie 96762, telephone 341-0788, E-mail: management@gunstockranch.com, www.gunstockranch.com.

Gunstock Ranch is a 400-acre working ranch at the base of the Koolau Mountains, minutes from the Turtle Bay Resort. Founded by Max Smith, a former state veterinarian, it is still owned and operated by his family. The ranch offers a wide range of riding experiences, including 20-minute pony rides for children two to seven years old; morning, sunset, and four-hour lunch rides for all skill levels ages seven and up, and advanced trail rides for experienced riders. Guided moonlight rides are offered each full moon. Boarding, stud services, trailer hauling, and other services are also available. For reservations, call 341-0788 or E-mail management@gunstockranch.com.

POLO

The Hawaii Polo Club

68-411 Farrington Highway, Waialua 96791, telephone 637-7669, www.hawaiipolo.com.

Polo Match at Mokuleia

The Hawaii Polo Club holds polo matches at its oceanfront polo field every Sunday from May to September. This is a great, inexpensive entertainment for a Sunday afternoon. The gates open at 11:00 a.m. for tailgating and ocean swimming. The main event begins at 2:00 p.m. with the pony parade and first match. There are delightful half-time activities like horse races, rugby matches, and skydiving exhibitions. After the second match, the band keeps playing, the bar and food outlets stay open, and the party continues until sunset.

The Polo Club hosts inter-island matches and teams from around the world. The fast-paced action makes polo an exciting spectator sport. The field consists of ten acres of grass, 300 yards long by 160 yards wide, which is equivalent to ten football fields. A match consists of six periods or "chukkers," each seven minutes long. Play begins with a throw-in of the ball by the umpire at the opening of each chukker and after each goal. Only injuries or penalties can stop a polo match. Except for tack repair, no time-outs or substitutions are allowed.

The admission fee is nominal. Parking is available on both sides of the field. If you want to swim in the ocean, drive around to the *maikai* side of the field. If you want to meet people and use the concessions, park on the *mauka* side. The **Hawaii Polo Beach Bar & Grill** serves gourmet plate lunches. There is a *pupu* (appetizer) menu and full bar from noon to sunset. Lunch wagons also serve food and beverages, or you can bring your own picnic and tailgate.

SHOPPING

It isn't possible to list or rate all the wonderful little shops in northern Oahu. For what it's worth, here are our favorites.

Art

Haleiwa Art Gallery

66-252 Kam Highway, Haleiwa 96712, telephone 637-3368, www.haleiwaartgallery.com, open 10:00 a.m. to 6:00 p.m. daily.

Haleiwa Arts Festival

Held in Haleiwa Beach County Park on the third weekend of July.

Bakeries

Ted's Bakery

59-024 Kam Highway, Sunset Beach, telephone 638-8207.

Waialua Bakery

66-200 Kam Highway, Haleiwa, telephone 637-9079.

Gifts and Souvenirs

Oceans in Glass

North Shore Marketplace, 66-250 Kam Highway, Haleiwa 96712, telephone 637-3366.

ꞈ Creations & Interiors
66-079 Kam Highway, Haleiwa 96712, telephone 637-1505, www.globalcreationsinteriors.com.

Foodland
59-720 Kam Highway, Pupukea, telephone 638-8081.
Laie Village Shopping Center, 55-510 Kam Highway, Laie, telephone 293-4443.

Polynesian Cultural Center Gift Shops
55-350 Kam Highway, Laie, telephone 293-3000.

Groceries

Foodland
59-720 Kam Highway, Pupukea, telephone 638-8081.
Laie Village Shopping Center, 55-510 Kam Highway, Laie, telephone 293-4443.

North Shore Country Market
Sunset Elementary School parking lot (across Kam Highway from Ehukai Beach Park), Saturdays 8:00 a.m. to 2:00 p.m., www.northshorecountrymarket.com: local produce.

Tamura's Market
Hauula Kai Shopping Center, 54-316 Kam Highway, Hauula, telephone 232-2332: seafood, poke, sushi, and produce.

Hawaiian Arts and Crafts

Treasures of Polynesia
Turtle Bay Resort, 57-091 Kam Highway, Kahuku 96731, telephone 293-6000.

Polynesian Cultural Center Gift Shops
55-350 Kam Highway, Laie, telephone 293-3000.

Jewelry

Jeanie's Jewelry

Turtle Bay Resort, 57-091 Kam Highway, Kahuku 96731, telephone 293-9049.

Ladies' Clothing

Silver Moon Emporium

North Shore Marketplace, 66-250 Kam Highway, Haleiwa 96712, telephone 637-7710.

Oogenesis

66-249 Kam Highway, Haleiwa 96712, telephone 637-4580.

Kohala Bay Collections

Turtle Bay Resort lobby, 57-091 Kam Highway, Kahuku 96731, telephone 293-6000.

Men's Clothing

Kohala Bay Collections

Turtle Bay Resort lobby, 57-091 Kam Highway, Kahuku 96731, telephone 293-6000.

Octopus Ink

Turtle Bay Resort lower level, 57-091 Kam Highway, Kahuku 96731, telephone 293-6000.

Sports Equipment

Barnfield's Raging Isle Surf & Cycle

North Shore Marketplace, 66-250 Kam Highway, Haleiwa 96712, telephone 637-7707.

Surf 'n' Sea

62-595 Kam Highway, Haleiwa 96712, telephone 637-SURF (7873).

Surfing Memorabilia

North Shore Surf and Cultural Museum

North Shore Marketplace, 66-250 Kam Highway, Haleiwa 96712, telephone 637-8888.

Strong Current Surf Design

66-214 Kam Highway, Haleiwa 96712, telephone 637-3406.

Surf Wear and Beach Wear

North Shore Swimwear

North Shore Marketplace, 66-250 Kam Highway, Haleiwa, 96712, telephone 637-7000, 1-800-24SUITS, www.northshore-swimwear.com.

Patagonia

North Shore Marketplace, 66-250 Kam Highway, Haleiwa 96712, telephone 637-1245.

SKATEBOARDING

A skateboard park on the North Shore is still in the planning stages. In the meantime, **Crank and Carve,** Haleiwa Shopping Center, 66-165 Kam Highway, Haleiwa, telephone 637-2121, serves as "a community-based skateboarding center."

SOCCER

Waialua District Park, 67-180 Goodale Avenue, Waialua, telephone 637-6061, has indoor and outdoor soccer facilities. **Sunset Beach Neighborhood Park**, 59-360 Kam Highway, Sunset, telephone 638-7051, and **Kahuku District Park**, 56-170 Pualalea Street, Kahuku, telephone 293-5116, have outdoor soccer facilities.

SOFTBALL

Softball fields are located in **Haleiwa Beach Park**, 62-449 Kam Highway, Haleiwa; and **Kahuku District Park**, 56-170 Pualalea Street, Kahuku, telephone 293-5116.

TENNIS

The Turtle Bay Resort Tennis Center

57-091 Kam Highway, Kahuku, www.turtlebayresort.com, Tennis Court & Pro Shop telephone 293-6024. The resort has ten plexi-pave courts. Individual lessons, tennis clinics for all levels and a player match-up service are available.

The Kuilima Condominiums

Each condo community has tennis courts available for residents and guests. For information, call the resident manager, telephone 293-8217.

Public Tennis Courts

Play is subject to regulations and time limits. Courts may be reserved by written permit issued by the Department of Parks and Recreation.

Wahiawa District Park

1139-A Kilani Avenue, Wahiawa: four lighted courts, backboard available, director Fred Sohl, telephone 621-5663.

Waialua District Park

67-180 Goodale Road, Waialua: four lighted courts, backboard available, director Laura Whittaker, telephone 637-9721.

Sunset Beach Neighborhood Park

59-360 Kam Highway, Haleiwa: two lighted courts, director Tom Walsh, telephone 638-7051.

TROPICAL GARDENS

Wahiawa Botanical Garden

This 27-acre collection of tropical horticulture is located at 1396 California Avenue, Wahiawa, telephone 621-7321. The garden dates back to the 1920s, when the Hawaii Sugar Planters Association leased the land from the state for an experimental arboretum. Many of the trees planted then are still growing in the garden. The property was transferred to the county in 1950 and opened as a botanical garden in 1957. Today, it is part of the Honolulu Botanical Gardens, featuring tropical flora that thrive in the cooler, shady, humid habitat of this tropical rain forest. An effort has been made to develop the collection of native Hawaiian plants. To reach the Garden, take the Kam Highway straight into the center of Wahiawa and turn *mauka* (east) on California Avenue. There is a sign before the intersection in the northbound lane of the Kam Highway. Call in advance to arrange a guided tour.

Dole Pineapple Plantation

This attractive tourist stop at 64-1550 Kam Highway, telephone (808) 621-8408, www.dole-plantation.com, a few miles north of Wahiawa, offers an interesting walking tour through a tropical garden and the "world's largest maze" with nearly two miles of paths lined by over 11,000 colorful Hawaiian plants. The Dole Pineapple Plantation is open daily from 9 a.m. until 5:30 p.m. See Chapter III.

Waimea Valley Historical Nature Park

Waimea Valley is not to be missed. Located at 59-864 Kam Highway, Waimea, telephone 638-7766, this exquisite park features world-class botanical collections in 35 separate gardens representing flora from different parts of the world and different groups of plants. The gardens contain over 5,000 taxa of tropical plants, all of them carefully documented and tracked. Stroll through the Hawaiian collection and enjoy an assortment of plants found only in Hawaii. Many of them are very rare; those marked with a red label are endangered. The Hawaiian ethnobotanical garden contains one of the best collections of Polynesian plants found anywhere. Call 638-7766 or check the bulletin board outside the gift shop for the schedule of guided tours and other events. See Chapter III.

Laie LDS Temple Gardens

The LDS Temple at 55-600 Naniloa Loop, Laie, telephone 293-9297, has extensive tropical gardens that are open to the public from 9:00 a.m. until 8:00 p.m. The Visitors Center is also open for tours.

VOLLEYBALL

Lighted volleyball courts are located in **Haleiwa Beach Park**, 62-449 Kam Highway, Haleiwa; **Pupukea Beach Park**, 59-727 Kam Highway, Pupukea, telephone 638-7213; and **Sunset Beach Neighborhood Park**, 59-360 Kam Highway, Sunset, telephone 638-7051. Unlighted courts are located in **Kahuku District Park**, 56-170 Pualalea Street, Kahuku, telephone 293-5116. Beach volleyball is available at **Waimea Bay Beach Park**, 61-031 Kam Highway, Waimea, and **Kuilima Cove at the Turtle Bay Resort**.

VII. ACTIVITIES IN THE AIR

*Dillingham Airfield and Gliderport is the center of airborne
activities in northern Oahu. Be sure to check the license,
qualifications, and safety record of the vendor in advance.*

AIR TOURS

At least three air tours operate at the Dillingham Airfield and
Gliderport in Mokuleia. **Eco Air Tours**, telephone 839-1499 or 1-
888-773-0303, offers air tours of six islands. **Interisland Airways,**
telephone 836-8080, offers a narrated tour that includes overhead
views of six islands plus a land tour on the Big Island of Hawaii. **Surf
Air Tours**, telephone 637-7003, offers airplane flights in Cessna
172s or 206s for 30 minutes along the North Shore or a longer circle-
island tour. **Paradise Helicopters** at the Turtle Bay Resort, telephone 293-2570, offers custom helicopter tours of Oahu and other
islands.

BIPLANE RIDES

Stearman Biplane Rides, Dillingham Airfield and Gliderport
in Mokuleia, telephone 637-4461 or 561-6389, www.peacock.com/
biplane, E-mail loopdloop@hawaii.rr.com, offers open cockpit flying
in a fully restored 1941 Stearman bi-plane. The bi-plane carries only
one passenger, who sits in the front cockpit with the pilot in the rear.
You can choose a scenic ride over the North Shore or other parts of
Oahu, a historic tour of Pearl Harbor retracing the Japanese bombing
route, or a combination of both. Aerobatics are optional.

GLIDING

A glider ride over the North Shore is an unforgettable experience. With average visibility of 30 to 40 miles, the views of the mountains, shoreline, and ocean are breathtaking. Bill Star and Sam Bleadon introduced gliding on the North Shore in 1970, when they came to Hawaii fresh out of college and started the Honolulu Soaring Club. They have operated continuously at Dillingham Airfield ever since. **Glider Ride Hawaii,** telephone 637-0207, www.gliderride-hawaii.com, now has three Schweizer SGS 2-32 high performance gliders for one and two-passenger scenic rides; two Schweizer SGS 2-33s for one-passenger scenic rides, instructional training of student pilots, and rental to qualified glider pilots; a two-seat Schleicher A-S-K-21high performance glider for aerobatics, and three tow planes. Passengers can take a scenic tour, a mini-lesson ride with hands-on flight controls, an aerobatic soaring flight with loops and rolls, or a combination. Glider Ride Hawaii operates from 10:00 a.m. to 5:30 p.m. daily, and sometimes later in the summer months when the days are longer. Reservations are advisable.

HANG GLIDING

Paradise Air, telephone 497-6033, www.paradiseairhawaii.com, offers power hang-gliding in two-seat ultralights powered by an 80 h.p. engine with a hang-glider type wing. It offers instructions seven days a week, weather permitting. Training flights typically head up the North Shore and around to the Windward Shore. When the winds are right, flights may explore the Leeward Coast along Makaha and Kaena Point. Paradise Air is located in the white hangars at the southwest corner of Dillingham Airfield. Reservations are required. **North Shore Hang Gliding and Ultralighting,** telephone 637-3178, also offers hang gliding and ultralighting at Dillingham Airfield.

HELICOPTER TOURS

Paradise Helicopters is located at the Turtle Bay Resort, Kahuku, telephone 293-2570. Three tours of Oahu, ranging from 20 to 60 minutes, are available. Custom tours can be arranged.

SKYDIVING

Skydive Hawaii, 68-760 Farrington Highway, Mokuleia, telephone 637-9700, www.hawaiiskydiving.com, offers tandem skydiving and aerobatics as well as aerobatic stunt plane rides. **Pacific International Skydiving Center**, telephone 637-7472, E-mail: skydivectr@aol.com, www.pacific-skydiving.com, offers skydiving lessons, high altitude jumps for one person or groups, and tandem skydiving from a PAC-750 aircraft. Professional jumps and exhibitions are available.

VIII. DINING

Northern Oahu's rich ethnic mix has produced a fascinating culinary heritage, with its own foods, flavors, sauces, and techniques. Local specialties include teriyaki chicken and beef, Japanese bento boxes, Korean barbecue, Chinese and Filipino specialties, Portuguese sausage, locally raised shrimp, fresh seafood, and Kahuku corn and fruit. Garden farms have taken over old sugar and pineapple fields, adding to the variety of fresh foods available. A traditional plate lunch includes a healthy portion of meat or fish, two scoops of white rice, and a serving of macaroni salad. Some eateries now offer a "healthy plate lunch" with fewer carbs and a green salad instead of macaroni salad. For those who missed World War II, this is your opportunity to savor spam; it was a staple on the island during the War and never lost its popularity. Suggestion: If you are on a tight budget, have a plate lunch and pick up huli huli chicken, Kahuku shrimp, or prepared food from a grocery, wagon, or stand for dinner, or enjoy a picnic or barbecue supper at a beach park as the sun sets.

Please consider this information a starting point. Check on current hours, prices, and other factors that are important to you. There is no guarantee that the food, pricing, and service at any establishment will be the same as we found them. We can promise, however, that none of the restaurants we tested knew that we were writing a guidebook or had any reason to treat us differently than other customers.

This Guide uses two simple symbols:
- * for the author's favorites, and
- $ for eateries that are reasonably priced for the level of food and service they provide.

Six categories are listed:

1. Luaus
2. Restaurants (quality cuisine with table service)
3. Cafes (home-style food and local specialties with table service in a casual setting)
4. Outdoor Dining (wagons and snack bars with outdoor seating)
5. Fast Food (local take-out food and fast food chains)
6. Other Specialties (shave ice, coffee shops, etc.)

For travelers' convenience, all the categories except luaus are separated into five geographic areas:

1. The Central Plateau
2. Haleiwa Town
3. Haleiwa to Kahuku
4. Laie Town
5. Hauula to Kaaawa

Note that some of these businesses do not accept credit or debit cards. Check before you order. There are plenty of ATMs available if you don't want to carry cash or travelers' checks.

SHORT LIST OF GREAT EATERIES

Though wildly diverse in cuisine, amenities, and cost, the following eateries remain constant favorites because they consistently offer excellent food, good service, and pricing that is appropriate for their food, service, and clientele:

Breakfast
Café Haleiwa, Haleiwa
Ted's Bakery, Sunset Beach
Hukilau Café, Laie

Sunday Brunch
The Turtle Bay Resort

Lunch
Giovanni's Aloha Shrimp Truck, Haleiwa and Kahuku
The Grass Skirt Grill, Haleiwa
Kua Aina, Haleiwa
Shark's Cove Grill, Pupukea
Ted's Bakery, Sunset Beach
Hukilau Café, Laie

Dinner
Phuket Thai Restaurant, Mililani Shopping Center
Cholo's Mexican Restaurant and Margarita Bar, North Shore
Shopping Plaza
21 Degrees North, Turtle Bay Resort
Lei Lei's Bar & Grill, Turtle Bay Resort

Takeout
Laie Chop Suey, Laie Shopping Center

LUAUS

If you want to experience a true Hawaiian luau, skip the overcrowded buffets in Waikiki and enjoy one of these delightful Hawaiian feasts on the North Shore.

Turtle Bay Resort
The Turtle Bay Resort, 57-091 Kam Highway, Kahuku, telephone 293-8811, www.turtlebayresort.com, hosts the "Voyages of Polynesia Luau" every Friday evening. The luau is held on the Kahuku Lawn Terrace, where there are spectacular ocean and sunset views, an elevated stage, and protection from the wind. A banquet room inside the hotel provides a backup for rainy evenings. Reservations are required. The cocktail reception begins at 6:00 p.m. The traditional Hawaiian

feast is followed by a Polynesian show featuring the traditional music and dances of the different cultures of Polynesia.

The Polynesian Cultural Center

The Polynesian Cultural Center in Laie, telephone 293-3333, www.polynesia.com, offers the most authentic *luau* and Polynesian review on Oahu. Held in three venues, it celebrates the ancient tradition of Hawaiian royalty, including a reenactment of the royal court procession, the traditional ritual of removing a roasted pig from the *imu* (fire pit or oven in the ground), a delicious feast of traditional Hawaiian dishes, and Hawaiian songs and dances. The food and entertainment are very good. The *luau* is followed by the spectacular evening show. You can buy a ticket for just the *luau* and/or the evening show without buying an all-day package. Alcoholic beverages are neither available nor allowed inside the Polynesian Cultural Center.

THE CENTRAL PLATEAU

Restaurants

*Assaggio

Assaggio, 95-1249 Meheula Parkway, Mililani, telephone 623-5115, is a popular white tablecloth Italian restaurant with a full bar on the south end of the Mililani Shopping Center. If you want great Italian food in northern Oahu, this is the place. The menu includes an extensive selection of Italian seafood, meat and pasta specialties. The food is excellent. There is a full bar. The service is deliberately paced for leisurely dining, Italian-style, so let your waiter know if you are in a hurry. Also bring a sweater—Assaggio's air conditioning is so cold you may think you are in Alaska rather than Hawaii.

*$Phuket Thai

Phuket Thai, 95-1249 Meheula Parkway, Suite A-6, Mililani, telephone 623-6228, is a white tablecloth restaurant located within the Mililani shopping center. It serves delicious Thai cuisine in a lovely, refined atmosphere. The service is excellent and the prices are very reasonable. Wine and beer are available.

Cafes

Chili's Grill & Bar

Chili's, 95-1245 Meheula Parkway, Mililani, telephone 627-0888, is located on the northern end of the Mililani Shopping Center parking lot. It offers the standard menu and décor of the popular national chain. Not tested—why go to Chili's when we're in Hawaii?

Ruby Tuesday's

Ruby Tuesday's is located on the northern end of the Mililani Shopping Center parking lot, 95-1249 Meheula Parkway, Mililani, telephone 623-4949. It is another multistate chain offering standardized fare. Not tested—again, why eat mainland chain food when we're in Hawaii?

$Zippy's

Zippy's has three locations in the Central Plateau:

- 94-1082 Ka Uka Blvd., Waipio (a few blocks west of Costco), telephone 671-1865.
- 95-1249 Meheula Parkway, Bldg. B, Mililani, telephone 623-1110.
- 100 N. Kam Highway, Wahiawa, telephone 622-4166.

Zippy's is a Hawaiian chain that serves a wide selection of local and diner-style food at reasonable prices. Each location has a sit-down restaurant and quick-service window. The sit-down restaurants are clean and attractive and the service is good. Zippy's is open 24 hours a day, making it a reliable place to stop on the way to and from the airport. You can even order online at www.Zippys.com.

Outdoor Dining

See **Zippy's** above.

Fast Food

Burger King

The Town Center of Mililani (in the Mililani Shopping Center parking lot), telephone 625-5711

Kentucky Fried Chicken

The Colonel has two locations in the Central Plateau:

- The Town Center of Mililani (in the Mililani Shopping Center parking lot), telephone 623-5555.
- 609 California Avenue, Wahiawa, telephone 621-7836.

Maui Mike's Fire-Roasted Chicken

Maui Mike's, 96 S. Kam Highway, Wahiawa (across the street from McDonald's), telephone 622-5900, is a fast-food joint serving slow-cooked meals. Additive-free chicks turn in a rotisserie. The juices dripping into the gas-fueled fire produce delicious, moist chicken. Six dipping sauces are provided. Sandwiches and side dishes like fries and baked beans are also on the menu. Eat in or take the whole thing with you to the Wahiawa Freshwater State Recreation Area or the North Shore for a picnic. Maui Mike's is open Monday to Saturday from 11:00 a.m. to 8:30 p.m.

Mc Donald's

114 S. Kam Highway, Wahiawa, telephone 622-3962

Subway Sandwiches and Salads

Subway has four locations in the Central Plateau:

- 94-1235 Ka Uka Boulevard (just west of Costco), Waipahu, telephone 678-3838.
- 95-1249 Meheula Parkway, Suite D2B (Mililani Shopping Center), telephone 623-1900.

- 823 California Avenue, Wahiawa, telephone 621-9555.
- Kemoo Farms, Wahiawa (north of Wahiawa on the Kam Highway), telephone 622-4555.

Other Specialties

*$Dole Pineapple Plantation

This attractive tourist stop at 64-1550 Kam Highway, Wahiawa, telephone 621-8408, www.dole-plantation.com, serves delicious pineapple confections. It is open daily from 9:00 a.m. until 5:30 p.m.

HALEIWA

Restaurants

*$Cholo's Homestyle Mexican Restaurant & Margarita Bar

Cholo's is located in the North Shore Marketplace, 66-250 Kam Highway, Haleiwa, telephone 637-3059. This charming little establishment serves delicious Mexican food for indoor and outdoor dining and take-out. There is a full bar with the best margaritas in town. Interesting Mexican art and handicrafts decorate the interior and are available for sale. In many ways, Cholo's is the most original, creative restaurant on the North Shore. The food and service are terrific. Readers of *Honolulu Magazine* voted it "Best Mexican Restaurant." Cholo's is open daily from 10:30 a.m. to 9:30 p.m. Reservations are only taken for parties of eight or more.

This Woody surf wagon marks the location of Cholo's.

Haleiwa Joe's Seafood Grille

Haleiwa Joe's is located between the Rainbow Bridge and the Haleiwa Boat Harbor at 66-011 Kam Highway, Haleiwa, telephone 637-8005. It serves a nice surf and turf menu with indoor and outdoor seating. There is a full bar where pub fare is served. The bar is usually packed with locals who meet there to drink, eat, and socialize. Reservations are not taken, and the wait for a table can be long. The food is generally good, but the service is inconsistent. The pricing is a little high for the level of the food and service. Haleiwa Joe's is open for lunch and dinner from 11:30 a.m. until 11:00 p.m. Monday to Thursday and 11:30 a.m. to midnight Friday and Saturday. The patio offers a nice view of the Haleiwa Boat Harbor. Live entertainment is occasionally provided on Friday evening. This is a great place to hang out if you have time to spare, but the unpredictable wait time makes it difficult for customers with children, seniors, or schedules.

*Jameson's By The Sea

With its popular lanai overlooking Waialua Bay at 62-540 Kam Highway, Haleiwa, telephone 637-4336, Jameson's has been one of the most popular restaurants on the North Shore for decades. The comfortable lanai is a lovely place to enjoy the sunset. There is a full bar. The menu focuses on fresh seafood. The food is good if not exciting. The service is excellent, and reservations are taken and honored. Prices are a little high for the level of the cuisine. Jameson's is open weekends from 9:00 a.m. to 9:00 p.m. and weekdays from 11:00 a.m. to 9:00 p.m. Try the crab and shrimp sandwich for lunch and the seafood specials for dinner.

Cafes

Killer Tacos

Killer Taco's is located on the south end of Haleiwa Town at 66-560 Kam Highway, Haleiwa, telephone 637-4573. Not tested.

*$Café Haleiwa

Located at 66-460 Kam Highway, Haleiwa, telephone 637-5516, this funky café has been serving breakfast and lunch to surfers, swimmers, and tourists from all over the world for more than 20 years. It is a comfortable place to enjoy good American or Mexican fare. Open daily from 6:00 a.m. to 2:00 p.m.

Paradise Found Café

Tucked in a charming, hand-painted corner of Celestial Natural Foods at 66-443 Kam Highway, telephone 637-4540, this tiny café serves vegetarian fare, including smoothies, organic soups, fresh-pressed vegetable juices, sandwiches, and healthy plate lunches. It is open from 9:00 a.m. to 5:00 p.m. Monday through Saturday and 9:00 a.m. to 4:00 p.m. on Sunday. Credit and debit cards are not accepted.

Breakers Restaurant & Bar

Breakers is open for lunch, dinner and late-night snacks from 11:00 a.m. to 2:00 a.m. in the North Shore Marketplace, 66-250 Kam Highway, Haleiwa, telephone 637-9898. There is a full bar, with daily drink specials. The food is tasty and the surf décor and videos are fun. Live entertainment is often provided on weekends. Unfortunately, poor management and maintenance problems make Breakers an unreliable choice for a nice meal. Best bet: eat outside on the patio or stop in after dinner for drinks and entertainment.

Kono's

This cute little cafe is located next door to Breakers in the North Shore Marketplace, 66-250 Kam Highway, G110, Haleiwa, telephone 637-9211. Kono's is open from 8:00 a.m. to 4:00 p.m. for breakfast and lunch, with limited seating inside and outside. The surf videos and friendly service make up for fairly ordinary food.

*$Grass Skirt Grill

This charming little café at 66-214 Kam Highway, Haleiwa, telephone 637-4852, serves delicious food at reasonable prices. Seating inside and outside is limited, but the tables are waited quickly and cleaned meticulously. The food is fabulous. Try the mahiburger or shrimp plate. Credit and debit cards are not accepted.

Rosie's Cantina

Rosie's was THE Mexican restaurant in Haleiwa before Cholo's came along. Located in the Haleiwa Shopping Plaza, 66-197 Kam Highway, Haleiwa, telephone 637-3538, Rosie's is most popular for its low-priced margarita specials. Mediocre food and service have made it a distant also-ran to Cholo's for those who savor Mexican cuisine.

Pizza Bob's

Pizza Bob's is a spacious eatery with a full bar in the Haleiwa Shopping Plaza, 66-197 Kam Highway, Haleiwa, telephone 637-5095. The menu focuses on pizza, pasta, sandwiches and salads. The prices are reasonable, but the food is mediocre and the service is slow. Pizza Bob's is open from 11:00 a.m. daily.

Kainoa's Sports Bar & Restaurant

Located in the Haleiwa Shopping Plaza, 66-197D Kam Highway, Haleiwa, telephone 637-7787, Kainoa's is basically a bar with a limited menu, but a barbecue and seafood menu are in the works. Not tested.

*$Kua Aina Sandwich Shop

Located at 66-160C Kam Highway, Haleiwa, telephone 637-6067, Kua Aina is nearly always full of loyal customers enjoying charbroiled burgers and sandwiches with fresh-cut fries. The mother ship of a growing chain, Kua Aina claims to serve the world's best hamburger. Service is quick and pleasant. Seating is available inside and outside on an attractive lanai. Credit and debit cards are not accepted.

*$Haleiwa Eats-Thai Food

This interesting café at 66-079 Kam Highway, Haleiwa, telephone 637-4247, serves terrific Thai cuisine in a funky North Shore setting. The food and service are very good.

Kaala Café and Juice Bar

Sandwiches, wraps, salads, fresh squeezed juices, smoothies, and gourmet espresso are served up with holistic remedies and massages at this café within the Kaala Healing Arts Center, 66-216 Farrington Highway, Waialua, telephone 637-4177. It is open weekdays from 6:00 a.m. to 6:00 p.m. and weekends from 8:00 a.m. to 4:00 p.m.

Outdoor Dining

Macky's

Macky's shrimp truck, telephone 780-1071, was featured on Rachel Ray's $40 a day in 2006. It was last seen parked on Kam Highway next to the 7-11. Not tested.

*$Giovanni's Aloha Shrimp

After 10 years in Kahuku and recognition by Travelocity as one of Hawaii's "best finds," Giovanni's installed this second lunch wagon in a shady grove on the east side of Kam Highway north of Paukauila Stream (immediately south of the Chocolate Gecko and Café Haleiwa), telephone 293-1839. Giovanni's serves three terrific shrimp dishes: tasty garlic, hot and spicy, and lemon butter shrimp. Believe them when they tell you how hot the hot and spicy version is (really hot!)— if you order it and wimp out you will not get a refund or replacement. Don't forget to sign the wagon! Open daily 11:00 a.m. to 5:30 p.m.

*$Thai lunch wagon

An excellent Thai lunch wagon is located in the same grove as Giovanni's Aloha Shrimp, east of Kam Highway and north of Paukauila Stream. The food is very good. The other wagons in the grove have not been tested.

Banzai Sushi Bar

Located at the north end of the North Shore Marketplace at 66-246 Kam Highway, Haleiwa, telephone 637-4404, Banzai Sushi Bar serves sushi and sashimi in an open air facility Tuesday to Sunday from 5:00 p.m. to 10:00 p.m. Not tested.

Spaghettini's

This outdoor stand at 66-200 Kam Highway, Haleiwa, telephone 637-0104, serves thin-crust, New York-style pizza, pastas, and sandwiches to eat at a handful of outdoor tables or take out.

Fast Food

Mc Donald's
66-457 Kam Highway, Haleiwa, telephone 637-6106.

Pizza Hut
The Pizza Hut behind the Hawaiian Moon Gift Shop at 66-437 Kam Highway, Haleiwa, telephone 637-6248, offers carry out and delivery.

Subway Sandwiches and Salads
66-437 Kam Highway, Suite 104, Haleiwa (next to the post office), telephone 637-5000.

L & L Hawaiian Barbecue
This island chain outlet in the Haleiwa Shopping Plaza, 66-197 Kam Highway, #11, Haleiwa, telephone 637-4700, serves local specialties like plate lunches, teriyaki chicken and beef, and "loco moco" (a hamburger with an egg). Founded 30 years ago in Honolulu, L & L now has over 180 locations in eight states. It provides lots of carbs for the surfer crowd. The Haleiwa location does not have a drive-through window.

Other Specialties

Chocolate Gecko Espresso
An addict's paradise, this little shop at 66-470 Kam Highway, Haleiwa, focuses all its attention on chocolate and coffee.

*Coffee Gallery Hawaii
Coffee Gallery Hawaii in the North Shore Marketplace, 66-250 Kam Highway, #C101, Haleiwa, telephone 637-5571, is a charming café and roastery. The seating area is hand-painted, the rafters are covered with poetry, and the coffee is good. Freezes, shakes, and smoothies are available if you're too hot for coffee. Watch out for the webcam in the corner.

Aloha General Store

This is a convenient spot to stop for a shave ice or smoothie while shopping at the North Shore Marketplace, 66-250 Kam Highway, Suite C130, Haleiwa, telephone 637-2288. Not tested.

Storto's Deli & Sandwich Shop

Pick up a lunch or buy the ingredients and make it yourself. This is the only standalone deli in Haleiwa, at 66-215 Kam Highway, Haleiwa, telephone 637-6633. Not tested.

North Shore Country Okazu & Bento

This little shop serves Japanese specialties for takeout only. It's a great place to pick up a bento box to take home or to the beach. It is located in the Haleiwa Shopping Plaza, Haleiwa Shopping Plaza, 66-197 Kam Highway, Haleiwa, telephone 637-0055, open 6:00 a.m. until 2:00 p.m.

Flavormania Ice Cream Parlor

This old-fashioned ice cream parlor is located next to Pizza Bob's in the Haleiwa Shopping Center, 66-197 Kam Highway, Haleiwa.

Aoki's Shave Ice

Located near the more famous Matsumoto's Shave Ice at 66-117 Kam Highway, Haleiwa, telephone 637-7017, Aoki's also serves authentic shave ice as well as ice cream, shakes, smoothies, and snacks.

*$Matsumoto's Shave Ice

Matsumoto's has been serving shave ice at 66-087 Kam Highway, Haleiwa, telephone 637-4827, as long as most North Shore residents can remember. It is easily the most famous Japanese shave ice shop on the North Shore. Read the history of Matsumoto's in the Drive Guide, and have your picture taken on the bench outside.

HALEIWA TO KAHUKU

Fine Dining

*21 Degrees North

This signature restaurant of the Turtle Bay Resort, 57-091 Kam Highway, Kahuku, telephone 293-8811, is named for its latitude—21 degrees north of the equator. It is the only true epicurean establishment on the North Shore. Frommer's reports that the food is so fabulous, people drive from all over Oahu to eat there. Chef Andrew Anion-Copley is famous for his sumptuous Pacific Rim cuisine. In addition to a wide diversity of menu items, there is a five-course tasting menu with wine pairings that is a gourmet's delight. An excellent cocktail bar features 21 signature martinis. Enjoy cocktails on the lanai as the sun sets, then come inside for dinner. Pricing is a little higher than other North Shore restaurants, but the food and service are in a different league. Reservations are recommended. Note that reservations for a window table with a view are not always honored no matter how far in advance they are made.

Restaurants

*Lei Lei's Bar & Grill

Located on the Fazio golf course, next to the Turtle Bay Resort's golf shop, Lei Lei's, telephone 293-2662, offers consistently good surf and turf fare in a casual, friendly atmosphere. The open-air bar is half in and half out of the building, giving customers a choice of sitting inside or outside. Breakfast, lunch and dinner are served in the paneled dining room and the pleasant lanai on the golf course. The sashimi, Caesar salad, ono, and prime rib are terrific. Parents can relax and enjoy a leisurely meal while the kids play on the grass. Reservations are taken and honored, and the service is good. The only problems are the distracting television sets and noise inside, and the waiters' persistent attempts to sell extra drinks, desserts, and other items you didn't order. If it isn't raining, ask for a table outside on the golf course.

*Ola's

The beachside restaurant at the Turtle Bay Resort, telephone 293-0801, www.olaislife.com, combines the ambiance of old Waikiki with a menu focused on Hawaiian cuisine. With tiki torches aglow and the surf along the reef lit with spotlights, this attractive, indoor-outdoor pavilion is the most romantic dining spot on the North Shore. Chef Fred DeAngelo has won awards for his innovative cuisine. The menu includes a wide range of food featuring fresh local ingredients. Reservations are taken and honored. However, the food and service are somewhat inconsistent. During the day, a full bar and pupu menu is available for beachgoers to enjoy at tables or take back to their lounge chairs.

The Palm Terrace

Turtle Bay Resort, 57-091 Kam Highway, Kahuku, telephone 293-8811, www.turtlebayresort.com. The Palm Terrace serves breakfast, lunch, and dinner with comfortable seating overlooking the Resort's pool terrace. It offers a diverse menu and good service, but the pricing drives most dinner guests to Lei Lei's and Ola's, which offer superior cuisine and ambiance at a comparable cost. The Sunday brunch with live entertainment is a popular tradition.

Cafes

The Bay Club

Located off the southern end of the Turtle Bay Resort's lobby, this spacious nightclub offers wonderful views of Kuilima Cove. Hotel guests collect there after dinner, and live entertainment is provided on weekends. The mai tais are excellent. The menu offers pupus, pizza, sandwiches and salads at ridiculously high prices.

Outdoor Dining

*$Waimea Valley Grill

Waimea Valley Grill, 59-864 Kam Highway, telephone 638-7766, serves lunch on the terrace next to the gift shop at the Waimea Valley Historical Nature Park. It offers delicious salads, sandwiches, and plate lunches at reasonable prices. Try the kalua pork or teriyaki chicken plate lunch.

*$Shark's Cove Grill

Shark's Cove Grill, 59-712 Kam Highway (across the street from Pupukea Beach Park), telephone 638-8300, isn't just another lunch wagon. Established by a woman with serious culinary training, the colorfully painted lunch truck serves delicious meals, such as shrimp and teriyaki skewers with rice and salad, at reasonable prices. It is now open for breakfast, lunch, and dinner, with seating at picnic tables. If the dining area is too rough for you, take your meal across the street to the Pupukea Beach Park and get a table with a view! Shark's Cove Grill is open daily from 8:30 a.m. to 8:30 p.m.

*$Ted's Bakery

The mere thought of Ted's Bakery, 59-024 Kam Highway, Sunset Beach, telephone 638-8207, fax 638-5188, makes locals' mouths water. Ted's serves breakfast, lunch and fabulous desserts, which can be taken out or eaten on the comfortable deck. The food is wonderful and the prices are reasonable. Try the beef teriyaki or the hot crab and bacon sandwich with a delicious guava smoothie. Besides the amazing chocolate haupia pie that Ted invented, haupia cream, pineapple macadamia, guava and other fruit pies, pineapple macadamia cheesecake, and other confections can be purchased by the slice or in their entirety. The breakfast pastries are to die for. Special cakes for birthdays and other occasions must be ordered in advance. Ted's is a terrific part of the North Shore community. Ted lives in the white and blue house on the hill and keeps a close eye on the operation. His parents started the business as a Mom and Pop store many years ago. Their pictures still hang inside, and Mom often comes in to arrange flowers and make sure everything is shipshape. Ted's is open from 7:00 a.m. until 4:00 p.m. Monday through Thursday and 5:00 p.m. Friday through Sunday.

Hang Ten Surf Bar

This poolside bar at the Turtle Bay Resort serves pupus, sandwiches, salads and specialties from the poolside grill until 5:00 p.m. A crowd gathers nightly to enjoy the sunset. The mai tais are excellent and the food and wait service are good, but the ocean breeze can be pretty strong.

Blue Water Shrimp & Seafood Co.

This blue lunch wagon in Tanaka's Polynesian Village, at the entrance to the Kahuku shrimp farms, telephone 293-9376, serves seafood platters including shrimp, prawns, clams, snow crab, and scallops, from 10:30 a.m. until 5:30 p.m. daily. Not tested.

Romy's Kahuku Prawns & Shrimp

Romy Aguinaldo operates a 40-acre shrimp farm with 31 ponds of prawns and 13 acres of hatcheries in the wetlands between the Kam Highway and the ocean. The prawns and shrimp harvested from the family's ponds are served steamed, fried, sweet or spicy, with garlic and butter, at the green stand on the west side of the Kahuku sugar mill shopping area, 56-781 Kam Highway, Kahuku, telephone 232-2201, www.romyskahukuprawns.com.

*$Giovanni's Aloha Shrimp

Giovanni's white truck has been parked in the lot east of the Kahuku Sugar Mill Shopping Center for more than a decade. After tasting the delicious lemon butter, garlic, and spicy shrimp, Travelocity rated this modest truck a "Find." Believe them when they tell you how hot the hot and spicy shrimp are (really hot), and don't forget to sign the truck. Open daily from 10:30 a.m. to 6:30 p.m., telephone 293-1839.

Other Specialties

Starbucks Coffee
Starbucks is located inside the Pupukea Foodland, 59-720 Kam Highway, Pupukea, telephone 638-8081.

LAIE

Cafes

*$Hukilau Café
This cute little café at 56-662 Wahinepee, Laie, telephone 293-8616, is a popular gathering place for Laie residents. This is a great place to sample local fare. The cafe is open for breakfast and lunch Tuesday through Friday and breakfast only on Saturday. Be sure to notice the photos of the old hukilaus and other local events.

*$Laie Chop Suey
This nondescript little restaurant in the Laie Village Shopping Center, 55-510 Kam Highway, Laie, telephone 293-8022, serves an amazing selection of authentic Chinese food to eat in or take out. The décor isn't fancy, but the food is excellent and the service is very friendly. Pick up an order and enjoy wonderful Chinese food at one of the nearby beach parks or in the comfort of your hotel or condo.

Fast Food

L & L Drive-In Chopstick Express
This express version of the L&L chain is located in the Laie Village Shopping Center, 55-510 Kam Highway, Laie, telephone 293-8887. Local and Oriental favorites are served at the drive-through window.

Pizza Hut

Every college town needs a pizza joint. The Pizza Hut in the Laie Village Shopping Center, 55-510 Kam Highway, Laie, telephone 643-1111, www.pizzahuthawaii.com, offers the standard menu to eat in, take out, or have delivered. Delivery to the Turtle Bay area is available.

Subway Sandwiches and Salads

Subway is located next to Foodland in the Laie Village Shopping Center, 55-510 Kam Highway, Laie, telephone 293-0444. An outdoor eating area is in the works.

Taco Bell

Taco Bell is open late in the Laie Village Shopping Center, 55-510 Kam Highway, Laie.

Mc Donald's

McDonald's is located south of the Laie Village Shopping Center, at 55-406 Kam Highway, Laie, telephone 293-8561, north of the Polynesian Cultural Center.

Other Specialties

Angel's Ice Cream

Ice cream, shave ice, and smoothies satisfy Laie's sweet tooth at the Laie Village Shopping Center, 55-510 Kam Highway, Laie. An outdoor eating area is in the works.

HAUULA TO KAAAWA

Restaurants

Crouching Lion Inn

The days when people drove from all over the island to dine at the Crouching Lion Inn may be gone, but the handsome old restaurant at 51-666 Kam Highway, Kaaawa, telephone 237-8511, is still a nice place to stop for a simple meal with a nice view of Kahana Bay. It is open for lunch, dinner, and cocktails.

Cafes

*Hawaiian Seafood Grill & Bar

The Hawaiian Seafood Grill & Bar in the Hauula Kai Shopping Center, 54-316 Kam Highway, Hauula, is a pleasant, breezy, clean place to dine. The appealing menu features seafood. The whole fish in a crispy batter is especially delicious. Non-Mormons who feel a little parched after a day in Laie may enjoy the bar, which stocks a good selection of beer, wine, and other alcoholic beverages. The prices are a bit high for the local trade, which gravitates toward Papa Ole's.

Papa Ole's Kitchen

This popular spot for plate lunches and other local dishes is located in the strip mall section of the Hauula Kai Shopping Center, 54-316 Kam Highway, Hauula, telephone 293-2292.

Tropicaina Bar & Grill

Don't be misled by this establishment's name. No alcoholic beverages are served here. Local fare and smoothies are the mainstay. The picturesque, ramshackle old building at 53-138 Kam Highway, Punaluu 96717, telephone 237-8688, has a great view of the Koolaus from the back patio. The service can be slow.

Uncle Bobo's Smoked BBQ

This longtime local establishment is located at 51-480 Kam Highway, Kaaawa. Not tested.

Fast Food

Domino's Pizza

Domino's offers another pizza alternative at the Hauula Kai Shopping Center, 54-316 Kam Highway, Hauula.

IX. LODGING

The North Shore is not lined with high-rise hotels, which is why we love it so. First-class accommodations are available at the Turtle Bay Resort and the adjacent Kuilima condominiums.

THE TURTLE BAY RESORT

This destination resort at 57-091 Kam Highway, Kahuku, telephone 293-8574 or 1-800-203-3650, fax 293-9094, www.turtlebayresort.com, has 375 guest rooms and 26 suites, all with ocean views. In addition, there are 42 beach cabanas lining Turtle Bay and luxury villas on Kuilima Cove. The lobby is furnished in soft pastels, with a huge glass wall cantilevered over Kuilima Cove. Conference and catering facilities are first rate. Dining options range from the sumptuous 21 Degrees North and weekly "Voyages of Polynesia Luau" to the romantic Ola's, attractive Lei Lei's, practical Palm Terrace, poolside grill and Hang Ten Surf Bar, and late night snacks at the Bay Club. Coffee and tea are available from a kiosk in the lobby each morning. Wine and tea are served in the afternoon as guests returning from their daytime adventures or conferences enjoy the magnificent ocean view and traditional Hawaiian music. A children's club is available on certain days to introduce young hotel guests to Hawaiian culture. The *keiki* (children's) program includes reef walks, *lei* making, Hawaiian arts and crafts, and beach activities. The Spa Luana offers first-class spa and fitness services. Horseback riding, tennis, golf, surf lessons, and other activities are available.

View of the swimming pool and Turtle Bay from a hotel balcony

THE KUILIMA CONDOMINIUMS

Twin condominium communities are located adjacent to the Turtle Bay Resort. Within these condo complexes, there are five swimming pools, four regulation tennis courts, and barbecue and picnic facilities. The condos range from studios to three-bedroom units. All are equipped with full kitchens, washers and dryers, and cable television. The main floor units have pleasant lanais opening to small lawns adjoining the golf course. Del Webb built the condos in the 1970s, at the same time as the hotel. Some of them have been completely refurbished, while others are the worse for wear. The most prominent rental agency is **The Estates at Turtle Bay,** 55-565 Kam Highway, Kahuku (next to the Post Office at the Kahuku Sugar Mill), www.turtlebay-rentals.com, telephone 1-888-200-4202 or 293-0600, fax 293-0471, E-mail trtlbayest@aol.com, which represents 115 condos. It identifies each listing as a one star (economy), two star (good), or three star (luxury) unit, with appropriate price differentials. **Turtle Bay Vacation Rentals,** telephone 293-7530, manages several Kuilima condos and beachfront villas. Other rental agents and individual owners list Kuilima condos for rent on **www.vrbo.com** and other websites.

OTHER ACCOMMODATIONS

Ke Iki Beach Bungalows, Ke Iki Beach

Ke Iki Beach Bungalows is a beachfront enclave on Ke Iki Beach, just north of Shark's Cove, at 59-579 Ke Iki Road, Haleiwa, telephone 638-8229 or 1-866-638-8229, fax 637-6100, E-mail info@keikibeach.com, www.keikibeach.com. There are eleven units—six three-bedroom units, four one-bedroom units, and a studio – grouped in several buildings. They are not luxury accommodations, but five of them open directly on the beach and the other six open on a pleasant garden only a few steps from the beach. The Ke Ala Pupukea bike path runs past the enclave. Guests can walk out the door and along the beach to surf, or watch the surfing, at Ke Waena and the Banzai Pipeline, or walk along the bike path to Shark's Cove and Three Tables to swim and snorkel.

Santa's By The Sea, Banzai Pipeline

If you would like a one-bedroom B&B with a living room and kitchen located on the beach at the Banzai Pipeline, investigate Santa's by the Sea, 59-461 Ke Waena Road, Haleiwa, HI 96743, telephone 638-7837, 985-7488 or 1-800-262-9912. The name refers to a collection of Santa furnishings.

Backpackers Vacation Inn and Plantation Village, Pupukea

Economy hostel bunks, private rooms, cottages, and apartments near Pupukea Beach Park are available from Backpackers Vacation Inn and Plantation Village, 59-788 Kam Highway, Haleiwa 96712, telephone 638-7838, fax 638-7515, E-mail info@backpackers-hawaii.com. Be sure to check out the room before you pay for it.

Shark's Cove Rentals, Pupukea

More economy units in the Pupukea area are located at 59-672 Kam Highway, Haleiwa, 96712, telephone 779-8535 or 638-7980, lanej003@hawaii.rr.com

Hale Kimo, Sunset Beach

This beachfront property has been in the same family since 1947. The lucky heirs have built two lovely beachfront homes there. You can rent one large home for up to 8 people or rent the whole complex and have a family reunion. Contact Hale Kimo Ohana, 139 Ohana St., Kailua, HI 96734, telephone 358-5786 (Steffany), fax 262-8080, E-mail hkimo@halekimo.com or halekimo@gmail.com.

Malaekahana State Recreation Area, Laie

Camping facilities ranging from bare tentsites, to furnished yurts and cabins, and even a little grass shack on the beach can be rented from Friends of Malaekahana, 56-335 Kam Highway, P.O. Box 305, Laie 96762, telephone 293-1736, fax 293-2066. See the Camping Section of Chapter VI for more information.

Laie Inn Hukilau Resort, Laie

The Laie Inn is an old-fashioned, two-story motel located adjacent to the Polynesian Cultural Center at 55-109 Laniloa St., Laie, HI 96762, telephone 293-9282 or bestinn@hawaii.rr.com. It is in serious need of refurbishing, but it is close to the beach and Polynesian Cultural Center and the prices are reasonable.

Gigi's Oceanfront Paradise, Punaluu

A large condo building and some beachfront cottages on the condo's *makai* side are available from Gigi's Oceanfront Paradise, P.O. Box 939, Hauula 96717, telephone 277-0516, fax 293-4934, E-mail info@gigiparadise.com.

Pat's at Punaluu

Apartments in the large "Pat's at Punaluu" condo building and several beachfront homes can be rented from Heidi Hawaii, telephone 778-8374, E-mail heidi@heidihawaii.com. Check on the status of extensive repairs on the condo building before renting. A beach cottage in the same location is available from Paul Kepka, telephone 497-6809, E-mail sunrisebeachcottage@yahoo.com.

AGENTS

The following agents handle vacation rentals in northern Oahu:

- **Team Real Estate,** 66-250 Kam Highway, Suite D-103, Haleiwa, HI 96712, telephone 637-3507 or 1-800-982-8602, fax 637-8881, www.teamrealestate.com.
- **Sandsea, Inc. Vacation Homes,** 61-815 Papailoa Road, #A, Haleiwa, HI 96712, telephone 637-2568 or 1-800-637-1974, www.sandsea.com.
- **Sterman Realty,** 66-250 Kam Highway, Suite D-100, Haleiwa, HI 96712, telephone 637-6200.

The following agents handle B & Bs:

- **All Islands B&B,** 463 Isiwahi Loop, Kailua 96734, telephone 542-0344.
- **Hawaiian Islands B & B,** 1277 Mokolua Drive, Kailua 96734, telephone 261-7895, 800-258-7895.
- **B & B Honolulu,** 3242 Kaohinani Drive, Honolulu 96817, telephone 595-7533, 800-288-4666, www.hawaiibnb.com.
- **B & B Hawaii,** P.O. Box 449, Kapaa 96746, telephone 822-7771, 800-733-1632, www.bandbhawaii.com.

X. HAWAIIAN WORDS AND PHRASES

English and Hawaiian both were declared the "official language" of Hawaii in 1968. Since then, there has been a tremendous resurgence in the use of the Hawaiian language. Your visit to Hawaii will be enhanced if you familiarize yourself with some of the frequently used Hawaiian words and phrases.

The Hawaiian language has 13 letters: five vowels and eight consonants. The vowels (a, e, i, o, and u) are pronounced as "clean vowels," like they are in Spanish. They are not mixed with other vowel sounds, as in English.

a =	Ah, as in bah
e =	Ay, as in hay
i =	Ee, as in tree
o =	Oh, as in obey
u =	Oo, as in room

The first six consonants (h, k, l, m, n, and p) are generally pronounced like they are in English. The last two (w and ') cause a lot of confusion.

The Hawaiian "w" is usually pronounced like the English "w," but not always.

- When "w" follows a, it can be pronounced as either "w" or "v" (Hawaii=Hah wai ee or Ha vai ee.
- When "w" follows i, it sounds like "v" (Haleiwa=Ha lay ee va).
- When "w" follows o or u, it usually sounds like "w."

The 'okina (') or glottal stop is a consonant. It signifies a breath break, as between the two parts of the English term "oh-oh." Lately some writers have begun to insert the okina in numerous Hawaiian words, although this runs counter to modern technological practice. The kahako is a macron over a vowel indicating that the vowel sound should be held longer. The kahako does not change the quality of the sound. This book follows the modern technological practice of omitting both the 'okina and the kahako.

The accent in Hawaiian words is usually placed on the next to last syllable (aloha = a LO ha, mahalo= ma HA lo).

Here are some Hawaiian words and phrases you are likely to encounter in this book or your travels in the islands:

aa	rough lava rock
aawa	yellow wrasse once abundant on Oahu
ahi	tuna
a hui hou	until we meet again
ahupuaa	geographical subdivision of a moku (for example, Waimea was an ahupuaa of the moku of Koolauloa)
aina momona	sweet or fruitful land
alii	person of royal or noble heritage
aloha	hello, goodbye, welcome, love
ama ama	mullet, a fresh water fish
anae holo	salt water mullet
enui nui	rainbow
hale	house
hale nui	grass shack
haole	Westerner, foreigner
haupia	coconut pudding
he alii	noble or chief with godlike spiritual power
heenalu	surf
heenaluor	surfing, wave sliding
heiau	temple or shrine made of stones
honu	Hawaiian green sea turtle
huki	hook

hukilau	method of cooperative fishing in which fish are driven into a large net
hula	Hawaiian dance, the dancer, or the chant used to dance
huli huli	sauce made of lime juice, soy sauce, and other ingredients
imu	oven
ipukai	platter
kahuna	priest
kahuna nui	chief priest
kai	salt water, ocean, sea
kamaaina	native, local resident
kane	man
kapu	taboo, rule establishing prohibited conduct
kapu moe	rule requiring commoners to prostrate themselves in the chief's presence
keiki	child
kii akua	tiki gods or idols
kilo	lookout used to spot fish
kilo ia	fish spotter
kohala	humpback whale
konohiki	head man, subordinate chief of *ahupuaa*
kuapa	open sea ponds enclosed with rock walls
kuleana	small lots commoners could buy
kupuna	grandparent, elder
lanai	porch

lau	fish
lei	flower garland worn around the neck
limu	seaweed
luau	Hawaiian feast
luakini heiau	*heiau* used for government as well as spiritual matters
luna	supervisor
mahalo	thank you
makai	toward the sea
mana	spiritual power
manini	small reef fish with stripes
mauka	inland, toward the mountain
mea hee nalu	surfer
mele	song, happy state of mind
menehune	legendary small people
moana	ocean
moi	salt water fish, desirable dinner food
moku	geographical district
moli	Laysan albatross
muliwai	pond of standing, brackish water, usually where a stream is blocked by a sandbar, also the mouth of a stream or estuary
muumuu	loose gown
naia	dolphin
nalu	wave, surf
ono	delicious, good
oopu	Hawaiian goby, Hawaii's only native freshwater fish

pali	cliff, precipice, steep hill
paniolo	cowboy
papa heenalu	surfboard
peheaoe	How are you?
pohaku	stone or rock
poke	cubed raw fish served as an appetizer
puone	inland fishpond formed when brackish water flowed through porous lava and filled depressions in the rock
pupu	appetizer, hors d'oeuvre
puuhonua	place of refuge for those who broke *kapu*
umu	kiln
wahine	woman

XI. DIRECTORY OF SERVICES

For each service, providers are listed in alphabetical order. Items covered in other chapters are not repeated here. For police, fire, and ambulance emergencies, dial 911.

ACUPUNCTURE

Barbara Fisher
66-590 Kam Highway, Haleiwa, telephone 637-8500.

AIRLINES

ATA
Telephone 1-800-435-9282, www.ata.com.

Air Canada
Telephone 1-888-247-2262, www.aircanada.ca.

Air New Zealand
Telephone 1-800-262-1234, www.airnewzealand.com.

Air Pacific
Telephone 1-800-227-4446, www.airpacific.com.

All Nippon
Telephone 1-800-235-9262, www.anaskyweb.com.

American
Telephone 833-7600 or 1-800-433-7300, www.aa.com.

China
Telephone 955-0088 or 1-800-227-5118, www.china-airlines.com.

Continental

Telephone   1-800-523-3273   (U.S.)   or   1-800-231-0856 (International), www.continental.com.

Delta

Telephone 1-800-221-1212, www.delta.com.

Go

Telephone   1-888-435-9462   (1-888-IFLYGO2),   www.iflygo. com

Hawaiian

Telephone   838-1555   or   1-800-882-8811,   www.hawaiianair. com.

Island Air

Telephone 484-2222, www.islandair.com.

Japan

Telephone 521-1441 or 1-800-525-3663, www.jal.com.

Korean

Telephone 836-1711 or 1-800-438-5000, www.koreanair.com.

Lan Chile

Telephone 941-2552 or 1-866-435-9526, www.lan.com.

Lufthansa

Telephone 1-800-645-3880, www.lufthansa.com.

Molokai-Lanai

Telephone 833-5492.

Northwest/KLM

Telephone   1-800-225-2525   (U.S.)   or   1-800-447-4747 (International), www.nwa.com.

Omni
Telephone 834-4557 or 1-877-718-8901, www.omniair.com.

Pacific Air Charters
Telephone 839-3559, www.pacificaircharters.com.

Pacific Wings
Telephone 1-888-575-4546, www.pacificwings.com.

Philippine
Telephone 1-800-435-9725, www.philippineairlines.com.

Qantas
Telephone 1-800-227-4585, www.qantas.com.

United
Telephone 1-800-864-8331 (U.S.) or 1-800-538-2929 (International), www.united.com.

AIRPORT TRANSPORTATION

North Shore Limousines
Telephone 293-1447.

North Shore Shuttle
Telephone 637-5300.

Oahu Airport Shuttle
Telephone 681-8181.

Star Taxi Hawaii
Telephone 942-7827 or 739-1300.

Turtle Bay Limousines
Telephone 222-8711.

ART GALLERIES

An artists' studio tour is conducted in May. The Haleiwa Art Show is held on the third weekend in July. Individual artists open their studios year-round by appointment. See www.hawaiinorthshoreartists.com.

Britton Art Gallery

North Shore Marketplace, 66-250 Kam Highway, Haleiwa, telephone 637-6505.

M. Goodwill Fine Arts

68-234 Au Street, Waialua, telephone/fax 637-8934, margo@mgoodwillart.com, www.mgoodwillart.com, by appointment only.

Haleiwa Art Gallery

66-252 Kam Highway, Haleiwa 96712, telephone 637-3368, www.haleiwaartgallery.com, open 10:00 a.m. to 6:00 p.m. daily.

Iwa Gallery

Kam Highway across the street from the Haleiwa Art Gallery, Haleiwa.

Kim Taylor Reese Gallery

53-866 Kam Highway, Hauula, telephone 293-2000.

Lance Fairly Gallery

53-839 Kam Highway, Hauula, telephone 293-9009.

Lee Ceramics

68-474 Crozier Drive, Waialua, telephone 637-4207, www.leeceramics.com

Tabora Gallery

66-160 Kam Highway, Haleiwa, telephone 637-7881.

Wyland Galleries

North Shore Marketplace, 66-250H Kam Highway, Haleiwa, telephone 637-8729.

BAKERIES

Ted's Bakery

59-024 Kam Highway, Sunset Beach, telephone 638-8207.

Waialua Bakery

66-200 Kam Highway, Haleiwa, telephone 637-9079.

BARBERS AND BEAUTY SALONS

Billy's Barber & Beauty Shop

66-447 Kam Highway, Haleiwa, telephone 637-5550.

Honolulu Airport Barber Shop

Telephone 836-3029.

Kahuku Barber & Hair Salon

56-565 Kam Highway, Suite C-3. Kahuku, telephone 232-2323.

Salon Atlantis

Haleiwa Shopping Plaza, 66-145 Kam Highway, Haleiwa, telephone 637-2511.

Spa Luana at the Turtle Bay Resort

57-091 Kam Highway, Kahuku, telephone 293-8811, www.turtlebayresort.com.

The Haircut Store

Laie Village Shopping Center, 55-510 Kam Highway, Bay 3, Laie, telephone 293-2223.

BICYCLE RENTALS

Barnfield's Raging Isle Surf & Cycle

North Shore Marketplace, 66-250 Kam Highway, Haleiwa, telephone 637-7707.

Country Cycles

59-059 Pupukea Road (across the street from Foodland), Pupukea, telephone 638-8866.

Planet Surf

Corner of Pupukea Road and the Kam Highway, Pupukea, telephone 638-5060.

BIKE TRIPS: SEE CHAPTER VI

BOAT CHARTERS: SEE CHAPTER V

BUS TRANSPORTATION

Oahu Transit Services, Inc. (The Bus)

Telephone 848-5555 from 5:30 a.m. to 10:00 p.m. daily for current routes and schedules, 848-4500 for customer service, www.thebus.org.

CAMPING: SEE CHAPTER VI

CAR RENTALS

Alamo

Honolulu Airport, telephone 833-4585 or 1-877-603-0615, www.alamo.com.

Avis
Honolulu Airport, telephone 1-800-831-2847, www.avis.com.

Budget
Honolulu Airport, telephone 1-800-527-0700, www.budget. com.

Dollar
Honolulu Airport, telephone 1-800-800-4000, www.dollar.com

Enterprise
823 California Avenue, A-4, Wahiawa, telephone 622-0024, www.enterprise.com.

Hertz
Honolulu Airport, telephone 831-3500 or 1-800-654-3011, www.hertz.com.

National
Honolulu Airport, telephone 739-8888 or 1-888-868-6207, www.nationalcar.com.

Thrifty
Honolulu Airport, telephone 831-2279, local reservations 952-4238 or 1-800-367-5238, www.thrifty.com.

CHIROPRACTORS

A Tsutsui Chiropractic
66-560 B Kam Highway, Haleiwa, telephone 637-9752.

CHURCHES

Non-Denominational
A non-denominational service is held at the Turtle Bay Resort in the chapel on Kuilima Point Sunday at 9:00 a.m.

Catholic

St. Joachim Church

53-536 Kam Highway, Hauula, telephone 293-8590.

St. Michael's Church

67-390 Goodale Avenue, Waialua, telephone 637-4040, Masses Saturday evening at 5:00 p.m., Sunday at 7:00 a.m. and 10:00 a.m., weekdays at 7:00 a.m.

Sts. Peter & Paul Church

59-810 Kam Highway, Waimea Bay, telephone 637-4040, Masses Sunday at 7:30 and 9:30 a.m.

St. Roch Church

56-350 Kam Highway, Kahuku, telephone 293-5026, Masses Sunday at 7:30 a.m., Wednesday and Friday at 9:00 a.m.

Protestant

Assembly of God

Haleiwa Assembly of God

66-113 Kam Highway, telephone 637-1923.

Waialua Assembly of God

1057 Ehoeho Avenue, Waialua, telephone 621-0923.

Baptist

First Baptist Church of Haleiwa

66-415 Haleiwa Road, Haleiwa, telephone 637-4847.

North Windward Baptist Chapel

53-075 Halai, Hauula, telephone 293-9887.

Church of Christ

Hauula Church of Christ

54-024 Ahinalu Place, Hauula, telephone 293-9606.

Liliuokalani Protestant Church

66-090 Kam Highway, Haleiwa, telephone 637-9364, Sunday service 10:00 a.m., Sunday school 9:00 a.m.

Sunset Beach Church of Christ and Christian School

59-578 Kam Highway, Sunset Beach, telephone 638-0019, service Sunday at 9:00 a.m.

Waialua United Church of Christ

67-174 Farrington Highway, Waialua, telephone 637-5934.

Congregational

Hauula Congregational Church

54-311 Hauula Homestead Road, Hauula, telephone 293-2122.

Episcopal

Holy Cross Episcopal Mission

56-356 Kam Highway, Kahuku, telephone 293-7330.

St. Stephen's Episcopal Church

1679 California Avenue, Wahiawa, telephone 621-8662.

Evangelical

Haleiwa Evangelical Mission,

66-130 Walikanahele Road, Haleiwa, telephone 637-9347

Jehovah's Witnesses

Sunset Beach Congregation

59-0488 Kam Highway, Sunset Beach, telephone 638-8028.

Methodist

Kahuku United Methodist Church

56-449 Kam Highway, Kahuku, telephone 293-5036, Sunday service in English at 9:30 a.m., in Tongan at 3:00 p.m.

Pentecostal

Greater Mt. Zion Holiness Church

53-776 Kam Highway, Hauula, telephone 293-2261.

Haleiwa Evangelical Mission

66-130 Walikanahele Road, Haleiwa, telephone 637-9347.

Seventh Day Adventist

Hauula Seventh Day Adventist Church

54-029 Waikulama, Hauula, telephone 293-8754.

Other

North Shore Christian Fellowship

66-437 Kam Highway, Haleiwa, telephone 637-6225.

Waialua Christian Church

68-031 Aweoweo, Waialua, telephone 637-9333.

Waialua International Christian Mission

66-388 Kaamooloa Road, Waialua, telephone 637-1255.

LDS

Laie Temple Gardens and Visitor's Center

55-600 Naniloa Loop, Laie, telephone 293-9297, open daily from 9:00 a.m. to 8:00 p.m.

Wards

Hauula 1st Ward

54-208 Hauula Homestead Road, Hauula, telephone 293-5253.

Hauula 2nd Ward
53-958 Kam Highway, Hauula, telephone 293-1845.

Hauula 3rd Ward
54-208 Hauula Homestead Road, Hauula, telephone 293-5044.

Hauula 4th Ward
54-208 Hauula Homestead Road, Hauula, telephone 293-9445.

Hauula 5th Ward
53-958 Kam Highway, Hauula, telephone 293-2279.

Hauula 6th Ward
53-958 Kam Highway, Hauula, telephone 293-2354.

Kahuku 1st Ward
56-589 Puuluana Place, Kahuku, telephone 293-1804.

Kahuku 2nd Ward
56-589 Puuluana Place, Kahuku, telephone 293-2166.

Kahuku 3rd Ward (Tongan)
56-589 Puuluana Place, Room 20, telephone 293-2941.

Laie 1st Ward
55-630 Naniloa Loop, Laie, telephone 293-2663.

Laie 2nd Ward
55-415 Iosepa, Laie, telephone 293-9710.

Laie 3rd Ward
55-415 Iosepa, Laie, telephone 293-1545.

Laie 4th Ward
55-630 Naniloa Loop, Laie, telephone 293-2263.

Laie 5th Ward
55-415 Iosepa, Laie, telephone 293-5085.

Laie 6th Ward

55-630 Naniloa Loop, Laie, telephone 293-1590.

Laie 7th Ward

55-630 Naniloa Loop, Laie, telephone 293-1009.

Laie 8th Ward

55-630 Naniloa Loop, Laie, telephone 293-1674.

Laie 9th Ward (Samoan)

55-110 Lanihuli, Laie, telephone 293-1404.

Waialua Ward

66-847 Kaukonahua Road, Waialua, telephone 637-5217.

Buddhist

Haleiwa Jodo Mission

66-279 Haleiwa Road #A, Haleiwa, telephone 637-4382.

Haleiwa Shingon Mission

66-469 Paalaa Road, Haleiwa, telephone 637-4423.

Kahuku Hongwanji Mission

Kahuku, telephone 293-5268.

Waialua Hongwanji Mission

67-313 Kealohanui. Waialua, telephone 637-4395.

Other

Church of Hawaii Nei

59-059 Pupukea Road, Pupukea, telephone 638-7841.

DELICATESSENS

Storto's Deli & Sandwich Shop

66-215 Kam Highway, Haleiwa, telephone 637-6633.

DENTISTS

Joe D. Flowers, DDS

56-117 Pualalea, Laie, telephone 293-9211.

Haleiwa Family Dental Center

66-125 Kam Highway, Suite 2, Haleiwa, telephone 637-9652.

North Shore Dentistry, Dr. John Dubiel, DDS

59-712A Kam Highway, Pupukea, telephone 638-7883.

Sunahara Dental, E. Devi Sunahara. DDS, Mike S. Sunahara, DDS

66-230 Kam Highway, Haleiwa, telephone 637-4550.

DOCTORS-SEE PHYSICIANS

DRUGSTORES-SEE PHARMACIES

DRY CLEANING

El'gant Alterations

90 S. Kam Highway, Wahiawa, telephone 622-4841, open Monday to Saturday 8:30 a.m. to 7:00 p.m., Sunday 8:00 a.m. to 5:00 p.m.

Laie Washerette

Laie Village Shopping Center, 55-510 Kam Highway, Laie, telephone 293-2821.

EQUIPMENT RENTALS

Barnfield's Raging Isle Surf & Cycle

66-250 Kam Highway, North Shore Marketplace, Haleiwa, telephone 637-7707: surfboards and bicycles.

Kite High

North Shore Marketplace, Haleiwa, telephone 637-0025: kite surfing equipment.

North Shore Equipment Rentals

67-016 Farrington Highway, Waialua, telephone 637-4600: tables, chairs, ice boxes, coolers, food warmers, tents, generators, contractor's and gardening equipment.

Planet Surf

Corner of Pupukea Road and the Kam Highway, telephone 638-5060: surfboards, snorkel gear, bodyboards, and umbrellas.

Surf 'n' Sea

62-595 Kam Highway, Haleiwa, telephone 637-9887, www. surfnsea.com: kayaks, surfboards, sailboards, snorkel equipment, scuba gear, windsurfers, and jet ski rentals.

The Watercraft Connection

Haleiwa Boat Harbor, telephone 637-8006, www.jetskihawaii. net: jet skis.

Tropical Rush

62-620A Kam Highway, Haleiwa, telephone 637-8886: surfboards.

Turtle Bay Resort

57-091 Kam Highway, Kahuku, telephone 893-8811, www. turtlebayresort.com, golf clubs, kayaks, snorkel equipment, beach chairs, and other items.

Wave Riding Vehicles

Kam Highway, Haleiwa, telephone 637-2020: jet skis and other wave riders.

FISHING CHARTERS: SEE CHAPTER V

FISHING SUPPLIES

Haleiwa Fishing Supply
66-519 Kam Highway, Haleiwa, telephone 637-9876.

FLOWERS

Alluvion Florist
61-676 Kam Highway, Haleiwa 96712, telephone 637-5041, fax 637-8836, E-mail: alluvion@aloha.net, www.alluvionhi.com. Open weekdays from 7:00 a.m. to 3:30 p.m., Saturday from 7:00 a.m. to 12:30 p.m.

Foodland
59-720 Kam Highway, Pupukea, telephone 638-8081.
Laie Village Shopping Center, 55-510 Kam Highway, Laie, telephone 293-4443.

Haleiwa Flower Shop
66-259 Kam Highway, Haleiwa, telephone 637-5144.

Island Impressions
Turtle Bay Resort, 57-091 Kam Highway, Kahuku, telephone 293-8811.

Rainbow Balloons & Flowers
Laie Village Shopping Center, 55-510 Kam Highway, Laie, telephone 293-9542.

GLIDING: SEE CHAPTER VII

GOLF: SEE CHAPTER VI

GROCERIES

Foodland

59-720 Kam Highway, Pupukea, telephone 638-8081.

Laie Village Shopping Center, 55-510 Kam Highway, Laie, telephone 293-4443.

Haleiwa Super Market-IGA

66-197 Kam Highway, Haleiwa, telephone 637-5004.

Malama Market

66-190 Kam Highway, Haleiwa, telephone 637-4520.

Tamura's Market

Hauula Kai Shopping Center, 54-316 Kam Highway, Hauula, telephone 232-2332.

HANG-GLIDING: SEE CHAPTER VII

HARDWARE

Ace Hardware Pioneer

66-134 Kam Highway, Haleiwa, telephone 637-6221.

Ace Hardware Pioneer

Laie Village Shopping Center, 55-510 Kam Highway, Laie, telephone 293-0999.

HEALTH FOOD

Celestial Natural Foods
66-443 Kam Highway, Haleiwa, telephone 637-6729.

Kaala Healing Arts Center
66-216 Farrington Highway, Waialua, telephone 637-4177.

HIKING: SEE CHAPTER VI

HORSEBACK RIDING: SEE CHAPTER VI

HOSPITALS

Kahuku General Hospital
56-117 Pualalea, Kahuku, telephone 293-9221.

Wahiawa General Hospital
128 Lehua Street, Wahiawa, telephone 621-8411.

KITESURFING: SEE CHAPTER V

LAUNDRY

Laie Washerette
Laie Village Shopping Center, 55-510 Kam Highway, Laie, telephone 293-2821.

Waialua Shopping Center
67-292 Goodale Avenue, Waialua.

LIBRARIES

Kahuku Public Library
56-490 Kam Highway, Kahuku, telephone 293-8935.

Waialua Public Library
67-068 Kealohanui Street, Waialua, telephone 637-8286.

LIMOUSINE SERVICE

North Shore Limousines
telephone 293-1447.

North Shore Shuttle
telephone 637-5300.

Turtle Bay Limousines
Laie, telephone 222-8711.

MASSAGE

Hooponopono Northshore Massage Therapy
Haleiwa, telephone 637-9734.

Kaala Healing Arts
66-216 Farrington Highway, Waialua, telephone 637-4177.

North Shore Natural Balance Massage
66-216 Farrington Highway, Waialua, telephone 636-2206.

North Shore Therapeutic Massage
62-620B Kam Highway, telephone 637-4277.

Turtle Bay Resort Spa Luana
57-091 Kam Highway, Kahuku, telephone 293-8811, www. turtlebayresort.com.

MEDICAL CLINICS

Haleiwa Family Health Center
66-125 Kam Highway, Haleiwa, telephone 637-5087.

Kaiser Permanente Kahuku Clinic
56-565 Kam Highway, Kahuku, telephone 432-3900.

North Shore Health Center
56-119 Pualalea Street, Kahuku, telephone 293-9231 (if no answer call 293-9221).

Poison Center
telephone 1-800-222-1222

Wahiawa Dialysis Center
850 Kilani Avenue, Wahiawa, telephone 621-5151.

MEDICAL DOCTORS-SEE PHYSICIANS

MOVIES

Laie Theater
Laie Village Shopping Center, 55-150 Kam Highway, Laie, telephone 293-7516.

NAIL SALONS

Amber Nails
Laie Village Shopping Center, 55-510 Kam Highway, Laie, telephone 293-8868.

NURSERIES

Alluvion Nursery

61-676 Kam Highway, Haleiwa, telephone 637-8835 or 1-800-909-8835, fax 637-8836, E-mail: info@alluvionhi.com. Open weekdays from 7:00 a.m. to 3:30 p.m., Saturday from 7:00 a.m. to 12:30 p.m.

Hibiscus Lady

69-240 Mahinaai Street, Waialua 96791, telephone 637-9995, E-mail: hibiscuslady@hawaii.rr.com.

Mokuleia Landscape Nursery

68-415 Kikou Street, Waialua 96791, telephone 637-6890.

Why Knott Nursery

P.O. Box 902, Waialua 96791, telephone 637-4150, fax 637-9660.

OPTOMETRISTS

Dr. Kevin Baize, O.D.

Laie Village Shopping Center, 55-510 Kam Highway, Laie, telephone 293-9500.

Dr. Clarence Murata, O.D.

66-210A Kam Highway, Haleiwa, telephone 637-5048.

Dr. Ken Nagahiro, O.D.

66-210A Kam Highway, Haleiwa, telephone 637-5048.

Hawaiian Eye Center

606 Kilani Avenue, Wahiawa, telephone 621-8448.

PHARMACIES

D.A. Pharmacy
Laie Village Shopping Center, 55-510 Kam Highway, Laie, telephone 293-1600.

Haleiwa Pharmacy
66-145 Kam Highway, Haleiwa, telephone 637-9393.

North Shore Pharmacy
56-119 Pualalea Street, Kahuku, telephone 293-9514.

PHYSICAL THERAPY

NORTH SHORE PHYSICAL THERAPY & SPORTS REHAB

56-565 Kam Highway, Kahuku, telephone 293-9885.

PHYSICIANS

Dr. Virginia Abshier, M.D
North Shore Health Center, 56-119 Pualalea Street, Kahuku, telephone 293-9231 (if no answer call 293-9221): Internal medicine.

Dr. Harry J. Ashe, M.D.
56-565 Kam Highway, Kahuku, telephone 293-2441: Family practice.

Dr. Miriam M. Chang, M.D.
56-565 Kam Highway, Kahuku, telephone 293-9216: Family practice.

Haleiwa Family Health Center
66-125 Kam Highway, Haleiwa, telephone 637-5087.

Hawaiian Eye Center

606 Kilani Avenue, Wahiawa, telephone 621-8448: Ophthalmology.

Kaiser Permanente Kahuku Clinic

56-700 Kam Highway, Kahuku, telephone 432-3900.

Koolauloa Health Center

56-565 Kam Highway, Kahuku, telephone 293-9216: Family practice.

Laie Country Doctor, Dr. Marc B. Shlachter, M.D.

Laie Village Shopping Center, 55-510 Kam Highway, Laie, telephone 293-2573: Family practice.

Physician's Exchange

telephone 524-2575.

POLO: SEE CHAPTER VI

PSYCHOLOGISTS

Dr. Dan Kehoe

Kahuku Hospital, 56-117 Pualalea, Kahuku, telephone 293-9221.

North Shore Mental Health

302 California Avenue, #212, Wahiawa, telephone 293-7979.

SCUBA DIVING: SEE CHAPTER V

SEWING

El'gant Alterations

90 S. Kam Highway, Wahiawa, 621-9314, open Monday to Saturday 8:30 a.m. to 7:00 p.m., Sunday 8:00 a.m. to 5:00 p.m.

SHOE REPAIR

El'gant Alterations
90 S. Kam Highway, Wahiawa, 621-9314, open Monday to Saturday 8:30 a.m. to 7:00 p.m., Sunday 8:00 a.m. to 5:00 p.m.

SHOPPING: SEE CHAPTER VI

SKYDIVING: SEE CHAPTER VII

SNORKELING: SEE CHAPTER V

SUICIDE INTERVENTION

Suicide and Crisis Center
telephone 832-3100

Suicide Hot Line
telephone 521-4555.

SURF AND WEATHER REPORT

Tropical Rush, 638-7874.

SURFING: SEE CHAPTER V

SWIMMING: SEE CHAPTER V

TENNIS: SEE CHAPTER VI

VETERINARIAN

North Shore Veterinary Clinic
67-292 Goodale Avenue, Waialua, telephone 637-6202.

VIDEO RENTALS

Foodland

59-720 Kam Highway, Pupukea, telephone 638-8081.

Laie Village Shopping Center, 55-510 Kam Highway, Laie, telephone 293-4443, closed Sundays.

Ohana Video

Laie Village Shopping Center, 55-510 Kam Highway, Laie, telephone 293-2327, closed Sundays.

WHALE WATCHING: SEE CHAPTER V

WINDSURFING: SEE CHAPTER V

INDEX

376 INDEX

MAPS